Business Prac

MW01519867

This is an international business study of Theravada Buddhist Southeast Asia. Using a cross-disciplinary approach, the book examines business practices within a political, cultural, economic, and religious context. It highlights those cultural and historical ties of the region that are shared because of a common religion. In analyzing business environments, economics, and government practices across the region, the book provides a deeper understanding of the influence of cultural values on work practices in Southeast Asia.

The author first offers an overview of the history of the region and the nature and guiding principles of Theravada Buddhism. The next sections of the book present the history and the business and economic environment of the four countries in Southeast Asia, along with some relevant case studies of Cambodia, Laos, Myanmar/Burma, and Thailand. The book analyzes business strategies and practices, management and marketing issues, as well as the characteristics of companies. The last part considers the political environment of the four countries and hints at future trends and developments. The book offers a framework for working in the region, and provides valuable insights into this unique business environment, which is significantly different from the Western context. Filling a gap in existing literature, this book provides an accessible study of actual business practices in Southeast Asia.

Scott A. Hipsher is currently associated with Anaheim University's Akio Morita School of Business in Tokyo, Japan. He is the author of *Expatriates in Asia: Breaking Free from the Colonial Paradigm* and *The Nature of Asian Firms: An Evolutionary Perspective*.

Routledge studies in the growth economies of Asia

Business Practices in Southeast Asia

An interdisciplinary analysis of Theravada Buddhist countries

Scott A. Hipsher

Routledge
Taylor & Francis Group

LONDON AND NEW YORK

First published 2010
by Routledge
2 Park Square, Milton Park, Abingdon, Oxon OX14 4RN

Simultaneously published in the USA and Canada
by Routledge
711 Third Ave, New York, NY 10017

Routledge is an imprint of the Taylor & Francis Group, an informa business

First issued in paperback 2012

© 2010 Scott A. Hipsher

Typeset in Times by Wearset Ltd, Boldon, Tyne and Wear

British Library Cataloguing in Publication Data
A catalogue record for this book is available from the British Library

Library of Congress Cataloging in Publication Data
Hipsher, Scott A.
Business practices in Southeast Asia: An interdisciplinary analysis of
Theravada Buddhist countries/Scott Hipsher.
p. cm.
Includes bibliographical references and index.
1. Business etiquette–Asia, Southeastern. 2. Theravada Buddhism. I. Title.
HF5389.H57 2010
658.00959–dc22

2009025826

ISBN13: 978-0-415-56202-7 (hbk)
ISBN13: 978-0-203-86223-0 (ebk)
ISBN13: 978-0-415-53355-3 (pbk)

Contents

Illustrations

Figures

Tables

1 Theravada Buddhist Southeast Asia

Introduction to the region

Southeast Asia is home to four neighboring countries, Cambodia, Laos, Thailand, and Myanmar/Burma, where the majority of the population are followers of Theravada Buddhism. This unique region of the world has long fascinated and perplexed foreign visitors. Situated between two of the world's most historically influential and populous civilizations, China and India, as well as more recently being influenced by Western and Japanese colonizers and businesses, it is not surprising complex cultures with contradictory features have emerged in these four countries.

Often a visitor's first impression of the region is of the gentleness of the people, yet violence is not unknown and one of the modern world's most brutal regimes, the Khmer Rouge, sprang to life out of the environments found in these lands. Theravada Buddhism emphasizes the spiritual and the forsaking of material possessions and yet crass materialism can easily be found. Both prostitution and celibate monks are fairly common in the region. Modern cities like Bangkok, with cosmopolitan populations, and remote villages, such as those found along the Thai–Burmese border where life has changed little in hundreds of years, can be experienced within a few hours' drive. Freewheeling capitalism in Thailand neighbors economies closely controlled by socialist governments in Myanmar/Burma and Laos. The populations of the Theravada Buddhist countries of Southeast Asia are filled with contradictions, complexities, and fascinating personalities.

While the people and cultures in the region have proven resilient to attempts by foreigners at stereotyping, there do appear to be some cultural ties that bind the people and cultures of the region together, as well as historical incidents that have resulted in the four nations evolving in some aspects into separate and distinct cultures.

Choosing a grouping of cultures or countries to draw a boundary around in order to limit a study is always a problematic and arbitrary decision. Each human has much in common with every other human on the planet; after all, we are all part of the human race. Equally true is the fact that each human is a unique individual, possessing a combination of attributes that makes him or her one of a kind. However, mankind has developed an insatiable capacity for classifying groups of humans between these two extremes. Common classifications used to study groupings of people include religious affiliation, race, nationality, income, gender, occupation, sexual preference, and countless others. It is acknowledged that grouping the people of the countries of Cambodia, Laos, Thailand, and Myanmar/Burma together has severe limitations. Although the majority in each of these nations adheres to the Theravada Buddhist religion, there are also sizable populations of Christians, Muslims, and other non-Buddhists in each country. Also, each nation has its own unique political system and history. Nevertheless, the majority of the populations of these four countries share a common religion and historical interactions within the region have allowed a connection to develop among the people of the region, which makes this region of the world different from the East Asian lands to the East, South Asia to the West, and the predominately Muslim nations to the South.

Tully (2005: 6) believed the boundary between Chinese-influenced East Asia and Indian-influenced Southeast Asia was one of the most distinct divisions found within Asia. Stuart-Fox (2003: 25) argued that the decision by the rulers of ancient China to refrain from sea travel opened the opportunity for inland Southeast Asia to become more heavily influenced by Indian civilizations, yet influence from trade and immigration from China has always been a major factor in shaping the cultures of the region. Being influenced in nearly equal portions by East Asian culture based on the technology of wet rice agriculture, Indian religions, modern globalization, and ancient indigenous beliefs and practices, makes the region a complex and exciting study.

As suggested by Kamrava (1999: 19), "Each national culture has two poles around which values cluster, one traditional and the other non-traditional." Therefore as the history of each of the four countries in the region is intertwined with the other three, it is not surprising that each of the countries of the region shares part of its traditional national culture with the others; while also having obtained more modern features of each of their cultures which have been shaped by global and local political influences.

This book will explore the cultural connections and common business and work practices found within these four nations, while always keeping in mind the individual differences between nations, organizations, and people found in the region. This book is intended for individuals in business, government employees, NGO workers, volunteers, educators, tourists, and others with an interest in exploring beneath the surface of one of the most charming, complex, and fascinating regions of the world.

Demographics

There are approximately 142.7 million people living in the four predominately Theravada Buddhist countries of Southeast Asia with around 14.2 million living in Cambodia, 5.8 million in Laos PDR, 57 million in Myanmar/Burma, and 65.7 million in Thailand. As a whole, the average gross domestic product (GDP) per capita in the region is in the neighborhood of 1,883 US dollars, but this is very unevenly distributed. Thailand, with approximately 46 percent of the region's population, produces over 91 percent of the region's GDP, while Myanmar/ Burma, with nearly 40 percent of the region's population, only produces a little over 4 percent of the region's GDP (Asian Development Bank 2008a: 12). While the fascinating cultures of these four countries have been the subject of numerous academic works in the fields of economics, literature, cultural studies, history, political science, and linguistics, the relatively small size of the economies may explain the lack of international business and management studies conducted in the region.

Mandalas

In the study of countries and cultures, the nation-state is usually used as the focus of study (McGrew 2004: 127). However, the modern nation-state is of relatively recent origin, and this is especially the case in Southeast Asia. Wyatt (2003: 1) stated, "The 'Thai' identity, along with its political, cultural, and linguistic components, has developed slowly through many centuries, and what the modern citizen refers to as 'Thai' existed only recently." In fact, interactions between various nationalities and ambiguity over nationality seem to be fairly common throughout the history of the region. For example, although normally considered one of the earliest capitals of a Thai kingdom, evidence shows an intermingling of Mon, Khmer, and Thai taking place in fourteenth-century Sukhothai (Vickery 2004: 31). Keyes (2002) made the case that interactions and intermarriage among people from different backgrounds have made it virtually impossible to draw clear historical boundaries around different modern ethnic groups in Southeast Asia and much of the written history of the region has reflected the political divisions of the region at the time of writing as opposed to actual historical ethnic divisions. Therefore, the history of any one country in the region can not be completely separated from the history of the region as a whole.

Modern nation-states are primarily defined by geographical boundaries. However, in inland Southeast Asia, geographical boundaries around kingdoms have traditionally been fairly ambiguous. Jumsai (2000: 2) claimed that, prior to French occupation, the people of Laos referred to their language as Thai and a Lao cultural identify that was separate from the Thais, as opposed to political identity, was mainly manufactured by the French and later built upon by the ruling Communist Party to promote and maintain a political division between Laos and Thailand. South (2007) explained how the construct of being ethnically "Karen" (an ethnic group living in both Myanmar/Burma and Thailand) is of fairly recent origin and the concepts of Karen nationalism and Karen unity are often used by the elite Christian segment of the community for political purposes even though there is little historical basis for the notion of the existence of a Karen "nation." Vickery (2004: 4) showed the borders of the ancient Khmer kingdoms of the thirteenth, fourteenth, and fifteenth centuries, and those of Cambodia today are radically different. Is the history of much of modern-day central and northeast Thailand the history of Thailand, Cambodia, or both? Chandler (2000: 99) claimed that, before the arrival of the French, Southeast Asian ideas about political control were not based primarily on geography and in fact there are no locally drawn maps of Cambodia from the early nineteenth century that have survived.

Instead of controlling land, power came from controlling people due to the historical low population density found in inland Southeast Asia and the introduction of the use of labor intensive wet rice farming techniques from East Asia (Chandler 2000: 16; Hill 2002; Jumsai 2000: 37). O'Connor (1995) made the case that by taking a longer-term view of Southeast Asian history, it becomes apparent the ethnic groups with cultures that used heavily Indian-influenced agricultural technologies, the Pyu, Mon, and Cham, lost their dominance to the Burmese, Tai, and Vietnamese, all of which used wet rice agricultural techniques similar to those used in East Asia, beginning approximately a millennium ago. While the South Asian religions and writing systems remained in much of Southeast Asia, the introduction of these new cultures that were based on wet rice farming resulted in inland Southeast Asia being transformed from being primarily South Asian influenced to being heavily East Asian influenced. The ethnic groups that brought the use of wet rice agriculture to the region from East Asia have remained dominant up to the present.

Diamond (1997) claimed that, in the evolution of civilization, societies go through four distinct stages: bands, tribes, chiefdoms, and nation-states. While the nation-state is a fairly recent development in Southeast Asia, the region has had political entities that were much larger than chiefdoms, according to Diamond's definition, since at least the time of the Angkor Empire.

Historians often use the term *mandala* to describe the historical political systems that fit between a chiefdom and nation-state that were found in inland Southeast Asia before the arrival of Europeans and the colonial system. "*Mandala* simply means circle in Sanskrit" (Dellios 1996). But Wolters (1982) used the term *mandala* to describe the political systems of Southeast Asia in precolonial days. *Mandalas* were in some ways similar to the feudal system that was seen in Europe in the Middle Ages, but in other ways somewhat different. A political *mandala* can be thought of as having a solid core where a kingdom or ruler's control over its subjects is at its strongest and control weakened the further one traveled from the political core. Two features that distinguished *mandalas* from modern nation-states were *mandalas* controlled subjects through personal relationships, as opposed to the concept of citizens belonging to a particular nationality, and physical borders between *mandalas* were not fixed, but flexible and often shifting. Along with ambiguity over borders, there was also ambiguity over which ruler controlled a particular individual or village. For example, Khmer rulers at times of weakness saw no contradiction in sending tribute to both kingdoms in Vietnam and Thailand; in fact it was often a smart political maneuver to play more powerful neighbors off one another. As another example, at times of strength, Vietnamese rulers were comfortable accepting tribute from Khmer leaders while accepting at a certain level Chinese claims of control over Vietnam. The *mandala* system often resulted in decentralized political structures (Chandler 2000; 19) and a lack of a true national identity for many of the people of the region. Evans (2002: 7) described the working of *mandalas* in Southeast Asia:

> Mandalas at their extremities waxed and waned, shading off into vassal states and peoples. During expansionary phases of a mandala, smaller states were drawn directly into its realm; when it contracted they regained their autonomy or perhaps became attached to an adjacent mandala. Sacred centres, and not sacred territories and boundaries, were the preoccupation of these politics, which were made up of personalized networks focused on the king rather than territorial units.

This lack of clear national identities resulted in extensive cultural borrowing and intermingling among the people of inland Southeast Asia. This has allowed the various ethnic groups in the region to develop cultures with much commonality. For example, Theravada Buddhism has become the dominant religion of the entire region although the religion is not indigenous to the region. This has also had an effect on the evolution of languages in the region as this religious influence explains why so much of the Burmese, Khmer, Lao, and Thai languages are built upon writing systems and vocabulary of the ancient Indian languages of Sanskrit and Pali, and also why the languages of the four nations have so much vocabulary in common (Goddard 2005: 2, 57). Kusakabe (2004: 59) found among those working in cross-border trade along the Thai–Cambodia border, some individuals still today have "an ill-defined sense of nationality," which suggests some of the ambiguity over political alliance that characterized the *mandala* system has not entirely disappeared despite relatively recent efforts by the national governments of each of the four countries to create separate and unique national identities.

Globalization

When one picks up a newspaper, academic journal or magazine reporting on current events, or switches on a news channel on television, most likely it will not be long before the term "globalization" will be encountered. While this term is ill-defined, the common consensus apparently is that it refers to the lessening of differences around the world. For example, Bishop (2008: 5) claimed "'Globalization' is shorthand for global integration. Most people focus on the economic dimension – namely international trade and investment – but globalization also includes social, cultural, linguistic, political, technical and environmental integration across borders." Cochrane and Pain (2004: 5) wrote

> There is a widely shared – almost taken for granted – view that the world is changing more rapidly and dramatically at the start of the twenty-first century than ever before. Although it may not be a term we all use, many of the changes seem to be associated with something that has been called "globalization."

Globalization has often been linked with Americanization or the spreading of western ideas, principles, and practices around the world (for an example, see Harris 2008). Ahmed (2007: 196) agreed with this assertion and wrote, "Globalization seeks to spread such cherished American ideas as democracy and human rights."

However, are a lessening of cultural differences and the Americanization of the world true reflections of ongoing trends seen around the world? Kamrava (1999: 22) believed the phenomenon was much more nuanced and wrote:

> In a sense, from a political perspective it makes no more sense to speak of a "national" culture than it does to speak of a "global" culture. Each culture has a core, a center that makes it unique and different from other cultures, At the national level, there are certain values and symbols that are held in common by the citizenry: values derived from a common past and a shared heritage; symbols articulated and expressed through the same linguistic medium; a common folklore; a set of values propagated by the political system, etc. But every culture also has outer edges, margins whose values and symbols overlap with those of other cultures, complement them or differ from them only marginally; where symbolic and valuative communication across cultural boundaries is the easiest.

This concept of diminishing cultural difference associated with globalization has greatly affected international business education and the study of business conducted across international borders. For example, Griffin and Putsay (2005: 309) made the claim, "To survive in today's global marketplace, firms must be able to quickly exploit opportunities presented to them anywhere in the world." But do the majority of firms in Myanmar/Burma have the resources and capabilities to exploit opportunities in Iceland or Peru? In their textbook, Daft and Marcic (2004: 83) proclaimed, "business is becoming a unified global field as trade barriers fall, communication becomes faster and cheaper, and consumer tastes in everything from clothing to cellular phones converge." Is this true? Is doing business in New York basically the same as doing business in the mountainous regions of Northern Thailand and Laos? Even if we accept that consumer tastes are converging, it is obvious that differences in economic development and individual purchasing power ensure markets differ around the world. It is questioned whether the assumption that globalization has made the world into a single indistinguishable market where national borders and culture no longer matter is accurate.

Many scholars have questioned how far economic globalization has actually progressed; these individuals are often labeled as inter-nationalists (Mackay 2004: 69). Masson (2001) looked at aspects often associated with globalization (e.g., current account surpluses, reductions in transportation costs, and immigration) and found the current level of globalization may actually be lower than was seen in the pre-World War I era. Ghemawat (2003) advocated taking a more historical look at the concept of globalization, and then one would see that the international interconnection of our current era is not as unique as often reported. He believed the term semi-globalization was a more accurate view of the world's economies in this era in which we live in. Instead of being something radical and new, many scholars have proposed that globalization is more of an evolutionary rather than a revolutionary phenomenon (Bordo *et al.* 1999; Wallerstein 2000).

Another view of globalization is that of the transformationalists, who believe there is a trend toward worldwide economic integration but also argue that national boundaries and local conditions will continue to be important factors in the lives of individuals around the globe. Transformationalists point to the regional nature of most international business as evidence of a different type of globalization than one of a single unified worldwide economy led by the United States (Kelly and Prokhovnik 2004: 104). There is significant empirical evidence that most international business is actually regional in nature as opposed to global. (For examples, see Chortareas and Pelagidis 2004; Collinson and Rugman 2008; Rugman and Brain 2003; Rugman and Verbeke 2004; Rugman and Verbeke 2008). There is also significant evidence of the regional nature of much of the trade within Southeast Asia. (For examples, see Areethamsirikul 2008; Freeman 2002; Maekawa 2004; Maneepong and Wu 2004; Masviriyakul 2004; Wattanapruttipaisan 2003).

It is questioned whether the concept of being part of a "global" economy accurately reflects the actual business, economic, political, and social environments found in Cambodia, Laos, Thailand, and Myanmar/Burma. It is believed global influences are felt in every corner of the world, including the Theravada Buddhist nations of Southeast Asia. However, it is believed downplaying the national, regional, and local conditions and cultures in which businesses practices are implemented is unlikely to produce optimal results for businesses operating in the region.

Historical regional connectivity and segregation

Chanthanom (1998: 33) wrote, "The name 'Southeast Asia' is a modern construction based on western knowledge of geography, geology, biology, anthropology and political science." People of the region have historically rarely thought of themselves as being from a particular region of the world, instead they have generally indentified themselves as belonging to various villages, kingdoms, linguistic groups, and more recently nations. However, the connection from a shared Buddhist faith, as well as sharing similar agricultural practices, has limited the amount of foreignness felt when cross-border personal interactions have occurred.

The peoples living in different areas of Southeast Asia where Theravada Buddhism dominates have a history of both connectivity and separation. Freeman (1910: 21) claimed it had been reported that mutually understandable dialects of the "Tai" (an ethnic group, as opposed to "Thai" which is a nationality) language could be heard throughout much of Southeast Asia, as well as inside the area of

China bordering Laos at that time, demonstrating a common heritage between Tai speakers throughout Southeast Asia. However, the geographical separation resulted in different Tai speaking groups developing separate forms of political organization.

A nationality is generally thought of as being part of a continuous geographic region, but the features of the land made travel throughout the region difficult in times past. Therefore individuals living alongside rivers and other transportation routes were often better connected to other individuals living a considerable distance away along transportation routes than those individuals who were connected to some other individuals in closer geographical proximity but separated by a lack of transportation routes (Hill 2002: 3–4). This separation due to geographical terrain may have delayed the creation of a sense of nationality based on geographic location within the region.

Although there have been historical interactions between people of different nationalities and linguistic backgrounds in the region, there have also been more recent periods where connectivity has been constrained. During the colonial era, for political purposes, the French emphasized the connection between the peoples of Vietnam, Laos, and Cambodia, and actively encouraged Vietnamese immigration in the Theravada Buddhist areas of Southeast Asia which the French controlled, while downplaying any historical connection areas of French Indochina had with Thailand (Chandler 2000; Evans 2002; Jumsai 2000). Additionally, after the end of the colonial era, differences in political ideology separated communist Laos and Cambodia from capitalist Thailand, resulting in fewer personal contacts and business transactions across borders within the region during the later part of the twentieth century; however, in recent times this trend of division is being reversed and business and exchanges between Thailand and its neighbors to the east are increasing (Stuart-Fox 2003: 194). To the west of Thailand, both the British colonial experience and the more recent isolationist policies of the military dictatorships in Myanmar/Burma have resulted in recent society and culture in the country evolving mostly independently from the rest of the Theravada Buddhist countries of Southeast Asia (Myint-U 2006). The Theravada Buddhist countries of Southeast Asia have deep historical and cultural ties with each other, but each country has also evolved and emerged into the modern world mostly without substantial interaction across the region until fairly recent times.

International trade and commerce were part of life in Southeast Asia long before the term "globalization" was coined. While historians do not have enough information to be sure of all the details, it is known the people populating present-day Thailand and other parts of mainland Southeast Asia were connected to trade routes that stretched from India to China and included many parts of modern day Indonesia during the period prior to the time when Tai speakers moved into the region. Along these trade routes, Indian languages, religious practices, and political ideology were transferred to a large portion of mainland Southeast Asia (Stuart-Fox 2003: 26). Furthermore, it was recorded that the "nation" of Funan (most likely a collection of mostly independent petty kingdoms), which appears to have been located in present-day Cambodia and spilled over into present-day Vietnam, had trade and tribute relations with the Wu Kingdom of China as far back as the Three Kingdoms period (AD 220–80) (Stuart-Fox 2003: 27–9). Being situated between and trading with these two great civilizations has resulted in the peoples of Southeast Asia being exposed to a variety of foreign ideas and business practices which have influenced their cultural and economic activities for centuries.

The ideas of nationalism in the region may be somewhat different than is found in other locations. In many heterogeneous societies, nationality is normally accepted based on originating or living for a considerable period within the geographical boundaries of a country. An immigrant can easily become an American, Canadian, or Australian, not only legally but also culturally and, in fact, is often encouraged to do so. But in general, individuals from the outside cannot immigrate into the region and become Thai, Lao, Burmese, or Khmer. For example, the people of Cambodia refer to their national identity by using the term "Khmer." Su (2003: 61) studied how Khmer people produced their sense of national identity and how Khmers were distinguished from non-Khmers. Su found the following seven criteria were used for identifying who is and who is not Khmer:

1   Ancestry: To be Khmer is to be born in Cambodia.
2   Religion/Philosophy: To be Khmer is to be Buddhist.
3   Language: To be Khmer is to speak Khmer.
4   Knowledge: To be Khmer is to know Khmer arts, literature, music, dance, and history.
5   Attitudes and Behavior: To be Khmer is to be respectful, polite, patient, gentle, modest, honest, and innocent.
6   Loyalty to and love for country: To be Khmer is to love Cambodia and the Khmer.
7   Flexibility: To be Khmer is to be flexible, to understand the impermanence of things, and thus to be able to adapt to changing situations.

Political environment

The state has become the political entity that has the most influence over the lives of people; however, the position of the state is often less well entrenched in developing economies and governments. In these areas, the state often has a weaker impact on guiding the evolution of a national culture than governments do in more advanced economies (Kamrava 1999: 95). Even in this era of "globalization," in which global citizenship is promoted, the nation-states retain their dominant position in the political and legal lives of their citizens, and nation-states are the political entities most people most closely identify with. For example, while the Lao speaking people of *Isarn* (the northeast region) in Thailand feel a cultural connection with the people living in Laos PDR, they primarily identify themselves as "Thai" and subjects of his majesty the King.

The nation-states of Theravada Buddhist Southeast Asia have a variety of political systems that are difficult to classify. Cambodia is now a "democracy" that has been ruled outright since 1985 by Hun Sen and the Cambodian People's Party (CPP). Hun Sen and his party won a resounding reelection victory in 2008, mostly with the support of rural voters. Despite claims by the Western media of election fraud and lack of an environment that allows opposition parties to seriously challenge the ruling party, it does appear the CPP is the choice of the majority of Cambodian voters. As in Cambodia, Thailand's recent divisive political environment is characterized by a division of politicians who win elections with the votes of mostly rural voters with opposition politicians primarily supported by urban elites. Thailand has a constitutional monarchy and has fluctuated since the end of the absolute monarchy in 1932 between some form of elected government and various military dictatorships. Laos PDR has been ruled by its communist party, dominated by a handful of members, since the middle of the 1970s, while Myanmar/Burma has been ruled by various military juntas since 1962. Each of these political systems has had a major impact on the business and economic environment found in each individual nation.

However, it is difficult for a nation-state and its citizens to ignore political connections with the outside world. The size of a country affects its ability to achieve foreign policy and international economic objectives (Gleason *et al.* 2008) and therefore smaller nations are often more receptive, or feel forced, to participate in international organizations. With the exception of Myanmar/ Burma, the governments of the Theravada Buddhist countries of Southeast Asia have been quite open in recent years to working within international frameworks while fiercely defending their sovereignty. Each of the Theravada Buddhist nations of Southeast Asia is a member of various international organizations. The Association of Southeast Asian Nations (ASEAN) and the Greater Mekong Subregion (GMS) are the two major international organizations within whose frameworks these four countries interact with each other.

ASEAN came to life in August, 1967 with the original members consisting six countries: Brunei, Indonesia, Malaysia, Singapore, Thailand, and the Philippines. Four other members, Vietnam, Laos PDR, Myanmar/Burma, and Cambodia all joined in more recent years (Kawai and Wignaraja 2007). Initially, ASEAN was created as a security alliance that was closely linked with the United States in response to a perceived threat from communist forces in the region. However, with the ending of the cold war, Southeast Asian states that have, or had in the past, socialist governments have joined ASEAN, and economic integration has become a main focal point of the organization's agenda (Ferguson 2004; Oldfield 1998: 53; Smith 2004).

Koh (2008) and Moeller (2007) have claimed that ASEAN is not taken very seriously by US and European politicians and diplomats. One of the principal critiques of ASEAN is that it does not do enough to promote democracy and human rights, but looking at the nature of the individual governments that make up ASEAN, this is not surprising. Instead of being an advocate for a specific set of values, a key feature of ASEAN is non-interference in the domestic politics of the member states (Emmerson 2007). Severino (2007) believed ASEAN had to be considered a success in the political arena, by often being able to keep regional issues from being dominated by outside political entities; however, its goal of economic integration has made less progress. Koh found that some of the criticisms of ASEAN have some validity, yet it was felt progress had been made by the organization in six areas. First, ASEAN has contributed to maintaining peace within the region; second, it has maintained the safety of the vital strategic sea lanes in which a large percentage of the world's trade passes through; third, it has created the concept of a single regional market and production base; fourth, it offers an excellent example of a functioning multicultural organization; fifth, it has been an active participant in creating new international structures in the post-cold war era; and sixth, it has set out its future course.

Agreements have been signed where the original six member states of ASEAN will eliminate all tariffs for products and services originating from other ASEAN nations by 2010, with the four newer members following in 2015 (Kawai and Wignaraja 2007: 6). However, intraregional trade within ASEAN has been more or less stagnant since 1995. On the other hand, due to a large percentage of unreported cross-border trade, actual trade among ASEAN nations may be higher than the reported 25 percent of total international trade in the region (Wattanapruttipaisan 2007). Wattanapruttipaisan also believed poor transportation connections, cross-border clearance difficulties, and varied and complex trade rules and technical regulations were factors limiting the amount of intraregional trade within ASEAN.

Areethamsirikul's (2008) research found the enlargement of ASEAN from six to ten members has had a positive impact on the growth of intra-ASEAN trade, but this has mostly come from the inclusion of Vietnam. The addition of Laos, Cambodia, and Myanmar/Burma into ASEAN has had little impact on regional trade patterns. Areethamsirikul also pointed out ASEAN's trade policies tend to lack details and ASEAN lacks any type of authoritative body with the power to ensure compliance with agreements and to administer rewards and punishments.

ASEAN is often considered to have a central role in proposals for larger Asian free trade agreements. China has proposed an ASEAN+3 (China, Japan, and Korea) framework, while Japan prefers a more inclusive arrangement that is referred to as ASEAN+6, including the ten current ASEAN nations, as well as China, Japan, Korea, Australia, New Zealand, and India (Kawai and Wignaraja 2007: 4). As ASEAN-China trade is rapidly increasing while Japan-ASEAN trade is not (Garrison 2005: 27), many see China as the natural center of a larger Asian free trade agreement instead of Japan; it has also been noted that China has been enthusiastically advocating the use of increased Asian political and economic integration through regional institutions to advance its own political agenda (Cheng 2004; Kuik 2005; Wang 2004). However, Ong (2003) believed anchoring an Asian free trade agreement in ASEAN, as opposed to China or Japan, would be easier to accept politically, both within and outside the region. Beeson (2003) did not see the moves toward regional free trade agreements in Asia as a proactive strategy of Asian leaders toward shifting trade focus from trade with Western governments to a more regional focus, instead he saw the moves as being reactive in nature, which suggests that any moves toward creating an Asian-wide free trade agreement that includes ASEAN may be dependent upon moves toward increased regional integration made by North American and European leaders.

ASEAN was initially created to counter the threat posed by nations that are now either part of ASEAN or are working closely with ASEAN. ASEAN has morphed from an anti-communist security organization into an organization that has a focus on economic issues. However, the vastly different political, linguistic, and cultural traditions found among the member states have slowed efforts to create any significant political integration. The "ASEAN way" refers to a core policy that is informal in nature, non-confrontational, and seeks consensus in decision making (Stuart-Fox 2003: 215). The ASEAN policy of non-interference in the internal political affairs of member states is most likely a necessary condition for the continued viability of the organization; on the other hand, this feature of the organization prevents creating deeper regional ties and is a source of criticism from the outside world.

The four Theravada Buddhist countries of Southeast Asia are also members of the Greater Mekong Subregion (GMS). The GMS is a creation of the Asian Development Bank and sprang to life in 1992. It comprises the nations of Cambodia, Laos PDR, Myanmar/Burma, Thailand, and Vietnam, as well as the Yunnan province of China (Krongkaew 2004). During colonial times, the region was divided into four distinctly different parts with differing political control and agendas, which limited trade and interactions. The four parts were French controlled (Cambodia and Laos), British controlled (Burma), independent (Thailand), and in the Chinese sphere of influence (Yunnan). During much of the cold war era, the region was divided into three separate areas, the first was aligned with the major socialist powers (Cambodia, Laos, Vietnam, and Yunnan), the second was US aligned (Thailand), and the third was neutral (Burma), which continued to limit the amount of intraregional trade and interactions. With the thawing of the cold war and the shift to more market-based economies in all the countries in the region, an increase in trade and interactions within the GMS countries has been seen (Than 2005: 38).

Menon (2005: 23) made the claim that the countries of the GMS have experienced some level of market integration but not necessarily institutional integration. However, it should be noted since the GMS framework has been implemented, intraregional trade has significantly increased (Maekawa 2004; Masviriyakul 2004; Menon 2005: 24). Strutt and Lim (2005) believed trade liberalization in the GMS could have a significant impact on poverty reduction. However, Krongkaew (2004) questioned the impact the GMS has actually had on increasing trade and reducing poverty and pointed out that the differences in levels of development and differences in political outlook of the different leaders functioning in different political systems would limit any future impact the organization could have. Menon (2005) saw the GMS as a possible tool to help bring the small economies of Cambodia, Laos, and Myanmar/Burma into contact with regional and international trade networks. On the other hand, Goh and Ang (2000) made the case that logistical problems are a major impediment to increased trade within the GMS, and while there have been some improvements in recent years, the cost of transporting goods across the region remains high, which limits the effectiveness of the GMS's attempts toward trade integration (Wattanapruttipaisan 2007).

Mills *et al.* (2004) believed there was a need for human resource capacity building throughout the GMS and this would be required in order for the political and economic agreements to work to their potentials. It was found, in Cambodia, Laos PDR, and Vietnam, that many of the senior public sector officials had received their higher education in the Soviet Union or in Eastern Europe and therefore often lacked the English language skills and understanding of market-based economies needed to perform effectively in working to reduce barriers to international trade and improve efficiencies in business environments. The authors also found some common human resource capacity building needs of government bureaucrats across all six political entities that make up the GMS. These included building leadership qualities, improving management style, understanding principles of good governance, ensuring transparency, accountability and corruption control, staff development, using technology transfers, understanding development theory, using performance management tools and decentralizing organizational structures.

Business environment

It would appear countries with less cultural distance between each other also have more similar business environments than they have with countries with larger cultural distances (Hutzschenreuter and Voll 2008), and therefore one would expect to see some similarities in business practices across the region. Further evidence that firms from countries within a single region have some similarities in business operations was provided by Qian *et al.* (2008) as they found firm value increased with regional diversification, up to a certain point, more than with more geographically distant diversification. The authors also found firms perform most effectively while operating in markets with similar economic and social-cultural conditions to their own. Onishi (2006) found there were limitations in transferring Japanese human resources (HR) management practices into operations of Japanese firms in Thailand, which suggests one can not think of all of Asia as a culturally homogeneous region. Research by Zhou *et al.* (2007) suggested that even basic strategic approaches that are effective in more developed economies do not produce the same results in lesser developed areas, which indicates a major difference in overall business environment. Therefore, many of the underlying assumptions of doing business in developed economies may not apply when looking at firms operating in the Theravada Buddhist countries of Southeast Asia.

Even with considerable recent economic growth, poverty still plagues all of the Theravada Buddhist countries of Southeast Asia to some extent. Research indicates that poverty reduction in developing economies in general has been the result of economic growth and macroeconomic policy that focus on freeing markets from constraints as opposed to programs specifically targeted at poverty reduction (Agrawal 2007; Hasan *et al.* 2007; Weiss 2005). However, while agreeing that economic growth is necessary for poverty reduction, some scholars have expressed the opinion poverty reduction can be further increased while inequalities of income are decreased in developing Asia by some government controls over the market (Ali 2007; Son 2007; Srivastava 2005). China's amazing feat in reducing poverty through economic liberalization (Wang 2005) is likely to be an inspiration and model to emulate in the future for the leaders of the Theravada Buddhist countries of Southeast Asia.

A unique feature of the business environment in some of the Theravada Buddhist countries of Southeast Asia is the widespread use of foreign currency domestically. In Cambodia, nearly 90 percent of currency in circulation is US dollars, while in Laos PDR it is estimated that approximately half of the currency used within the country is US dollars or Thai baht (Menon 2007). Although specific data for Myanmar/Burma is difficult to find and is often unreliable, it is generally reported that the use of US dollars is common in domestic business transactions and a thriving black market where Kyats can be exchanged for US dollars is operating throughout much of the country. In Thailand, although foreign currencies are not normally used locally, the US dollar is the currency most used in foreign trade and these transactions in US dollars make up a considerable amount of the nation's economic activities (Saicheua 2008). The dollarization of some of the economies, as well as trading activities that take place in US dollars or other foreign currencies, results in the economies in the region being greatly affected by events and economic policy decisions made outside each country's borders.

The economies of the Theravada Buddhist countries of Southeast Asia continue to rely heavily on agriculture. In 2006 it was estimated that agriculture accounted for 29.6 percent of the country's GDP in Cambodia, 47.4 percent in Laos PDR, 48.5 percent in Myanmar/Burma, and 8.9 percent in Thailand (Asian Development Bank 2008a: 285). With improvements in infrastructure, more access to markets, and the transferring of existing agriculture technology into the region, there are appealing opportunities in this sector of the region's economies. A change being seen in the agricultural sector is the moving away from being mostly informal and subsistence-based toward the use of contract farming where agro-business companies provide technical support, credit, and guaranteed markets (Setboonsarng 2008). This is making farmers more professional but, so far, has not resulted in the mass creation of large commercial farms. Instead, the single family remains the most common form of farm ownership. Contract farming appears to have had a positive effect on poverty reduction and is resulting in developing commercial agriculture in the region (Setboonsarng *et al.* 2008); however, the most poverty stricken farmers are possibly being left out of the system and are seeing no benefits (Cai *et al.* 2008). While the percentage of individuals engaging in agriculture across the region has been decreasing, due to population growth the actual number of individuals in the region working as farmers has not seen a major decrease (Hill 2002).

Chinese influence

The importance of the position of individuals of Chinese ancestry in the business environments in the Theravada Buddhist countries of Southeast Asia has been a major feature of the business environment for a considerable length of time (Carney and Gedailovic 2003; Clarke 1998; Keller and Kronstedt 2005; Naisbitt 1997; Shapiro *et al.* 2003; Suehiro and Wailerdsak 2004; Tsang 2001). Trade between China and areas of Southeast Asia has been going on since the time of the Shang dynasty (1766–1050 BC) (Stuart-Fox 2003: 23). Since that time, many people of Chinese ancestry have found their way to Southeast Asia in order to seek their fortune, and have often successfully done just that.

Hill (2002: 136–7) in referring to the entire Southeast Asian region wrote:

> In the 1930s it was estimated that Chinese owned a third to two-thirds of the modern, commercial sector in agriculture, fisheries and trade. They 'knew money.' They supported each other economically and socially. They were supported by the colonial powers.

The preeminent position of ethnic Chinese in business activities in the region may not always be evident to a new arrival to the region as for the most part, many ethnic Chinese families have taken Thai, Cambodia, Laotian or Burmese names and as many of these families have been in the region for generations, these ethnic Chinese families have for the most part adopted the local languages and cultural practices.

Technology, competitiveness, and impact of religion

Kao *et al.* (2008) measured the competitiveness of the business environments of ten Southeast Asian nations, using economic factors, availability of technology and infrastructure, human capital and costs, and managerial ability. The Theravada Buddhist nations of Southeast Asia did not fare very well. Not surprisingly, topping the list was Singapore, followed by Malaysia. Thailand was ranked third, while the other three nations of the region, Myanmar/Burma, Cambodia, and Laos were ranked in the bottom three positions, placing behind Indonesia, the Philippines, Brunei, and Vietnam.

The dominant religion or philosophy of a region and values associated with that religion or philosophy have subtle effects on many aspects of secular life, including organizational behavior; although often these effects go unnoticed by those from within the dominant religious tradition as they seem natural parts of life (Ali and Gibbs 1998). Christian values have been identified as playing a role in shaping business environments in Western countries (Anderson *et al.* 2000; Cornwell *et al.* 2005; Vinten 2000). It has been acknowledged that Islamic values influence the business, economic, and political environments in countries with majority Muslim populations (Abbasi *et al.* 1989; Ali and Al-Owaihan 2008). Confucian values have been associated with business practices in ethnic Chinese firms (Wang 2004; Yan and Sorenson 2004). Likewise, it would seem obvious that Theravada Buddhism shapes many features of secular life and business practices throughout the region where this religion/ideology dominates. For example, many leaders in the region believe Theravada Buddhism can be used as an ideological foundation to create a unique socioeconomic development method that can be used as an alternative approach to either pure market capitalism or socialism (Jackson 2003: 58). Theravada Buddhism is only one of many factors shaping the business, economic, and political environments in these four countries, but it is felt this common belief system binds the nations together in a way that makes this a distinctly recognizable region.

2 Introduction to Theravada Buddhism and the life of the Buddha

Theravada Buddhism

Theravada Buddhism plays an important part of the lives of the majority of people living in Cambodia, Laos, Thailand, and Myanmar/Burma. Buddhism is one of the most adhered to "religions" in the world and yet according to Davids (1894: 151) it is unlikely Gautama (the Buddha) "intended, either at the beginning or the end of his career, to be the founder of a new religion," instead it has been speculated the Buddha was interested in building upon the then existing Hindu religion as practiced in the area.

Is Buddhism primarily a religion or a philosophy? After all, "The Buddha did not create the world, is no longer alive and does not exist," (Kaw 2005: 27) and therefore the Buddha is not a supernatural being who can intervene in the lives of people living today. Metaphysics and questions such as the origin of the universe are not main concerns of Theravada Buddhism; instead Buddhism in Southeast Asia is primarily concerned with ethics (King 1964: 1) and Theravada Buddhism "has no dogmas, superstitions, necessary rituals, mediating priests or blind faith in an unknown (and unknowable) God" (King 1964: 2). Therefore Buddhism is sometimes classified as a philosophy instead of a religion. Yet, for many lay believers "praying" to and worshiping Buddha images is an extremely common practice (Schober 1989: 32); this practice would appear to have much in common with the Christian, Hindu, or Muslim concepts of religious prayer to the supernatural.

It needs to be kept in mind there is a wide divergence between doctrinal Buddhism and the popular Theravada Buddhism of the masses (Jackson 2003: 61, 306). This has been the case for a considerable amount of time; in 1922 Saunder (42) noticed, "There is a marked difference between the theoretical Buddhism of early days, reflected in the standard literature of Southern Buddhism [Theravada Buddhism], and the Buddhism of the present day." Studying the vast literature that comprises the Buddhist canons, as is done by Buddhist scholars and theologians, gives only a partial picture of Theravada Buddhism and how it affects millions of people living in Southeast Asia. One could not expect to understand modern Islam by solely studying the Koran, nor would one be expected to understand the part that Christianity has played in the history of Europe and North

America from only reading the Bible. The same principle applies to the study of the effects of Theravada Buddhism on the history of Southeast Asia and the lives of its citizens today.

The way Theravada Buddhism is interpreted and practiced in Southeast Asia is filled with contradictions, complexities, and nuances. Theravada Buddhism stresses the fact that the path to enlightenment is an individual endeavor and must be learned from within and cannot be taught, and yet to devote one's life to seeking enlightenment normally requires one to become a monk, live in a regimented communal environment, and strictly follow a large number of rules and regulations. Kaw (2005: 122) states, "critical or independent thinking is not at all foreign to traditional monastic schools," and yet "[i]n Theravada Buddhism there is more emphasis on correct practices, or orthopraxy, as the basis of authoritative presentations of doctrine than on correct belief" (Jackson 2003: 17). The seeking of enlightenment could be thought of as a selfish endeavor and "becoming a disciple-son of the Buddha may involve a considerable amount of personal struggle between what counts as good for oneself and what counts as good for the wider context" (Carbine 2004: 107). Furthermore, Theravada Buddhism is primarily a path for celibate monks who are striving for enlightenment by separating themselves from secular activities and yet a place for lay worshipers is necessary for the religion to thrive (Carbine 2004: 27).

Theravada Buddhism, in theory, is apolitical in nature; however, monks in Southeast Asia have often been involved in politics and, at times, even in military matters (Bode 1898: 61, Jerryson 2009; Kaw 2005: 122; McCargo 2009). It would appear the interpretation of core Theravada Buddhism values can differ to some extent depending on time, place, and individual interpretation; nevertheless the core of the religion/philosophy affects the actions, beliefs, and thoughts of millions of people across the region on a daily basis.

First and foremost, Theravada Buddhism is a path for celibate monks to search for enlightenment; however, in order for the religion to survive and thrive for over 2,000 years, a strong connection between monastic life and lay people has been necessary. Monks and lay people have very different religious goals. In theory, monks are striving to reach *nibbana* (nirvana) in this life, while the main focus of lay people is to strive to be born in the next life with higher status or on a higher level of existence (Crosby 2006). Another conflicting pressure comes from the need for Theravada Buddhism to balance maintaining the purity and traditions of the religion with pressures for the religion to adapt to an ever modernizing world. Schober (1989: 30) wrote:

> Religious practices among the lay community is largely confined to the lower stages of the path to enlightenment. Due to the inherent imperfections of lay life, a lay person who masters the exceedingly difficult task of becoming an *arahat* [Buddhist saint] may not continue to exist in the lay domain. He must either join the *sangha* [order of Buddhist monks] or become extinct and enter *parinibbana* [*nibbana*].

All forms of Buddhism are built upon the foundation of the life and teachings of the Buddha. It would appear that the histories taught of the Buddha's life (and previous lives as told in the Jataka Tales) are a mixture of elements based on facts as well as elements that were added after his death to create a mythical aura around the Buddha. Historically, the dates of the Buddha's life have been given as 563–483 BC; however, recently most scholars believe the evidence suggests it is most likely the Buddha died slightly later, around 400 BC (Prebish 2008). It has been speculated that at the time and in the area where the Buddha originally lived, written language was not used, and therefore it was a considerable amount of time after the Buddha died that his story was put on paper. Prior to the introduction of written language into the area where Buddhism was practiced, the Buddha's life story and teachings were handed down orally from generation to generation (Davids 1894: 9). It is probably impossible for modern scholars to accurately separate fact from fiction in regards to the life of the Buddha, but for the majority of the population of the region, what is taught about the Buddha's life, whether fact or myth, lays the foundation for their religious beliefs.

Life of the Buddha

The Buddha, often known by the name Gautama, was born in what is now modern-day Nepal around the fifth century BC and was named Siddhatta by his parents. Legend states that the Buddha's mother died during or shortly after childbirth, but he was raised by his mother's sister who was also a wife of his father. Siddhatta was born a prince and was raised as a member of royalty. Siddhatta married and had a son and was poised to take over his father's kingdom one day. However, Siddhatta was not satisfied with life and after seeing four signs in the forms of an old man, a sick man, a decaying corpse, and a dignified hermit, he decided to leave his life of privilege and set off on a life of wandering and searching for life's truths (Davids 1894: 25–32).

Siddhatta took along his servant, named Channa, and began his life as an ascetic monk. First he took up with a group of five monks who practiced severe fasting and self-mortifications. After about six years, the future Buddha became disillusioned with these severe practices and set out to find enlightenment on his own. Finally he sat down under a Bo-tree determined not to rise until he found enlightenment. This period of his life is often depicted as an epic struggle between the forces of good and the truth, and the forces of evil. Finally, he found enlightenment and became a Buddha (enlightened one). At first, the Buddha was not sure whether he should attempt to teach others or not, but finally his love of his fellow man won out and he set out to teach others the truths he had discovered (Davids 1894: 32–42).

Now referred to as Gautama, the Buddha began his career as a wandering teacher. He started his teaching career by addressing his former colleagues who were still attempting to find enlightenment through pain; the Buddha now rejected that path and laid out his four Noble Truths. Among the Buddha's first converts were many women. The Buddha traveled widely during much of the year; however, he stayed in one place during the rainy season, a tradition that is carried on to this day by members of the *Sangha* (order of Buddhist monks). During his lifetime, the Buddha laid down the fundamental rules of the *Sangha* and in his eightieth year, he uttered the words, "Mendicant! I now impress it upon you, decay is inherent in all component things; work out your salvation with diligence!" and then died (Davids 1894: 42–83).

After his death, many miraculous stories about his life and how he was destined for greatness from an early age have been added to the Buddha's life history (Davids 1894: 27). Also, the Jataka Tales, which show the previous lives of the Buddha as various animals, are used to teach morality and the path toward eventual enlightenment (Kaw 2005: 208; Saunder 1922: 2). It is obviously impossible to scientifically prove the Jataka Tales are an accurate history of the Buddha's previous incarnations; however, these stories are an important component of popular Buddhism.

Theravada Buddhism is one of the two main schools of Buddhism, the other being Mahayana. Theravada Buddhism is also referred to as the southern school, as it passed from Sri Lanka into Southeast Asia, while the spread of the Mahayana school took a northerly route through Tibet, China, and on to Korea and Japan. Theravada is a Pali word meaning "Way of the Elders" or "Doctrine of the Elders" (Dhammapia 2003: 10). In general, Pali is the language of Theravada Buddhism, while the Mahayana school uses pronunciations based on Sanskrit. The different schools within Theravada Buddhism generally have less variations of practices or ideology than seen in Mahayana Buddhism. While Theravada Buddhism teaches that the path to enlightenment comes from one's own efforts, Mahayana Buddhism places more emphasis on the belief of supernatural *bodhisattvas* (compassionate servants of humanity) leading people toward the ultimate goal (Saunder 1922: 47).

While Theravada Buddhism in general follows a strict interpretation of Buddhist scriptures, there are some different schools of thought within the religion. Davids (1894: 8) noticed that the religion took on a new set of characteristics that were acceptable to the local populations as it moved into Southeast Asia. An example of a different school of thought can be found amongst the Shwegyin Monks in Myanmar/Burma. The Shwegyin School of Theravada Buddhism arose at the time of, and possibly in response to, the British gaining more control over the country. While many schools of Theravada Buddhism place the highest priority on meditation as a means toward enlightenment, the Shwegyin School places more emphasis on the study and understanding of Buddhist scriptures. While members of the Shwegyin School, which has its center in Mandalay, are allowed to meet with members of the Sudhamma (also spelled Thudamma) School, which is the dominant form of Theravada Buddhism in Myanmar/ Burma, the two schools have completely separate hierarchical structures and a number of different practices (Carbine 2004; Schober 1989: 231–2).

History of Theravada Buddhism

Theravada Buddhism's introduction into Southeast Asia has transformed the region, but exactly how this Indian religion gained popularity in Southeast Asia remains a mystery to some extent. Baumann (2001) divided the history of Theravada Buddhism into three separate periods: canonical, traditional, and modern. Canonical Buddhism began during the time of the Buddha and lasted until the time when the famous and powerful Indian ruler, Asoka, adopted the Buddhist philosophy in the third century BC and created the first Buddhist kingdom. Traditional Buddhism began during the reign of Asoka and lasted up until the mid to late nineteenth century. The modern period began as a response to the colonial era and attempts at introducing Christianity into the region. However, despite many decades of efforts, Christianity made few inroads in mainland Southeast Asia during the colonial era (Freeman 1910: 19).

During the reign of King Asoka, Buddhist doctrine was written down and formalized, and Buddhism as a mass religion had its origin; additionally Theravada Buddhism was introduced into Sri Lanka around this same time (Bechert 1970). As time went on, Buddhism began evolving and divided into various schools of thought as the acceptance of Buddhism moved into both new geographical regions and into different historical eras (Dhammapia 2003: 9). However, Buddhism created a common connection between the different regions of Asia, and increases in trade and cross-cultural exchanges were stimulated by the introduction of this shared religion throughout much of East and Southeast Asia (Goh 2007: 25; Stuart-Fox 2003: 39).

Theravada Buddhist sects in different nations share identical doctrines; however, there are differences in monastic practices and it is generally believed that Buddhism as practiced in Myanmar/Burma is more orthodox than that practiced in the other countries of Southeast Asia (Chanthanom 1998: 308; Schober 1989).

Theravada Buddhism was well established in Myanmar/Burma before it spread to the rest of Southeast Asia (Stuart-Fox 2003: 69). Although there are Burmese legends that the Buddha actually traveled to lands which today are inside Myanmar/Burma and introduced the religion in his lifetime (Bode 1898: 21), this appears unlikely. The history of Buddhism in Southeast Asia most likely began when the Indian King/Emperor Asoka sent Buddhist emissaries to various parts of South and Southeast Asia to increase the number of converts (Carbine 2004: 101). Buddhism was well established in Pagan (Bagan) in present-day Myanmar/Burma when the legendary King Anawrahta, who was recorded to have been a great patron of Buddhism, helped to purify the religion and established Theravada Buddhism as the state religion; although whether King Anawrahta was an actual historical figure or a literary device used by Buddhist scholars to convey Buddhist concepts throughout the region remains uncertain (Goh 2007). In the twelfth century, Burmese Buddhism was divided into three branches: Mahayana, Theravada, and Sarvastivadin; and it was reported that in 1180, an elder monk and a novice were sent from Myanmar/Burma to

Sri Lanka and upon their return with four additional monks from Sri Lanka, instituted the Sinhalese form of Theravada Buddhism into the country (Goh 2007: 42). Buddhism continued to evolve, divide, consolidate, and dominate in the lands that today make up much of Myanmar/Burma from the twelfth century up until the colonial era (Bode 1898). Education was primarily conducted in the monasteries and this continued initially after the British incorporated Burma into their colonial empire. In general, the British did not actively oppose Buddhist practices during the colonial era; however, they did begin after a time to introduce secular education and this became the path toward much sought after employment within the British-controlled governmental system. Therefore Buddhist monasteries began to lose their place as the centers of education for the population and a gap was created between the majority of the population who held traditional values and the select few who had their training in missionary schools. Nevertheless, Buddhism has regained and retained its place in modern Burmese society and there continues to be a high level of respect given to those who have permanently taken up the life of wearing the robes (Kaw 2005).

As Tai speakers began to spread across the then Khmer-controlled land of what is now present-day Laos, the Tai language became dominant as did Theravada Buddhism (Evans 2002: 7). Prior to 1828, Vientiane was one of the most important religious centers in Southeast Asia, but with the sacking of the city by the Thais, a shift transpired of religious, and also political, alliance toward Bangkok of the Lao speaking peoples living in the Korat plane of present-day Thailand (Ivarsson and Goscha 2007). Although both the French and the subsequent Vietnamese-backed communist rulers have attempted to align Laos closer to Vietnam and away from Thailand and have attempted to downplay the importance of religious life, Theravada Buddhism remains a core feature of Lao culture and this shared religion is one factor tying the Laotian and Thai peoples close together.

Theravada Buddhism has traditionally been an important cornerstone of the national identity of Thailand. However, in Thailand, religion, politics, and the social order have always been closely intertwined. Initially, the most important distinction with the Tai as they moved into Southeast Asia was between the "civilized" Buddhist population and the "uncivilized" non-Buddhists (Evans 2002: 21). Buddhism has often been used to justify the status quo and "Buddhist intellectual culture in Thailand until the twentieth century can only be described as conservative and stagnant" (Jackson 2003: 17). However, the encroachment of colonialism and the introduction of the use of western scientific methods have been the catalyst for the fusion of Asian philosophy and western scientific analysis that is now seen in modern Theravada Buddhism within the country (Jackson 2003: 42–8). The concept of the connection between the monarchy, Buddhism, and the state was significantly strengthened during the reign of Rama VI (1910–25) (Evans 2002: 71) and this connection remains very much in evidence today.

"For as an integral part of the Thai social order, Buddhism has also been subject to extra-religious influences which have historically restricted intellectual speculation on matters of doctrine" (Jackson 2003: 24). Unlike the other nations of Southeast Asia that have majority Theravada Buddhist populations, Thailand chose to vigorously oppose socialism and communism and to protect the institution of the monarchy and, therefore, "In Thailand, Buddhism has been officially defined as anti-communist and communism as anti-Buddhist" (Jackson 2003: 29). Meanwhile in Myanmar/Burma, Buddhism and socialism have often gone together. Differences in the political and economic ideology of national governments have led to differences in the emphasis on which aspects of the religion are taught in different countries.

The Khmer Empire of Angkor originally was founded by individuals who were followers of Hinduism. However, artifacts indicate Buddhism was flourishing in the area prior to the emergence of the Khmer Empire. In the twelfth century, a shift toward Mahayana Buddhism occurred, most likely during the reign of Jayavarman VII, and in the thirteenth century, the Khmers began embracing Theravada Buddhism; although the forces behind the change were not well understood. Exactly what caused the change in religious philosophy of the region continues to be debated; however, it was reported by Zhou Daguan, a Chinese envoy who visited the city of Angkor in 1296–7, that many aspects still associated with monastic life, for example shaved heads, wearing yellow robes with one shoulder bare, and going barefoot, were already practiced during this period (Chandler 2000: 69–71; Sharrock 2009; Tully 2005).

Buddhist philosophy

"Buddhism is a religious tradition with a distinctive theoretical history in which notions of argumentation, methods of reasoning and the place of reason in human knowledge differ markedly from the situation in the Western tradition" (Jackson 2003: 6). In many ways Buddhism is similar to other religions, for example, Christianity has its ten commandments while Buddhism has its five precepts (avoid taking life, avoid stealing, avoid illicit sexual relations, avoid lying, and avoid intoxicants). But, there is also a difference in interpretation of the basic religious "rules" and the five precepts are not seen as commandments that it is a sin to break, but could be considered as sage advise or "counsel to the wise" (King 1964: 140).

At the core of Buddhist philosophy are the four Noble Truths, which the Buddha conveyed to his followers in his first formal lecture in the Deer Park at Sarnath near Varanasi, reportedly in 528 BC, and have been taught to Buddhists worldwide ever since (Sumedho 1992: 7).

The first Noble Truth is there is suffering. Every living human suffers. Always and in all times, every human suffers, grows old, and dies, no matter how rich or poor. The second Noble Truth is the origin of suffering, which is attributed to attachment and desires. People are unhappy because they do not have what they want. There is desire for sense pleasures, desire to become, and desire to be rid of tangible or intangible things. The third Noble Truth is that the cessation of suffering is possible through the release of attachment and desire.

One who wants nothing is never disappointed. The fourth Noble Truth deals with the method to achieve the cessation of attachment and desire called the Eightfold Path (Sumedho 1992).

The eight elements of the path are broken down into three sections:

Wisdom (right understanding, right aspiration)
Morality (right speech, right action, right livelihood)
Concentration (right effort, right mindfulness, right concentration).

(Sumedho 1992: 51)

The four Noble Truths are at the heart of Theravada Buddhism and are all inward looking and stress the fact that achievement of enlightenment comes from the efforts of the individual. The four Noble Truths are about cultivating the spirituality of the individual and are not especially concerned with the betterment of society or helping one's fellow man.

The primary method to achieve right mindfulness and right concentration is through meditation. Theravada Buddhism emphasizes meditation as the means to gradual enlightenment, which sharply varies from the Zen concept of abrupt awakening (Jackson 2003: 190). While, in general, few lay people meditate with the hopes of achieving *nibbana*, the number of people meditating has been expanding with the growth in popularity of urban meditation centers and instructional books on meditation written by respected monks (Kaw 2005: 21). For lifelong monks, the ultimate goal of mediation is to achieve enlightenment, while for the lay person it is normally to find a level of inner peace and calm in one's daily life.

"In practical terms, *karma* [*kamma*] – not *nirvana* [*nibbana*] – is the central concept among Theravada Buddhist" (Keyes 1977: 286). Achieving *nibbana*, enlightenment, is a distant goal, and unattainable in this lifetime for the vast majority of Theravada Buddhists, therefore achieving merit to ensure a good rebirth is the actual religious objective of the overwhelming majority of followers of Theravada Buddhism (Curtis 1903: 189; Davids 1894: 102; King 1964). Merit can be achieved in a variety of ways, but it is considered essential meritorious to build temples and feed and care for the monks. This concept of merit makes the monastic and lay communities mutually interdependent. The monks rely on the lay population for their material needs, while the lay community needs the monastic community to achieve merit in order to have a successful birth in the next life (King 1964; Schober 1989).

The concept of *kamma*, or *karma*, is more or less like a running balance sheet of good (credits) and bad (debit) deeds. Good and bad deeds are weighted, with some deeds being deemed to be especially meritorious, while others bring less merit. At the end of the current life, an individual's good and bad deeds will be measured and added up, and where one starts one's next life will be decided by the balance one has acquired. This balancing is a natural law and is not the decision of a supreme being. Generally, one never has enough merit and therefore merit-making is considered a lifelong endeavor (Schober 1989: 99).

There do seem to be some inconsistencies as doctrinal Buddhism rejects the existence of a permanent soul and advocates the notion of impermanence; "The self is temporary in nature" (King 1964: 6). Therefore, if there is no permanent soul, what is reborn into the next life? Davids (1894: 114) explained Buddhist thoughts on the topic as follows:

> The life of man, to use a constantly recurring Buddhist simile or parable, is like the flame of an Indian lamp, a metal or earthenware saucer in which a cotton wick is laid in oil. One life is derived from another, as one flame is lit at another; it is not the same flame, but without the other it would not have been.

Therefore, unlike Christianity, where faith and asking for forgiveness for one's sins can clean the slate, for a Theravada Buddhist, a meritorious action is needed to balance a bad deed, such as breaking one of the five precepts. In Theravada Buddhism, perfection in behavior is not expected, but it is the on-balance feature of the religion that moderates an individual's actions. Demerit moves one farther away from enlightenment; however, while merit is necessary to move closer to the ultimate goal, merit alone will not lead to enlightenment (Schober 1989: 80). For most lay people, acquiring merit has more to do with improving one's station in their current life, and future lives when reborn, than it does with achieving *nibbana*.

Theravada Buddhism stresses the importance of the concept of impermanence and the ever changing nature of the world. "For practical purposes, Buddhism views the universe as an eternal process in which worlds, and individuals in them, rise and pass away in endless succession and in infinite numbers" (King 1964: 37). The feature of impermanence has been associated with kings and political players in the region often taking a wait-and-see attitude as a change in power structure in the future was considered inevitable and did not need to be rushed by overly hasty actions (Stuart-Fox 2003: 31–2). Davids (1894: 88) explained the Buddhist belief that

> The whole kosmos – earth, and heavens, and hells – is always tending to renovation or destruction; is always in a course of change, a series of revolutions, or of cycles, of which the beginning and the end alike are unknowable and unknown.

The concept of impermanence and constant change would appear to conflict with the concept of one's fate having been fixed due to one's *kamma* earned in previous lives. King (1964: 19) explained how Buddhist beliefs blend these two seemingly contradictory concepts together, "to a great extent my present existence is filled with and determined by my past, yet each moment is new and contains elements of freedom with that newness."

Doctrinal Theravada Buddhism stresses enlightenment coming from within and downplays any associations with magical occurrences. However, Theravada

Buddhism as practiced by the majority of lay people is filled with prayers directed toward images of the Buddha, magical objects, protective amulets, and a belief in a multitude of spirits.

This mixture of Buddhism and belief in spirits has been reported by a number of observers, for example, "Buddhism as a pure theology provides little practical guidance for the everyday uncertainties of love, fertility and death, and hence humans seek clues to the future and solicit assistance through magical objects, or people such as spirit mediums" (Evans 2002: 12); "Buddhism, the nominal religion of the Laos, absolutely forbids any worship of the evil spirits … Yet all the Laos people worship the spirits, and the Buddhist monks themselves are very often the leaders in the worship" (Freeman 1910: 45); and "A belief in supernormal powers, magic, and the existence of supernatural beings is an integral part of the life of lay Buddhists in Burma" (Kaw 2005: 150).

Although the Buddha apparently did not himself focus on metaphysical issues, there are various heavens and hells described in some of the Buddhist canons but these are not endless existences as is the case with Christian and Muslim versions. Instead, inhabitants of the various heavens and hells also eventually die and are reborn; there is also support in some of the Buddhist scriptures for the belief in the existence of ghosts and spirits (Dhammapia 2003). There continues to be a divergence of opinion about the role of magical phenomena in Buddhism, with some Buddhist scholars condemning many popular Buddhist practices as superstitions, which the Buddha preached against following (Jackson 2003: 129). There is the Theravada Buddhism of the monks and Buddhist theologians, which is a path of enlightenment through one's individual effort; this coexists with the Theravada Buddhism of the common people, which includes prayers to spirits, wearing of protective amulets, and various other elements that conflict with the actual teachings of the Buddha.

Curtis (1903: 224) believed Buddhism made inroads into Southeast Asia as it did not require converts to drop old beliefs and superstitions, while Christianity did not have success in gaining converts in the region as Christianity required the acceptance of a single god and the denouncing of traditional spiritual practices. Therefore, the populations of Southeast Asia were able to "convert" to Buddhism without having to abandon their traditional animist practices.

In Christianity, the ultimate religious goal to be attained in one's life is to reach heaven after death. In Theravada Buddhism, the ultimate goal is to reach *nibbana*. In Christianity, it is generally believed one has a single life and therefore only one chance to reach heaven. However, in Theravada Buddhism, with its belief in rebirth, one can make progress toward the ultimate goal with the hope that further progress in future lives will help to achieve *nibbana* and therefore the current existence is not an all-or-nothing affair and will not necessarily result in achieving the ultimate goal or being considered a failure. There are varying degrees of success that can be obtained. Therefore, lay people can postpone seeking *nibbana* in this life without rejecting it as their ultimate goal (Kaw 2005: 36).

The concept of what exactly to expect upon reaching *nibbana* is not clear. Sometimes it is described as complete annihilation and the end of the cycle of rebirth, while at other times it is described as a great calm in which all passion and desire have been extinguished (Dhammapia 2003: 39; Sauder 1922: 8). Dhammapia (2003: 25) claimed the term *nibbana* is a Pali form of the verb, *nibbanti*, which means to be extinguished or blown out, as in a candle light that has been blown out. However, "the exact meaning of *Nibbana* has not been settled in Buddhism" (Dhammapia 2003: 2).

Dhammapia (2003: 49) made the case that there are some fundamental differences in the concept of *nibbana* found in Buddhism's two main branches. Followers of Theravada Buddhism generally see *nibbana* as a potential that can be reached through self-discipline and meditation, while followers of Mahayana Buddhism are more likely to think of *nibbana* as something already inside everyone and reaching *nibbana* is thought of as a return to one's original and true condition. Nevertheless, both branches of Buddhism emphasize *nibbana* is the freedom from illusion and ignorance.

Dhammapia (2003) found that from a Buddhist point of view, *nibbana* can not be adequately explained by the use of words and needs to be experienced to be understood, and the primary path to that understanding comes through meditation.

While debatable, a case could be made that the core Buddhist belief that has the most impact on the day-to-day lives of ordinary people living in the Theravada Buddhist countries of Southeast Asia is the teaching of the "middle path" and the avoidance of extremes. Although this concept originally came from the Buddha's teachings to his followers to avoid both "the extremes of an austere asceticism and a spirit of worldliness" (Saunder 1922: 37) in order to reach enlightenment, the concept also has application in secular life. Generally, in western society, being extremely ambitious is thought of as a virtue; however, this is not necessarily the case in the Theravada Buddhist countries of Southeast Asia, although on the other hand being lazy is also looked down upon. Wealth and material possessions are coveted worldwide; however, within the region it is not considered good manners to openly express the concept that one is overly concerned with financial matters. In daily practice, the middle path means to be serious in one's work and studies, but not too serious, and to ensure one also enjoys one's life. It means one should be virtuous, but one does not have to be without sin.

The concept of the middle path fits well into the overall Buddhist teachings which emphasize impermanence and the near endless series of lives one has through rebirths. Believing everything is going to change, in an often unpredictable manner, can result in individuals having a fairly low locus of control and since one believes one does not have absolute control over the future, or the present due to past *kamma*, there is little reason to expend extreme amounts of effort to "get ahead." However, Theravada Buddhists generally believe they do have some level of control over their present and future situations and therefore they do not entirely leave their present and future situations up to fate (Harvey 2007). They are therefore often inclined to follow the middle path and work for the future, but not become overly obsessed with working toward material success. This moderation in ambition in the indigenous population has often been cited as the primary reason that Chinese and other minorities whose ambitions are not moderated by religious beliefs often dominate business activities in the region.

Buddhism teaches life continues not for a single lifetime, but for a multitude of lives and spiritual development follows one life after another. This belief can often create a lack of urgency in individuals (King 1964: 35–6). If one does not reach *nibbana* or one of the Buddhist heavens, or a rebirth at the top end of society at the end of this life, there is still a chance during the next life or the one after that and so on. Again, this fits into the concept of the middle path. Buddhist teachings stress the importance of moving forward, but there is no need to rush to achieve the goal, instead one should take the middle path and one will eventually get there.

The concept of the middle path has also driven the political history of the region. For example, "While Buddhist ideology tolerates the use of force when necessary, the ideal is to govern through non-violence" (Goh 2007: 48), and the idea that rulers need to follow the middle path and find a balance between being harsh, cruel, and hated, and being soft and not respected, has been around in the region for a considerable amount of time (Goh 2007: 56).

It can be speculated the concept of much of one's present life being pre-determined by one's *kamma*, the belief in the impermanence of all things, the teaching of the middle path or moderation in all things, as well as the belief in the influence of spirits and "magic" may result in the population of the Theravada Buddhism countries in Southeast Asia having a relatively lower locus of control than populations in most other regions of the world. Personal observation would appear to indicate individuals, including business managers and owners, are more reactive and less proactive than is advocated in Western societies. It would appear to be highly likely that the religious and philosophical beliefs associated with Theravada Buddhism contribute to this relatively more reactive behavior in professional situations which has been observed in the region.

Theravada Buddhism values in secular life

It would appear the influence of Theravada Buddhism has had a significant impact on the evolution of the cultures found in these four countries. Boyd and Richerson (2005: 6) wrote, "Culture is information capable of affecting individuals' behavior that they acquire from other members of their species by teaching, imitation, and other forms of social transmission." Boyd and Richerson also made a strong case that the evolution of culture comes from both learning arising from individual innovations as well as copying behaviors and beliefs of the majority without analysis. Therefore culture is a combination of constant change and holding on to traditions; and "Religion, often the most traditional of cultural elements, provides a ready example of the continued hold of tradition on cultures" (Kamrava 1999: 9).

Therefore, religions worldwide are often instruments used to justify the status quo and reinforce the social hierarchy, and some elements of Theravada Buddhism make this especially true in Southeast Asia.

> Karma [*kamma*] as an inexorable natural law of moral cause and effect provided an explanation for both individual fortune and social status. The king ruled as king because through previous lifetimes he had accumulated the necessary karma to do so. In this way karma powerfully reinforced social hierarchy, for everyone was born into the social situation they deserved.
>
> (Stuart-Fox 2003: 32)

King (1964: 64, 231) also expressed the idea that *kamma* results in reinforcing the existing social hierarchy and allows individuals to ignore the plight of the poor with a clear conscience. Stuart-Fox (2002: 10) reflected on the connection between political office and social status and how religious merit was used as a justification for acceptance of the power and arbitrary decisions of various rulers in Laos. Jackson (2003) claimed Theravada Buddhism has a long tradition of supporting the existing social order in Thailand. While Kaw (2005: 108–49) reported on how the military junta in Myanmar/Burma use Buddhist teachings to instill a sense of obedience to authority in order to control expressions of dissent.

While Theravada Buddhism teachings are often used to support non-democratic and non-egalitarian practices, individuals at the top of the hierarchy have social obligations and other responsibilities as well. Davids (1894: 146–7) listed the responsibilities under Theravada Buddhism of both masters and servants, while Evans (2002: 105) described how the concept of constant change also influenced the social hierarchy, and those at the top of the social hierarchy distribute wealth, dispense patronage, and continuously display their status to reinforce the image that they are not in the process of losing *kamma* in this life. The Theravada Buddhism concept of *kamma* gained in previous lives determining the social order of the present is moderated somewhat by the concept of constant change. Therefore it is not surprising the organizations and businesses found in the Theravada Buddhist countries of Southeast Asia are more hierarchical in nature than is the norm in Western organizations. However, to think of workers and farmers who make up the majority of the populations as extremely docile and unquestionably accepting of their fate would not be accurate either. Theravada Buddhist ideology provides justification for individuals to begin life at different stations in life, as well as justification for changes in individual fortune as life proceeds.

In the majority of the different sects of the monolithic religions there is a clear separation between clergy and lay people and one does not become a part of the ordained clergy without years of study. Moreover, traditionally the majority of the clergy came from the segments of society that were able to afford to provide advanced education to their sons. However, while many aspects of Theravada Buddhism are hierarchical in nature, joining the *Sangha*, the order of Buddhist monks which could be considered to be more of less the equivalent to the clergy found in Christianity and Islam, is very egalitarian. All males, from members of royalty to the poorest boy in the most remote village, have the same right to join the *Sangha* and in theory would be treated equally.

While joining the clergy or a monastery in Christianity is generally considered a lifelong calling/occupation, this is not necessarily the case in Theravada Buddhism. While many do join the *Sangha* for life, many others join for temporary periods, which traditionally was for a single rainy season of around three months (Dautremer 1913: 83), but now is often as short as seven days. Therefore the separation between being a part of the clergy and a lay person is not so great and having spent time in the *Sangha* has traditionally been considered part of the process of moving from childhood into manhood.

Since joining the *Sangha* is limited to males in Southeast Asia, although ordination of females is allowed in Theravada Buddhism in Sri Lanka (Ekachai 2008), Theravada Buddhism is often thought of as a patriarchal religion. However, for lay people, women have traditionally played a very important religious role that may account for the success in the spreading of Theravada Buddhism across Asia (Andaya 2002). The prominent role of women in Theravada Buddhist societies, at least among the common people, was noticed by visitors in the early twentieth century (Dautremer 1913).

Theravada Buddhism would seem to play a significant role in shaping attitudes about work and the pursuit of material wealth of the citizens of the region. Theravada Buddhist beliefs have been proposed by some scholars as a contributing factor in the relative poverty of the region (Piker 1993). For many followers of Theravada Buddhism, religion and material wealth go hand in hand, with some adherents believing material wealth is a goal of collecting *kamma* in both this present life and future lives (King 1964). This belief that being virtuous can have both material and spiritual rewards contrasts with the ideology that permeates in many Western societies about the separation between spiritual and secular life. In the Theravada Buddhist nations of Southeast Asia, religious philosophy has an impact on nearly all the behaviors of much of the population; however, because of the emphasis on the middle path, that influence should not be thought of as promoting extreme piety.

It is proposed the influence of Theravada Buddhism encourages the creation of the following five features in organizations, politics, and personal lives in the region: (1) hierarchical, but paternalistic in nature; (2) flexibility; (3) a low locus of control; (4) moderation and taking the middle path; and (5) a focus on the individual. While these features are found in other locations to varying degrees, it is felt the unique combination of these ingredients that are used in the variations of recipes used in life in the Theravada Buddhist countries gives life and work in the region a distinct flavor unlike that tasted in other locations.

3 Cambodia

Khmer history

In the nineteenth century, Adams (1879: 171) wrote, "Unhappy is the Cambodian! Hemmed in between the Siamese on the one hand, and the Annamites
[Vietnamese] on the other." But it has not always been that way. At one time the
Khmers (Cambodians) were at the top of the regional hierarchy and created the
first major political power and advanced civilization in Southeast Asia (Jumsai
2001: 17–19).

The details of the pre-historical period of life in the lands that make up the
Cambodia of today remain mostly unknown to historians (Chandler 2000: 9), but
it appears humans have been living in the area surrounding the Tonle Sap in
present-day Cambodia for at least tens of thousands of years; however, it is
unknown if the original human inhabitants were ancestors of the present-day
Khmers. However, the evidence does suggest Khmer-Mon people have lived in
the area since at least the third century BC (Tully 2005: 7–8). By the first century
AD, the people living in present-day Cambodia had created a high-level civilization patterned on the Indian model (Tully 2005: 8); but it should be kept in mind
that "Indian influence in Cambodia was not imposed by colonization or by force.
Indian troops never invaded Cambodia, and if individual Indians enjoyed high
status, as they often did, it was partly by convincing local people that they
deserved it" (Chandler 2000: 12). Prior to the creation of the Angkor Kingdom,
a nation referred to as Funan was reported to have existed and offered tribute to
China; however, it is most likely that Funan was not a united kingdom but a
group of loosely connected tribes that banded together to make tribute in order
to fit into the Chinese worldview and therefore facilitate international trade
(Chandler 2000: 15).

The Angkor period is usually marked as starting in AD 802 and ending in 1431
(Chandler 2000: 29); however, recent research on the sediment profiles of the
moats surrounding Angkor Wat appears to indicate that a large-scale organized
workforce was in the area long after the date normally provided as the end of
that period (Penny et al. 2007). There is some ambiguity over the length, beginning, and ending of arguably the region's greatest civilization, and ambiguity
has continued to be an integral feature of the history, politics, and daily lives of

individuals in the Theravada Buddhist countries of Southeast Asia up until the present.

King Jayavarman II is considered the founder of the Angkor Kingdom. Not much is known of this monarch and there are no known inscriptions that he authorized still in existence today. Nor is the motivation for moving the kingdom from the Mekong Valley to the northwest region adjoining the Tonle Sap known. However, it has been reported that Jayavarman II performed some type of ritual where he became a "universal monarch," and that he reigned for almost 50 years and founded a lasting dynasty that was to become one of the most advanced in the world during its existence (Chandler 2000: 34; Jumsai 2001: 19; Tully 2005: 15, 20).

By the late eleventh century AD, the Angkor Kingdom had become politically fragmented, and then Suryavarman II came to power and reunited the kingdom. Suryavarman II is best known as the ruler who commissioned the building of the world-famous Angkor Wat, which is the great symbol of Khmer power and whose image can today be seen on the country's currency and national flag. Angkor Wat was built in devotion to the Hindu god, Vishnu, and was not completed until 1150, after the death of Suryavarman II (Chandler 2000: 49–50; Tully 2005: 26).

Life in Angkor and the attitudes of its citizens were most likely quite different from what is seen today in modern Cambodia; however, the builders of Angkor are believed to be the direct ancestors of the Khmers of the twenty-first century. The majority of the population of Angkor were slaves; however, slavery during that time period appears to have been quite nuanced, not all slaves fell into a single category and absolute control by a master was apparently not universal. Evidence indicates that both pre-Angkor and Angkor societies were split into the elites, who understood Sanskrit, at least in its written form, and the masses, who only understood the Khmer language. As no popular literature of the period has survived, what is known about Angkor almost entirely comes from the elite's perspective. Angkor was a multi-ethnic empire that was dominated by a single ethnic group, the Khmers (Chandler 2000: 21, 23, 47, 48; Tully 2005: 17, 21).

By the end of the twelfth century, Jayavarman VII came to power and a major shift from Hinduism toward Mahayana Buddhism took place. It is thought that the Angkor Kingdom reached its zenith during Jayavarman VII's reign, with the empire extending throughout Southeast Asia into the present-day countries of Myanmar/Burma, Laos, Thailand, and Vietnam. Many impressive structures were built during this period, including the incredible Bayon found at Angkor Thom. The Bayon was initially built as a Buddhist structure, a fact that was not rediscovered until the 1920s due to the subsequent reworking of the structure in order to hide its Buddhist origins by more traditional Hindu elements of the Empire in the years following the death of Jayavarman VII. Angkor might have been the largest city in the pre-industrial world, with evidence the population might have been as high as one million (Chandler 2000: 56, 61, 67; Sharrock 2009; Tully 2005: 26–7, 39, 44).

"The largest change affecting Cambodia in the thirteenth century was the conversion of most of the people to the Theravada variant of Buddhism" (Chandler

2000: 68). This conversion may have been the result of an increasing number of Tai speakers into the regions controlled by Angkor and the influence of Mon Buddhist missionaries. While Theravada Buddhism had many features in common with Mahayana Buddhism as practiced at the time in Angkor, there were also some differences. Theravada Buddhism taught that one's own actions carried out while living a humble and modest life would lead to *nibbana*, while Mahayana Buddhism placed more emphasis on achieving *nibbana* via appeals to various *bodhisattvas*, or "Buddhist saints" for want of a better term (Chandler 2000, 69: Tully 2005: 39).

The demise of Angkor is a mystery that has not been solved to the satisfaction of all historians. The Siamese (Thais), who had previously been vassals of the Khmers, apparently launched a large-scale and successful assault on Angkor around 1431, which seems to have played a part in the moving of the capital of the Khmer civilization to Phnom Penh. Other factors given for the decline of Angkor include ecological degradation and the impact of Theravada Buddhism on the population. Although conventional wisdom has been that Angkor was suddenly abandoned, evidence indicates that Angkor Thom was only abandoned in 1629, nearly 200 years after the attacks by the Siamese, and other parts of Angkor were rebuilt as late as 1747 (Tully 2005: 17, 49; Vickery 2004).

From the beginning of the fourteenth century until the middle of the sixteenth century, there are very few surviving inscriptions of life in the Khmer Kingdom. Although decline is the common term used to refer to this time period, Chandler (2000: 78–9) cautioned against taking an overly negative view of the era. Change from a centralized political structure that built massively in stone to a more decentralized political system may not have had a seriously negative effect on the majority of the population even if it makes this later period of less interest to historians and archeologists. However, the loss of the Saigon (Prey Nokor) and the Mekong Valley in the 1620s to the Nguyen (Vietnamese) had the effect of cutting off the Khmer Kingdom from maritime trade, which weakened the country politically and may have resulted in Cambodia losing some sovereignty to its two neighbors, Vietnam and Thailand. In general, Cambodia's historical relations with Thailand have been different and less confrontational than its relations with Vietnam, which may be attributed to the sharing of a common religion. It has been speculated that the current situation, where the majority of the Khmer population are mostly occupied with activities related to agriculture, monastic life, and roles in the government, and where most commercial activities are carried out by ethnic minorities, can be traced back to the days before French colonization and can be partially attributed to the conversion of the population to Theravada Buddhism (Chandler 2000: 77, 95, 100, 115; Tully 2005: 56, 62).

The French colonial period of Indochina began in 1858 when French marines came ashore near Saigon under the pretense of protecting French Catholic missionaries and Vietnamese converts to Catholicism; the Vietnamese military forces were no match for a modern European army and the French military victory set the stage for the mission of protection that would evolve into outright occupation. The French established a protectorate in Cambodia in 1863 and this gradually evolved through various stages into Cambodia becoming a fully fledged French colony. At first, the French preferred to rule through the traditional system; however, King Norodom proved to be a less than reliable puppet and was in 1884 forced under the threat of physical harm to revise the original treaty giving France complete control over administrative, judicial, and commercial matters (Chandler 2000: 137; Tully 2005: 80–8).

The French ruled and viewed Cambodia through a colonial prism and Cambodian opinions were mostly discounted. Most of the French literature of the colonial era takes a romantic view of the Khmer people and refers to them as lazy, obedient, and in need of French protection. The costs of running the colony in Cambodia were consistently higher than the income it provided and this fact was often blamed by the French on the Cambodian royal family and local administrators. King Norodom was blamed by the French for holding up reforms; however, after 40 years a new ruler, King Sisowath, came to power and modernization progressed somewhat under programs including those to abolish slavery, update the legal code, limit corruption, create a civil service workforce hired by merit, and improve the nation's infrastructure. Similar to what was seen in Laos, over time a significant number of Vietnamese become important in the administration of the country, which may have been a factor in developing a stronger sense of Cambodian nationalism that became more evident in the twentieth century (Chandler 2000: 139; Tully 2005: 88, 92, 103).

Up until the time of World War II, there was not a substantial anti-French Cambodian national movement, yet there was an uprising against the French of considerable scale in 1885–86 that required the French to back down on some demands for reforms in exchange for King Norodom's support in restoring peace and stability. Most rural Khmers had no direct dealing with the French and complaints were mostly directed at local Khmer administrators, not toward the central government controlled by the foreigners. The image of Cambodia during French rule that most likely springs to mind in western observers is of a peaceful backwater filled with charming peasants. But, there was also a dark side to the period as the French allowed the police to use brutal methods, squeezed the population through heavy taxes, and brought in Vietnamese civil servants to run much of the day-to-day government operations, therefore lessening the opportunities for Khmers to advance professionally and gain skills while under French rule. While it is popular these days to demonize all aspects of the colonial rule in Asia and other locations, the population of Cambodia probably increased four-fold during the period of French rule, which would appear to indicate the country made significant "progress" in the fields of health, agriculture, and other areas that were needed to support a larger population during this period (Chandler 2000: 4; Tully 2005: 89, 97, 99, 103).

World War II was obviously a turning point for colonialism in Asia, and this was also true in Cambodia. The Japanese controlled Indochina through the existing French administration until March 9, 1945 when the Japanese military government easily crushed the French resulting in the Japanese government decreeing the independence of the Asian nations under its control, possibly to gain allies in a final attempt to come to some form of victory, or at least a stalemate in the war. King Sihanouk was placed on the throne in 1941 because the French believed they could easily manipulate this young and inexperienced member of the royal family. In 1945, he declared Cambodia's independence as directed by Tokyo. However, after the war finally ended, the French quickly returned (Chandler 2000: 167; Tully 2005: 104, 109–10).

The defeat of the British, French, and American colonial powers by the Japanese, albeit temporary, destroyed the myth of the superiority of the "white man." However, this was not immediately evident to the government leaders in Europe. The French attempted to reestablish their position as colonial master in Indochina after the end of World War II; however, resistance to a return to the old order was fierce and, following the French military defeat by Vietnamese forces at the Battle of Dien Bien Phu in 1954, the French reluctantly agreed to the conditions of the peace conference held in Geneva in 1954. The Franco-Khmer treaty of 1949 established Cambodia as an independent nation within the French Union; however, Cambodia's sovereignty was severely restricted under this treaty. Sihanouk began his royal crusade for independence in March 1953 and, by October of the same year, the French approved the right of the king to have authority over Cambodia's armed forces, judiciary, and foreign affairs. On November 9, 1953, the last French troops left Cambodia and independence was finally recognized on July 21, 1954 (Chandler 2000: 172, 177, 185; Tully 2005: 81, 103, 117, 119, 121).

A limited form of democratic-style politics began in Cambodia prior to independence and King Sihanouk was an active participant. The political party called the Democrats won a resounding victory in 1951 over the Liberals, who were supported by the King and the French. Shortly after this first attempt at democracy in Cambodia, a coup was launched against the Democrat government of Huy Kanthoul, who was removed from power, and Sihanouk again became the dominant figure in Cambodia's political life. Afterwards, Sihanouk was able to take the lion's share of the credit for Cambodia gaining its independence from France and Sihanouk leveraged this popularity into political power. In 1955, Sihanouk abdicated his throne in order to be able to directly run the country and the next period of political life in Cambodia was dominated by this single larger than life figure (Chandler 2000: 188–9; Tully 2005: 114, 117, 121, 128–9, 132).

Independence most probably meant little to the average person residing in Cambodia's villages. Life went on pretty much the same as before, and the common man believed politics were the concerns of the city and elites, and who ran the country had little to no effect on the lives of the vast majority. However, this was about to change, and the worldwide competition between the forces of market economies and democracies and the forces of communist ideology soon affected the entire population of the country. Initially, Sihanouk accepted US military aid but, in a major shift in policy in 1963, stopped receiving US aid in an attempt to appear neutral. Although some of the funding gap was picked up by China, this decision had major economic consequences for the nation. Sihanouk broke off diplomatic relations with the United States in 1965 and then entered into a secret alliance with the North Vietnamese in 1966. Slowly Sihanouk's iron grip on the nation began to slip and, on March 17, 1970, a coup took place that overthrew the government and a new government with Lon Nol as the head was formed. The National Assembly quickly made the change in government official and Sihanouk was no longer in control (Chandler 187, 191, 194, 200, 204; Tully 2005: 145, 148; 151).

Sihanouk, Communist China, and Communist North Vietnam quickly placed the blame for the coup on the United States and labeled Lon Nol as nothing but a Central Intelligence Agency (CIA) puppet. The coup opened a major rift in Cambodian society between those who supported the coup and opposed communism, and those who opposed the coup, mostly because of support for Sihanouk and the institution of the royal family, not necessarily because of support for Sihanouk's communist allies. By 1970, the influence of the communist party of Cambodia had increased rapidly and it was at the time controlling around 20 percent of the nation's territory. Only a week after the coup that caused his ouster, Sihanouk announced the formation of the National United Front of Kampuchea, which joined forces with the Khmer Rouge in the battle for the country. Although the leadership of the Khmer Rouge was dominated by hard-line communists, most support for the removal of the Lon Nol government was due to support for Sihanouk. The Lon Nol government had a number of weaknesses and, when a stroke robbed the government of the full facilities of its leader, problems mounted (Chandler 2000: 202, 296; Tully 2005: 154–8).

The war began to go badly for the Lon Nol Government and Phnom Penh fell to the communists on April 17, 1975. Within hours of taking over the city, the Khmer Rouge ordered the entire population of approximately 2 million in Phnom Penh to leave their homes and go to the countryside to begin growing rice. Democratic Kampuchea was formed and the Khmer Rouge ruled, or more accurately misruled, the country from April 1975 until January 1979. Prince Sihanouk was made the first head of state under the Khmer Rouge but was given no real power and, by 1976, he was forced to retire. On the day of the conquest of the Cambodian capital, Pol Pot issued the following eight points that emphasized the radical nature of the new rulers: evacuate people from all towns, abolish all markets, abolish the use of the Lon Nol regime's currency (and delay the issuing of the revolutionary currency that had already been printed), defrock all Theravada Buddhist monks and force them to labor alongside all others, execute all leaders of the old regime, establish cooperatives with communal eating as a major feature, expel all Vietnamese from the country, and dispatch troops to the Vietnamese border. It is impossible to know exactly how many people died due to the policies of the Khmer Rouge, but Tully believed 1.7 million was a reasonable estimate (Chandler 2000, 208–11; Tully 2005, 172, 178).

The brutality of the Khmer Rouge has been well documented, and it is felt there is no need to go into all the details in this volume. Furthermore, the debate about the cause of the Khmer Rouge's brutality has been an intensely emotional topic of debate with many with rather leftist political orientations placing the blame squarely on the shoulders of the US bombing campaigns in Southeast Asia prior to the Khmer Rouge's takeover (for an example, see Model 2005). Taking an opposing view, Eanes (2002) thought it was the mixture of a radical and untested communist ideology alongside various domestic factors that led to such awful consequences. Ear (1995) exposed the strong support many members of Western academia gave to the Khmer Rouge during the initial stages of its rule and speculated this support may have contributed to the outside world failing to respond rapidly to this tragedy. It is unlikely that any one factor can be singled out as the cause of this horrible period in time and it appears unlikely that the causes of the massacres and misguided policies can be identified to the satisfaction of all individuals at the present.

Although the Khmer Rouge attempted to isolate the country from the outside world, international political struggles would again change the country's history. Because of the constant purges of members of the Cambodian communist party, many members of the military and government, including Heng Samrin and Hun Sen, fled to Vietnam and began working with the Vietnamese to affect regime change back in Cambodia. Vietnam and its main ally, the Soviet Union, felt threatened by the expansion of Chinese influence in Southeast Asia (China was the Khmer Rouge's major backer) and on Christmas Day 1978 the Vietnamese military launched a well-planned and well-executed, lightening-quick attack that overran the Khmer Rouge's military forces and resulted in Vietnamese control of most of the country within three weeks (Chandler 2000: 222–5; Pribbenow 2006; Stuart-Fox 2003: 199; Tully 2005: 192–3).

While the overthrow of the Khmer Rouge ended this nightmarish period, the Vietnamese occupation of the country did not create the conditions needed for rapid economic growth and expansion. The establishment of a pro-Soviet Vietnamese regime in Cambodia upset the balance of power in Southeast Asia, which alarmed the United States, Thailand, China, and other ASEAN countries. This alarm resulted in outside influences keeping the Khmer Rouge alive as well as providing international support to opponents of the Vietnamese-backed government, including the remnants of the Khmer Rouge, in order to weaken the Vietnamese position in Southeast Asia. The new Vietnamese-controlled government led by Heng Samrin attempted to rebuild the country and actually spent considerable sums of money, even though this was a drain on Vietnam as at the time the Vietnamese economy was in disarray (Jeldres 1993: 105; Stuart-Fox 2003: 201; Tully 2005: 202, 209, 216).

In 1982, two non-communist groups joined with the Khmer Rouge to create the Coalition Government of Democratic Kampuchea, which was supported, both financially and diplomatically, by the United States, China, and ASEAN, and occupied Cambodia's United Nations (UN) seat despite being controlled by Khmer Rouge leadership. However, over time, the power of the Khmer Rouge faded away. The Vietnamese control over Cambodia also gradually declined throughout the 1980s and, with the ending of the cold war, led to the UN (UNTAC) mission that began in the country in 1992. The UNTAC mission was to help in the transfer of control from the Vietnamese-dominated government to a democratically elected Khmer government. This mission had a significant number of problems, attributed to the bureaucratic nature of the UN, the lack of Asian and Cambodian experience of the UN staff, and the perception of the locals of the arrogant and extravagant behavior of the UN staff, largely due to the huge income difference between the UN-paid foreigners and the local population (Chandler 2000: 228; Jeldres 1993).

The UN sponsored elections and the results could be considered unique and somewhat confusing. In 1993, over four million Cambodians went to the polls, but no single party gained a majority. FUNCINPEC, a loose coalition centered around a royalist theme, won the most votes but not a majority, while the party in power, the Cambodian People's Party (CPP), finished in second place. However, the ruling CPP refused to give up power. In a compromise that can only be considered bizarre, the UN approved a power-sharing plan where there were two governments, one led by First Prime Minister Ranariddh and FUNCINPEC, and another government led by Second Prime Minister Hun Sen and the CPP. The UN, after spending so much money and time to rebuild the country, moved out with Cambodia still divided and left it up to the Khmer people to sort out the situation. Hun Sen and the CPP controlled the military and therefore it is not surprising that in the end the Second Prime Minister was able to oust the First Prime Minister and take control of the nation (Tully 2005: 221–6).

Since that time, the CPP and Hun Sen have strengthened their grip on power and have won elections that appear to reflect the will of the people. While Hun Sen and the CPP have been targets of extreme criticism in the Western media, they have been able to guide the country through extremely turbulent times toward something resembling peace and stability, and they will likely be the dominant political force in the country for some time to come (Chandler 2000: 244; Downie and Kingsbury 2001; Header 2005).

Business and economic environment

General features

Cambodia is not a small country in a geographical sense, however its population is only around 13 million, with the population mostly living in rural areas (Tully 2005: 4). The vast majority of the country follows the Theravada form of Buddhism and extensive efforts by Christian missionaries to convert the population have met with very limited success. However, a large percentage of the commercial activities in the country are directed by people with ethnic Chinese or Vietnamese ancestry and ethnic tensions have been an important component driving Cambodia's recent history and business environment (Tully 2005: 2–6, 101).

The business and political environment of Cambodia has been shaped to a large extent by Cambodian's attitudes toward hierarchies and hierarchical relationships.

For most of Cambodian history, it seems, people in power were thought (by themselves and nearly everyone else) to be more meritorious than other people. Despite some alterations, this belief remained essentially unchanged between Cambodia's Indianized phase and the onset of Theravada Buddhism.

(Chandler 2000: 2)

The image of Cambodia that might be most prevalent in the world is one of extreme poverty and devastation left in the aftermath of the Khmer Rouge's rule; however, there have been considerable advances made in both political reconstruction and economic policies as the country has moved from being a centrally planned economy to one more or less based on market principles (Mahmood 2005: 1).

Economic conditions

In 2007, Cambodia was estimated to have experienced a very respectable 9.6 percent increase in GDP and an 11 percent average growth over a three-year period. The textiles, tourism, and construction sectors have been driving the economic growth and, while productivity in rice production has increased slightly, a decline in growth in harvesting of forestry products and the fishery industry has slowed overall growth in the agricultural sector. Inflation for 2007 was around 5.9 percent and the budget deficit was 3.2 percent of GDP, showing some government restraint in the use of monetary and fiscal policies. A number of structural reforms to improve the business environment based on international recommendations have been implemented, including the Commercial Arbitration Law of 2006, Law on Secured Transactions, and other laws designed to improve the ability of the financial sector to effectively serve the needs of the country (Asian Development Bank 2008b: 195–7). There is also a thriving informal sector of the economy that includes significant amounts of cross-border trade and therefore the accuracy of economic data collected in Cambodia is questionable (Roman 2004).

While the good economic news should not be discounted, there are still severe problems in the Cambodian economy and many obstacles for private industries to overcome in order to create quality jobs that can help fuel the economy and lessen the impact of poverty on the citizens of the country. The poor are overwhelmingly living in agricultural families, the agricultural sector of the economy has not experienced rapid long-term growth, and the average yields of Cambodia's rice harvest are the lowest in Southeast Asia. Literacy rates and educational levels in Cambodia are relatively low and many rural people work as unpaid agricultural workers on family farms, and this is especially true for women. Only about 15 percent of the total labor force works for wages. Furthermore, the industrial sector is highly dependent upon garment manufacturing, which makes up almost half of the sector (Mahmood 2005).

Poverty, while in decline, continues to be a major concern for Cambodia due to the lack of diversification of the country's industrial sector, which limits job

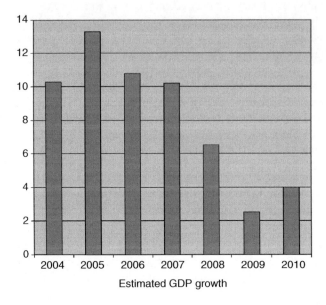

Figure 3.1 Cambodia's estimated annual GDP growth (%).

growth. Ninety percent of Cambodia's citizens live in rural areas, and poor infrastructure makes it difficult for rapid growth in these places. Also, a weakening global economy could harm the tourism industry and dampen foreign investment, which are key factors in the nation's economic development (Asian Development Bank 2008b: 195–7). Moreover, there have been some concerns expressed about the sustainability and unequal distribution within the country of income that is derived from tourism, an important and growing sector of the economy (Kaosa-ard 2006; Prachvuthy 2006).

Business practices

It has been reported that Cambodia is one of the most difficult and expensive countries in Southeast Asia in which to run a business, and Cambodia was given the last place rating in a study of Southeast Asian nations on having an effective business environment (Hasan, Mitra, and Ulubasoglu 2007). In another study of the ten ASEAN countries, Cambodia came in eighth, ahead of Myanmar/Burma and Laos, in managerial performance; ninth in national competitiveness, behind Myanmar/Burma and ahead of Laos; ninth in human resource performance, only ahead of the Philippines; and eighth in technology performance, ahead of only Myanmar/Burma and Laos (Kao *et al.* 2008). Ear (2009) reported that, while on the surface the government policies appear business friendly, the need to pay various forms of informal "taxation" makes doing business in the country difficult and expensive.

The educational sector has also been identified as having a number of challenges to overcome in order to effectively prepare an educated workforce, which will be needed for sustained growth; it has been reported that a low percentage of potential students are actually enrolled, and drop-out rates are high. There remains a pervasiveness of the informal practice of teachers demanding money from their students and the country has a social-cultural environment that does not foster transparency, accountability, and meritocracy; these factors may be contributing to the slow progress being made in improving Cambodia's educational system (Tan 2007).

One sector of the economy that has prospered is the garment sector. The garment sector contributes about 14 percent to the nation's GDP and 80 percent of recorded exports while being directly responsible for approximately 350,000 jobs and indirectly responsible for about an equal number. The garment industry is almost entirely controlled by foreigners, with individuals with direct connections to the government playing relatively minor roles, which is quite different than in many other industries. This lack of heavy involvement of government-connected individuals may result in the industry being more market-based and therefore more efficient than other sectors of the economy (Ear 2009).

Agriculture

Approximately 70 percent of all Cambodians earn their living primarily through agriculture; however, only about 30 percent of the country's GDP comes from this sector. During recent years the agricultural sector has been growing at almost the same pace as the broader economy. Nevertheless, it is in rural agricultural communities where the majority of the country's poverty can still be found. It's expected, from the examples seen in neighboring Thailand and

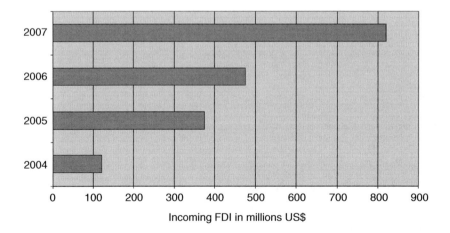

Figure 3.2 Cambodia's annual incoming foreign direct investment (US$).

Vietnam, small-scale family farms will continue to dominate the sector as the country continues down its path toward development. Suggestions for improvements in the agricultural sector include better infrastructure in rural areas, more access to credit, cheaper electricity, access to technical knowledge, and better education (United Nations Development Programme 2007).

The primary crop of Cambodia is rice. Approximately 78 percent of rural households grow rice. While the acreage devoted to rice planting has shrunk in recent years, rice remains the staple crop of the people and has the potential to become an important source of exports for the country. Cambodia has produced lower yields in rice production compared to the neighboring countries of Thailand and Vietnam. This has been attributed to the poor soils found in the country, low levels of technical expertise and research, and a failure to meet international quality standards. Cambodian rice is on average 35 percent broken, while long-grained Thai or Vietnamese rice is only 5 percent broken, resulting in Cambodians receiving lower prices for their exported rice compared to rice producers in other countries (Ear 2009).

Development overview

Cambodia's economic development has undoubtedly been slowed by its tragic history, but it is felt that Cambodia shares some aspects of its business environment with the other nations of Southeast Asia, where the majority of the population follow Theravada Buddhism. While Cambodia has made significant progress in economic development and poverty reduction in recent years, it continues to be one of the most underdeveloped nations in Asia and it is debatable whether the business, economic, and political environment are moving fast enough in a direction to ensure the majority of people in Cambodia will enjoy the same fruits from economic growth as the citizens of other nations in Asia have experienced.

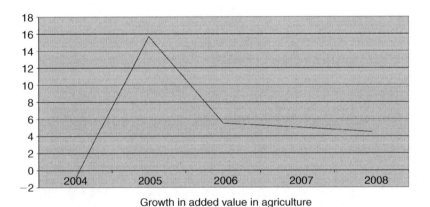

Growth in added value in agriculture

Figure 3.3 Cambodia's annual added value in agriculture growth (%).

Case studies

A Cambodian beverage company

In 1992, an ethnic Chinese Cambodian citizen began a company to join an international beverage import-distribution network. Currently the company imports and distributes a number of internationally branded beverages throughout the country. The company has made attempts at importing and distributing other products, but it has found that by concentrating on what it knows best, beverages, it can turn a profit in this highly competitive industrial sector.

The firm is 100 percent owned by a single owner and is part of a family-owned conglomerate in which different members of the family act as managers of branches using an unrelated diversification strategy. The beverage branch is managed by a son of the owner. Other branches of the company include karaoke nightclubs and hotels. The company feels unrelated diversification helps to reduce risk in the company and the family relies heavily on personal relationships in making business contacts. These business practices of having single-family ownership or control, following an unrelated diversification strategy, and using personal relationships with business networks are common features of ethnic Chinese firms throughout East and Southeast Asia (Carney and Gedai-lovic 2003; Keller and Kronstedt 2005; Shapiro *et al.* 2003; Suehiro and Wailerdsak 2004; Tsang 2001; Yan and Sorenson 2004).

The company competes in a highly competitive industry where price is a very important factor. The company's pricing is not the lowest in the industry; however, the company's competitive strategies include being able to supply a wide range of products (alcoholic and non-alcoholic) with internationally recognized brand names to which the company has exclusive distribution rights. The company competes against a fair number of similar sized firms, as well as against many smaller sized firms, many of which are involved in selling imported beverages while evading the tax system. In fact, the smuggling situation is so extensive that the company does not bother to attempt to distribute into a few of the border provinces as they can not compete against firms that pay no taxes. The company did not create the existing legal environment in Cambodia, which consists of a number of both arbitrarily enforced written laws and unwritten common practices. The managers of the company feel it would be virtually impossible for a company to follow all the written laws to the letter and survive within the current business environment found in the country. The firm also realizes it must retain good relations with government officials in order to conduct business in Cambodia, and maintaining these relationships comes with a price tag.

The company develops long-term relationships with its suppliers and has learned from experience that it is a necessity to have exclusive rights to distribute a particular brand in order to be profitable in the long term. The company uses a pull strategy by working with companies that can supply products with internationally recognized brand names and by promoting the brands locally, but the company believes this strategy needs to be complemented by the push strategy of having enough distribution capacity to ensure the products are on the shelves of as many outlets as possible.

All the firms owned by the family employ between 600 and 700 people in total. The beverage import and distribution branch has approximately 50 full-time staff members and also employs approximately 300 sales promotional staff (e.g., beer girls working the nightclubs and restaurants to convince customers to purchase a particular brand). Recruitment is normally informal and because of the low skill level need for this type of work, turnover is quite high. The company does not currently use any type of formal training program for staff members; instead it relies strictly on on-the-job training. The company was previously actively involved in a government-sponsored and international community-funded training program for the beer girls. The program was designed to provide the girls (who almost universally have little education or marketable skills) with a chance to develop skills needed to move on to more professional types of work, while avoiding being pulled into prostitution. However, as the girls are not full-time employees and the company could not force them to attend the program, only a very low percentage of the girls were willing to give up their free time to attend, and eventually the program faded away.

As manual labor is quite cheap in the country, the firm does not make use of much machinery or modern technology. For example, in the warehouse the company does not use fork trucks. To use fork trucks requires additional space, and the price of warehousing space is rising in Phnom Penh. Also the fork trucks themselves are expensive and fuel and repairs are costlier than using human muscle. However, the firm does supply meals to its full-time staff in addition to a salary as a form of paternalistic management.

The firm has had a lot of financial success and has grown alongside the Cambodian economy. Much of the firm's success was attributed to the patriarch of this one of thousands of rags-to-riches stories found in ethnic Chinese communities throughout Southeast Asia. It was reported the founder of the company has shown strong leadership and determination as well as flexibility and good business judgment. The company believes it is very important to be considered trustworthy within the business network it operates in. The company is looking to the future; the short-term future will definitely involve continuing within the beverage importing and distribution industry, but many international beverage firms are making plans to set up production in Cambodia, which will change the nature of the industry to a considerable extent, and at that time the company will devise a new strategy that may include continuing in the beverage industry or may include changing the focus of the firm. The company is taking a wait-and-see attitude.

It would appear quite evident the firm is hierarchical but paternalistic in nature and also exhibits a high degree of flexibility. While the owners and managers do not appear to have a low locus of control, the behavior of the employees, especially the beer girls, is consistent with having this attribute. While taking the middle path may not be obvious in the actions of the management, it is seen in the behavior of the employees, demonstrated by the beer girls' reluctance to attend after-hour training to enhance their professional opportunities. A considerable focus on the individual is evident, as the firm's policies and strategies are primarily the product of a single individual, the patriarch of the family.

Family-owned tailor shop

Located on a main thoroughfare in downtown Phnom Penh is an ethnic Chinese family-owned tailor shop that specializes in making business suits for men and women. The owner does not participate in the day-to-day management of the company, but her son is the top manager of the firm. Most of the shop's customers are from the local community, but a significant number of sales (approximately 30 percent) are made to foreigners, mainly tourists. The family started in the restaurant business, but seeing the success of a nearby tailor shop, decided to shift focus. The firm makes more men's clothing than women's, and focuses on making value-priced clothing as there is only a very small market for top-of-the-line business suits in Cambodia.

The company focuses on supplying individual walk-in customers as the profit margin for this type of customer is higher than producing shirts or uniforms in batches for special orders. The company does not attempt to make its own fashion designs; instead it relies on pre-existing styles and patterns.

The firm buys the majority of its supplies from abroad, with most supplies coming from Thailand. The company does not develop long-term relationships with suppliers; as an alternative it chooses suppliers by price. There are many direct competitors to the company, and the company mostly competes by keeping its prices competitive without being the absolute lowest, and also by keeping its completion time short (three to five days), while using the firm's very convenient and busy location as its primary marketing and promotional tool.

The company mostly uses informal recruitment and selection procedures. New recruits are mostly friends and family of existing employees and nearly all employees come from the same village outside of the city. This creates a real family atmosphere on the job and the feeling of attachment helps keep employees from seeking out new employment where the pay may be slightly higher. The company has no formal training programs; instead it relies solely on on-the-job training. The firm pays by the piece made, therefore encouraging employees to develop the ability to complete as many pieces of clothing as possible and as quickly as possible.

The company uses simple technology in its work and buys much of its equipment second hand. Although the firm may not be considered innovative or technologically advanced in the traditional sense, the manager of the firm does not lack energy, effort, or ambition. The young manager of the firm has developed a considerable amount of business savvy, evidenced by the growth of the company, and he has long-term plans to go from having a shop to owning a large garment "factory."

The ownership and management relationship with the employees would appear to be consistent with the hierarchical but paternalistic attitude found in other firms in the region. Changing focus from running a restaurant to a tailor shop shows considerable flexibility. The employee's behavior is consistent with having a lower locus of control and following the middle path, and as this is a family-owned and operated business, it is very personal and individualistic in nature.

Yaklom Angkor Lodge & Sawadee Food Garden

The Yaklom Angkor Lodge & Sawadee Food Garden in Siem Reap, Cambodia, as well as the Yaklom Hill Lodge in Ratanakiri, Cambodia, is owned and operated by Ms. Orapin Sritatera, who is a native of Thailand. There is a Khmer partner who owns a share of the operations but who is not actively involved in the day-to-day operations. This partner does, however, help to smooth over relationships with members of the local political and business community.

The business was founded in 1988 when Siem Reap was mostly a destination for adventurous tourists going off the beaten path instead of the major international tourist destination it is today. The business operations of the company include lodging and restaurants. The restaurants primarily serve Thai food, but they also serve some Western food during breakfast time, mainly for the guests staying at the company's guesthouses. This is the first business owned and operated by Ms. Orapin, she had never owned a business in her native country prior to launching this business in Cambodia. Prior to coming to Cambodia, Ms. Orapin worked as a marketing research manager in Thailand and she feels because of this experience she developed the habit of always keeping on the lookout for new business opportunities.

The company operates within the tourist segment of the economy. A large percentage of the company's customers are Thai, estimated at around 50 percent of total customers, with approximately another 20 percent being other foreigners, and the remaining 30 percent of the business comes from Cambodian nationals. The Yaklom Angkor Lodge & Sawadee Guest House has been positioned to attract a slightly upscale clientele, but still priced to be affordable for middle-class Thai tourists, who are known to enjoy a bit of luxury when traveling.

Ms. Orapin did not come to Cambodia to start a new business; instead, she came to accompany her husband who was working for a non-governmental organization (NGO) at the time. Ms. Orapin has said she became a business owner in a foreign country "by accident." In the 1980s, there were few professional positions available in Siem Reap for foreigners, and Ms. Orapin "needed something to do." Therefore, she used her previous training as a marketing research manager to identify an opportunity and used her entrepreneurial spirit to take advantage of the opportunity that was discovered.

The desire for financial rewards was an objective in starting the business, but there were other factors that influenced her decision. Owning a business was a viable solution to the problem of having a career while living in the same location as her husband. Furthermore, she used her position as a business owner to supply her brother, who had previously worked as a restaurant manager in Sri Lanka, with a position inline with his abilities and expectations. Family considerations played a major role in deciding to start this business.

The Yaklom Angkor Lodge & Sawadee Food Garden and its affiliated operations, including the Yaklom Hill Lodge and the Panida Restaurant, are mainly marketed toward Thai customers who are vacationing or on business in Cambodia, but these businesses also portray an international image which can be attractive to not only Thais but also to other foreigners and even to upper-income local customers. It would appear the company is primarily using a differentiation strategy, with its "Thai-ness" as its primary distinguishing feature.

The company does not necessarily see itself as being totally independent, but as part of an interdependent network of Thai-related tourist companies. The company mostly focuses on being a restaurant and guesthouse, while maintaining a close relationship with various Thai travel agencies and transportation companies, as well as local tour guides and souvenir shops. The network provides a complete package for tourists coming to Cambodia, although different components of the network are under different ownership.

Ms. Orapin feels there are a number of important factors a Thai company needs to be aware of to be successful in Cambodia. Understanding the different culture, relying on locals to deal with local problems, knowing the regulations and, above all, being patient were all reported to be critical, and it was reported many of these lessons were learned the hard way. Operating a business in Cambodia was in many respects thought to be very similar to running a business in Thailand: same religion, similar cultures, and both having cuisines built upon rice. On the other hand, many aspects were thought to be quite different because of the differences in economic development and political environment.

Ms. Orapin's brother is the main restaurant manager for the company and a Thai chef is employed to ensure the food is authentic Thai, which its Thai customers demand. The rest of the staff is Khmer. Ms. Orapin speaks fluent Khmer, but sometimes this does not prevent miscommunication as differences in cultural context can lead to misunderstandings. Also, the historical relationships between the Thais and Khmer have created some natural barriers between the Thai owner-manager of the company and its local employees that need to be overcome to ensure good working relationships.

The biggest obstacle to growth and success has been the cyclic and unpredictable nature of the tourism industry. The differences in income between different times of the year can be substantial. However, the family does not solely rely on income from this business and it is therefore easier to weather the ups and downs. Making money is important; however, profitability is not the sole, nor even the primary, reason why the company was founded and continues to operate.

The company has recently expanded and added another restaurant, the Panida Restaurant, to its portfolio of businesses, showing optimism and commitment to doing business in Cambodia. Apparently, the company does not want to grow beyond the size where the family can manage and finance it comfortably. As in so many businesses in the Theravada Buddhist countries of Southeast Asia, there is no separation between ownership and management, and factors other than economic factors affect business decisions. An expanding business requires more managerial energy and commitment; therefore, the amount of time and energy the owner is willing to expend will affect the expansion plans of this firm.

In many ways it appears this business is a one-woman show, which is hierarchical, paternalistic, and very individualistic. Ms. Orapin's moderate goals would be expected of one taking the middle path, and the lack of long-term planning would be consistent with having a relatively lower locus of control where one allows fate to take its course while retaining flexibility to respond to unforeseen events.

4   Laos

History of Laos

As in the rest of the countries of Theravada Buddhist Southeast Asia, the history of Laos and the history of the region can not be separated. It was reported nearly 100 years ago, "Laos is the name of a people, not of a political division" (Freeman 1910: 13); while Stuart-Fox (2002) wrote, "the Lao people have a history, Laos does not." The nations of Laos and Thailand share many qualities and "One wonders why the Thai and the Lao, though two people of different countries speak the same language? Why are both Buddhist? Why do the two people share the same cultural activities?" (Jumsai 2000: 1). In contrast, over a hundred years ago, Curtis (1903: 8) noticed: "Though the Laos and the Siamese are both Shans and have much in common, a stranger would note at once many marked differences in natures, habits, and customs of these two peoples."

Yet, even with a common history, today Laos is an independent country with its own government, and it has a unique place in the world so deserves to be examined in its own right. However, one needs to be aware that Laotian history has recently often been written through a political prism to support Marxist ideology and modern Laotian history, at least what is written in Laos, has had a political agenda with an emphasis on peasant uprisings and has deemphasized the role of royalty and the common cultural connection with the Thais (Gay 2002). It should also be kept in mind that French historians during the colonial era also tended to deemphasize Laos' connection with the people of Thailand in order to justify the annexation of Laos into French Indochina (Jumsai 2000: 6).

A common belief is that the "Tai" people, a linguistic grouping, supposedly originating in the region of southern Guangxi, China, were pressured by an expanding Chinese empire into moving southward. Today members of the Tai linguistic group include a number of "hill tribes" throughout Southeast Asia and Southern China, as well as the lowland majority peoples of the present-day countries of Thailand and Laos (Evans 2002: 2). Legend has it that prior to the coming of the Tai into Laos, giants controlled a kingdom called Sawa in modern day Laos (Phothisane 2002: 83–4). It has often been reported that the Kingdom of Nan Chao, in the present-day Yunnan province of China, was a Tai kingdom (Pholsena 2004: 237; Syamananda 1993: 14). However, the Chinese Chronicles of the period referred to the people living in Nan Chao as the "Payi" or the "Huans" (Jumsai 2000: 8).

The traditional theory of a conquering Tai race emigrating south from China to lay claim to the lands of present-day Laos and Thailand is being challenged, and an alternative explanation is being considered where the origins of the culture and peoples now inhabiting present-day Laos sprang up closer to home in the regions of present-day southern China, northern Vietnam, and upper Laos (Pholsena 2004). Nevertheless, the histories of Thailand and Laos are closely related and "prior to the nineteenth century it makes little sense to use the ethnic terms 'Lao' or 'Thai,' although it is common for national histories to project such entities into the distant past" (Evans 2002: 2).

A legendary figure from Lao mythology is the most famous ruler of Nan Chao, called Khun Borum of Boulom by the Lao and Pilawko by the Chinese, who was reported to have been the ruler from AD 729–49. It has been reported that Khun Borum ruled over a large united kingdom and along with Khun Lo were great kings of Nan Chao. However, subsequent kings were less competent and the kingdom went into steady decline until it was finally crushed during Kublai Khan's conquest of Yunnan in 1253, causing the inhabitants to scatter into areas previous controlled by the Khmer Empire (Jumsai 2000: 10–26). While much of the early history of the peoples living in what is present-day Laos is mostly unknown, it is known that: "Trade routes in the middle Mekong date from prehistoric times and trans Mekong commercial traffic was by no way new in the seventh century" (Hoshino 2002: 53). Therefore, it appears that for a considerable length of time the peoples living in the area that comprises present-day Laos were not completely isolated and were connected to people from other parts of the region.

It could be argued the first great "Lao" kingdom was the Kingdom of Lan Xang Hom Khao (a million elephants under a white parasol), normally referred to simply as Lan Xang, which was founded by King Fa Ngum, who most likely was of Khmer descent and a vassal of the Kingdom of Angkor (Evans 2002: 9). King Fa Ngum, who ruled from 1352 to 1371, "was considered by the Lao to be one of their greatest kings, He united the country into a powerful state and the extent of his country was probably the biggest known in Lao history" (Jumsai 2000: 98). The Lan Xang Kingdom was a *mandala* with Luang Prabang at the core. In 1356, King Fa Ngum and his army of around 48,000 men and 500 elephants conquered Vientiane and then later expanded the kingdom as far as the areas surrounding present-day Roi-Et in Thailand (Jumsai 103–5). However, King Fa Ngum fell out of favor and was forced into exile between 1371 and 1374 and died shortly thereafter (Evans 2002: 10; Jumsai 2000: 108). An interesting feature of this era of Laotian history is that Luang Prabang was effectively ruled by a woman, given name Kaeo Phimphen but commonly known as Maha Thewi, from 1428–38 (Phothisane 2002: 77–9) demonstrating the important role of women in Lao society, which was later remarked upon by Freeman in 1910.

Possibly the first Europeans to visit the land that now comprises the country of Laos were a group of Portuguese who accompanied a Burmese envoy around 1545. The Europeans who visited the area in the seventeenth century reported extensive trade and international trade disputes between the kingdoms located in what is today Laos, Thailand, and Cambodia. The Europeans in Laos at the same time also commented on the importance of the Theravada Buddhist religion in the lives of the people (Ngaosrivathana and Ngaosrivathana 2002).

In 1707, the "Lao" kingdom was divided into two independent monarchies, one in Luang Prabang and one in Vientiane (Phothisane 2002), and later another division came with the creation of the Kingdom of Champasak (Jumsai 2000: 86). In the late eighteenth century, various leaders in Laos took sides in the Vietnamese civil war and, as a result of the Lao-Tay-son alliance, parts of Laos were well connected to international trade routes through Vietnam for a short period of time (Breazeale 2002; Quy 2002).

After the fall of the Ayutthaya Kingdom in 1776, the Kingdom of Vientiane took advantage of the weakness of Siam and extended its geographical influence. However, beginning in 1778, Taksin, the leader who is often credited with re-uniting the Thais and driving out the Burmese, marched on and eventually sacked Vientiane with the help of the Kingdom of Luang Prabang. In the aftermath of the Thai invasion, thousands of families were taken out of Laos and resettled into Thailand in the areas around Saraburi. By 1782, the Chakri Dynasty was established in Bangkok and subsequently the Thais became the dominant power in the region and Lan Xang ceased to exist, although there was a major last stand uprising against the Thai dominance by Chao Anou, the King of Vientiane in 1827 (Evans 2002: 25).

The nineteenth and early twentieth centuries were an era when European dominance and the instilling of the colonial system overtook much of Southeast Asia. In 1899, the French extended their control over territories in Southeast Asia by adding Laos as one of its five associated regions of Southeast Asia, which also included Cambodia, Tonkin, Annam, and Cochinchina. The French justified their control over Laos by using quite vague claims of historical Vietnamese control over the region. Auguste Pavie was the first French governor of Laos. Although French presence in the country (the census of 1907 showed only 189 French in the country) and control over Laos were very light and had little immediate effect on the lives of most of the common people, changes did occur, such as the abolishing of slavery in the 1890s, and in the heavy use of individuals from Vietnam in the country's administration, which resulted in a major increase in the number of ethnic Vietnamese in the country (Evans 2002: 45–7, 59; Jumsai 2000: 234).

Laos, like most of its other colonies, was an economic burden on France and it has been suggested the possession and holding on to colonies may have had more to do with French nationalism and pride instead of economic interests. Although initially there were intentions of integrating Laos into the economy of the rest of Indochina, the reality was the majority of international trade in the region remained in the hands of Chinese merchants and was conducted through Thailand, not Vietnam. Prior to World War II, there were a few minor uprisings against the French but nothing that actually threatened French control over Laos (Evans 2002: 42, 49–59).

"When the French took over Laos there was no sense of a Lao nation among the population" (Evans 2002: 70). Curtis reported (1903: 5), "The term 'Laos' is an arbitrary one, being the French spelling of the name of a single tribe of Laos, namely the *Lao* tribe. But the Siamese call all the Laos in their kingdom and in French territory *Lao*." While Jumsai claimed (2000: 2), "Prior to the French occupation, the Laos referred to their language as Thai." However, a sense of Lao nationalism eventually grew within what even the French thought of at the time as "more a cartographic reality than a social or historical one" (Evans 2002: 71). Most of this sense of nationalism did not necessarily rise in opposition to French rule but to the increase of the influence of the Vietnamese in the country and "Anti-Vietnamese sentiment was central to the Lao nationalism that stirred in the 1940s" (Evans 2002: 70).

Although considered a backwater by most at the time, the history of the people of Laos was greatly affected by the events of World War II. As in most of the rest of Southeast Asia, Laos fell under the control of the Japanese, which had the effect of destroying the myth of the superiority of the white man over the Asians. The French continued to rule Laos through most of World War II; however, on March 9, 1945, the Japanese overthrew the French and on April 8, 1945, the king in Luang Prabang was forced to declare the independence of the country. However, in August of the same year, the Japanese surrendered to the allies, causing a rift between the king, who had already agreed to a return of the French, and Prince Phetsarath, the prime minister of the country, who held the important rank of viceroy and who was a supporter of Lao nationalism and believed the country's declaration of independence should stand even with the defeat of the Japanese. Prince Phetsarath is often thought of as the father of Lao nationalism, but he was actually in favor of joining Laos with Thailand and/or Cambodia, countries with similar cultures and religious traditions, in a loose federation, and opposed the French plan to incorporate Laos into the Indochina Federation with Vietnam, a country with which the people of Laos had limited cultural connections (Ivarsson and Goscha 2007).

After the Japanese surrender in August 1945, Prince Phetsarath declared the unification of an independent Lao kingdom, resulting in the King dismissing him from his posts as prime minister and viceroy (Evans 2002: 83). Prince Phetsarath was the eldest brother of Prince Souvanna Phouma and Prince Soupanouvong, the leaders of opposing forces who would seek to control an independent Laos in the years to come. The French returned to take control over Vientiane on April 24, 1946 and Luang Prabang on May 13, 1946 (Jumsai 2000: 276).

The return of the French sparked a Lao nationalist movement called Lao Issara. It does not appear that this movement was initially communist in nature, but there were substantial connections between many of its leaders and Vietnam, and future communists in Vietnam. For example, Prince Souphanouvong had worked in Vietnam and had a Vietnamese wife; while Kaysone Phomvihan was born in Savannakhet to a Vietnamese father and Laotian mother, but left Laos to study in Vietnam at around ten years of age. Although the Lao Issara movement was not successful, it was a training ground for future leaders of the communist movement in Laos (Evans 2002: 85–7).

With the return of the French, a form of democracy began taking shape in Laos. An election was held in December 1946 to form a Constituent Assembly, which met for the first time in March 1947 and endorsed a new constitution. Later in 1947, elections were held and the National Assembly chose Prince Souvannarath to become prime minister. However, real power remained in French hands; but that was soon to change. In July 1949, a general convention was signed between France and the Royal Lao Government (RLG) giving increased autonomy to Laos. The French colonial system in Southeast Asia was crumbling and full sovereignty was granted to the RLG in October 1953 (Evans 2002: 90–1).

As the French left Southeast Asia, the United States in their quest to stem the advance of communism began to move in, not as a colonial power, but often by becoming the primary source of financial support for the non-communist governments in the region. This funding led to a dependence on the United States that often resulted in Laotian governments having little choice but to conform to the wishes to the US Government. Additionally, the French withdrawal from Laos resulted in a mass exodus of the Vietnamese who had played such a vital role in the administrative and economic environment in Laos during the colonial era, leaving a talent gap. The RLG quickly became dependent on US financial aid and advice, especially to pay and train its armed forces. The armed forces of the RLG were important to the government as the Vietnamese-led communist movement had picked up a number of allies in Laos. Kaysone Phomvihan joined the Indochinese Communist Party in 1948, while Prince Souphanouvong joined in 1954 (Evans 2002: 94–104).

As the 1950s came to an end, King Sisavangvong, who had reigned for 50 years and had consistently sided with the French, passed away and the new monarch, King Savang Vatthana, took the throne. In the 1960s, a coup was staged, led by Army Captain Kong Le, who was aligned with neutralist Souvanna Phouma. However, the regime was to be short lived as troops loyal to the anti-communist Phoumi Nosavan took control over Vientiane in a bloody fight that led to the formation of a government led by Boun Oum (Evans 2002: 117–19).

Wanting peace, being pressured from the growing communist military advances in the country, and not wanting to be pulled into the Vietnamese civil war, many Laotian leaders sought a middle path solution, which would be expected in a country where the primary religion places such a high emphasis on compromise, peace, and the avoidance of confrontation. This policy became known as "neutralism." In January 1962, a compromise was reached by the three princes, Boun Oum, Souvanna Phouma, and Souphanouvong, and the United States withheld economic and military aid in an attempt to force the then-ruling Phoumi government to accept this agreement. In the meantime, the Vietnamese-led communist armed forces continued to make military advances in the country. Neutralism worked to the advantage of the communists and by 1964, when the second coalition government fell, the communists, now known as the Pathet Lao, controlled nearly half of the geographical area of the country (Evans 2002: 123–8).

Much has been written about the Laotian civil war and the involvement of the United States and outside communists, so it will be only touched upon briefly here. The civil war in Laos did not specifically arise from problems within Laos and a significant number of the combatants in Laos were not ethnic Lao. The US military's involvement in Laos was primarily motivated by the effort to stop supplies that were moved along the Ho Chi Minh Trail from reaching North Vietnamese troops in South Vietnam. Instead of openly violating the UN agreement restricting foreign troops from fighting in Laos, many members of the ethnic Hmong community were recruited by the US military to fight against the communists. The communist forces, which were led and made up primarily of North Vietnamese soldiers in open violation of the UN agreement, entered into Laos as a way to supply their forces located in Southern Vietnam, as well as a way to expand the war throughout Southeast Asia, therefore increasing the costs, economically as well as politically, to the United States in the hopes of ending its involvement in the conflict. During the war and up until 1978, the Chinese also supplied a large number of non-combat troops to build roads in Laos to support the Pathet Lao (Zhang 2002). In violation of international agreements, Vietnamese combat troops remained in the country in support of the Pathet Lao while the United States secretly trained fighters from the Hmong minority led by General Vang Pao. The United States also launched massive bombing raids in an attempt to stop the advancing communist forces and, as this was in the days prior to smart bombs, civilian casualties were numerous. After the withdrawal of US support, the RLG collapsed, and by 1975 Laos was under the control of the communist forces (Kurlantzick 2005: 115).

Unlike the Khmer Rouge takeover of Cambodia, the communist takeover was slow-paced and went through stages. There was not really a final military victory that brought the communist party to power; instead, it was a series of small military victories and the withdrawal of US support for the RLG that resulted in a communist victory. The Pathet Lao did not have much popular support in the country; however, the communists relied on the population's desire for peace and compromise, possibly due to the influence of Theravada Buddhism, to take over. Toward the end of 1975, the king abdicated and, in a secretly held meeting in Vientiane, the Laos People's Democratic Republic came into existence with Souphanouvong selected as president and Kaysone Phomvihan as prime minister (Evans 2002: 174–5).

The communist takeover of the country resulted in reshaping its demographics to a large extent. As with the Khmer Rouge in Cambodia, most of the leaders of the Pathet Lao movement were from the countryside and were considered ignorant country hicks, or in the language of Lao, *khon pa*, by the nation's elites. Therefore, there was much migration from the countryside into the capital, Vientiane, while there was also a mass exodus of the ethnic Chinese merchant class and educated Laotians across the border into Thailand. As life under communist rule became more oppressive and the economy continued its decline, the pace of the exodus of the best and brightest Laotians increased (Evans 2002: 178).

Although the scale of violence that accompanied the Pathet Lao's rise to power did not approach the scale of the Khmer Rouge in Cambodia, there was still considerable repression of the former members of the RLG and its army. More than a few former members of the RLG and its military were sent to reeducation camps and were never heard from again. However, the Hmong, who as a group had been most closely associated with the United States and who had already suffered very heavy casualties during the war, were often singled out on a scale that Evans (2002: 184–6) referred to as the equivalent of the "ethnic cleansing" seen in more recent conflicts.

The new Laotian communist government was closely aligned with Vietnam and was modeled after the Vietnamese communist government. In 1977, Laos signed a 20-year Treaty of Friendship and Cooperation with Vietnam and the government embarked on implementing socialist programs. As Laos had almost no manufacturing sector in its economy, the government instead made a few attempts at establishing farming collectives, but when this resulted in decreased production, increased dissatisfaction of the people, and further increases of people fleeing to Thailand, the government reversed course. Socialism as an economic system never took a strong hold in Laos and, as early as 1979, the government began moving toward market-based reforms. As communism crumbled around the world, Laos' connection with the broader communist world began to weaken and the final 45,000 Vietnamese troops left the country by the end of the 1980s (Evans 2002: 187–99).

Since independence, the economy of Laos has relied on foreign aid. First, the RLG was dependent upon US aid, later the communist government of Laos relied on aid from other communist nations and the USSR in particular, and with the collapse of communism in Europe, Laos has "opened up" to the outside world and now is a major recipient of development aid from developed countries, as well as extending its trade with China. Laos has moved away from Marxist principles and the opening up of the economy has led to increasing income gaps, especially between the major cities and the countryside. It should also be noted that the combination of a communist government alongside market activities has not surprisingly led to very high levels of corruption (Evans 2002: 200, 214, 218, 229).

However, a Lao identity that includes Laotians and peoples living in the *Isarn* region of Northeast Thailand, which is separate from a Thai identity, has emerged. People who are classified as Lao (whether Thai or Laotian citizens), identify themselves as Lao through dietary habits (eating sticky rice and fermented fish), music (playing the bamboo organ), and freely offering hospitality to others. Chanthanom (1998: 195) found when doing interviews on both sides of the border in the area that: "Every interviewee agreed that people in the [*sic*] northeastern Thailand are Laotian, not Thai. They are divided by laws, not by culture."

Business and economic environment

General features

Laos has produced few industries and, outside of the regional success of Beer Lao Brewery, industrial growth has been quite slow. Asia has been the home of the fastest growing economies in the late twentieth and early twenty-first centuries; however, "Only in Laos, it seems, has little changed, the same generation of leaders that battled the United States and its allies in the 1970s is still in power and still harboring old grudges" (Kurlantzick 2005: 14). Laos' underdevelopment makes it a cheap and "unspoiled" destination for backpackers and budget travelers, who often write glowing reports about the country; however, for those living in the country, this underdevelopment means life expectancies closer to those found in the poorest regions of sub-Saharan Africa instead of those found in the faster developing parts of Asia.

A key feature of the Laotian economy that potential foreign investors should be aware of is the use of multiple currencies within the domestic economy. It is estimated that about 50 percent of the money stock in Laos PDR is in kip (the Laotian currency), while around 30 percent is in the currency of the country's largest trading partner, Thai baht, and the remaining 20 percent is made up of US dollars. While there are some benefits to this use of foreign currencies, there are also costs, such as the government's lack of ability to have an independent monetary policy (Menon 2006).

Although previously Laos PDR had politically been closely aligned with Vietnam, the changing power structure in Asia has shifted focus and China is now becoming a major source of political backing and investment for the communist leaders of the country (Kurlantzick 2005). Also, as the legitimacy of communist economic policies continues to fade, it would appear the leadership of the country is making a shift to align itself closer with Lao traditional culture and is attempting to be identified as defenders of the Theravada Buddhist religion in order to retain power (Pholsena 2004; Tappe 2007).

Economic conditions

After years of stagnation, the twenty-first century is seeing some economic growth coming to the country. GDP grew by 8 percent in 2007, which built upon the respectable average of 6.8 percent GDP growth during the previous five years. Increased output from the country's hydropower plants, a rise in demand for the products of the country's mining industry, and a growing number of tourists have been the primary drivers of the country's economic growth. Also, inflation was held to 4.5 percent in 2007 and the country's foreign reserves have been growing steadily over recent years (Asian Development Bank 2008b: 205).

The private sector portion of the economy is growing and market reforms are continuing. Nevertheless, poor infrastructure continues to limit economic expansion and complying with excessive government regulations is a major cost burden for companies operating in the country. Another obstacle to continued growth is the lack of an efficient banking system as Laos' state-owned banks are burdened with excessive non-performing loans (Asian Development Bank 2008b: 206–8). Economic growth and increased migration from rural areas into Vientiane has also brought health and sanitary problems that need to be addressed (Khanal and Souksavath 2005).

Even with the recent economic growth, GNP per capita in the country is still only around US$500. Also, the agriculture sector of the economy, which is the largest and the sector where most people work, has seen very sluggish growth and this is causing a widening income gap between urban and rural residents. Furthermore, Laos' international trade, with the exception of tourism, is conducted almost entirely within the region of Southeast Asia and the country has very little connection with the more advanced economies of the world (Asian Development Bank 2008b), which is limiting the country's exposure to modern technology and business practices.

Business practices

In a study on the competitiveness of ten Southeast Asian countries, Laos was placed tenth overall; tenth in managerial performance; ninth in human resource performance, ahead of only Cambodia; and tied with Myanmar/Burma for last place in technology performance (Kao *et al.* 2008). These results confirm that Laos PDR is one of the most underdeveloped nations in the region and in the world and there are plenty of opportunities for improvements in the business environment in the country.

Slowly, Laos is starting to become more connected with the outside world. The government has been gradually opening the country to foreign visitors and investors and, equally, if not more importantly, increased road construction is linking the country and its abundant natural resources to the growing economies of Southeast Asia and China. A number of international donors, including Japan, the Republic of Korea, Australia, and the Asian Development Bank, have agreed to fund further road construction projects that will increase linkages between

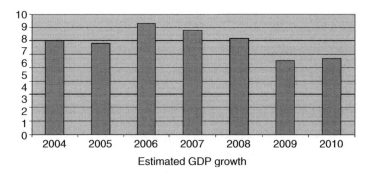

Figure 4.1 Laos' estimated annual GDP growth (%).

Laos and its neighbors (Gunn 2008). Research indicates that this improved transportation system can be expected to have a major positive impact on lowering the logistics costs of operating in this land-locked country (Banomyong 2004).

The business environment of the country has obviously been shaped by the political and economic systems (De Valk 2003), but the social-cultural environment where Theravada Buddhism is a central feature also appears to be a significant factor. For example, Hyakumura and Inoue (2006) reported on the importance of the social capital of a manager in the country in reducing non-productive conflict, which is consistent with the findings of other researchers on the personal nature of business and management in the region.

Laotian views of the "global" environment are mostly seen through a regional lens with much of the news of the outside world coming from the Thai media as most of the Laotian elites have access to news from Thailand and because of the similarities in languages can read and understand the Thai language (Chanthanom 1998: 72).

Although the country politically is controlled by the Communist Party, the private sector dominates the economy; 99 percent of firms and 94 percent of all employees are in the private sector. Not surprisingly as Laos PDR is a developing economy, small and medium enterprises (SMEs) and microenterprises comprise the vast majority of firms within the country. Some growth is being seen in firms in the handicraft, agricultural processing, timber production, textiles, trading, and internet service provider sectors (Southiseng and Walsh 2008).

Agriculture

Laos is primarily a rural agricultural country with approximately 70 percent of its labor force working in the agricultural sector of the economy. While rice remains the primary crop grown in the nation, growing coffee, raising livestock,

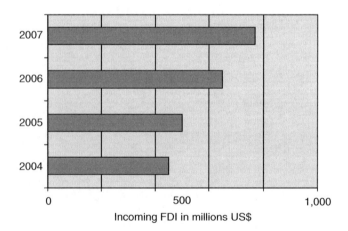

Figure 4.2 Laos' annual incoming foreign direct investment (US$).

and fish farming are increasingly becoming important agricultural activities (Asian Development Bank 2009: 236).

Most of Laos is mountainous and unsuitable for growing rice in paddy fields. Therefore, much of the rice in the country, especially in the highland areas, is grown using the swidden method. However, due to economic concerns and pressure from the government's programs designed to protect forests, swidden agricultural methods are beginning to be replaced by continuous sedentary farming techniques and tree plantations. Therefore, in upland areas there is a move away from subsistence farming to the growing of cash crops, which include Job's tears (a grain used in various Asian cuisines), fruits, maize, and raising fish grown in fishponds. However, upland farmers have little access to price information or markets for their crops, making the shift from subsistence farming based on swidden methods to the more environmentally friendly practices of growing cash crops a risky proposition (Yokoyama *et al.* 2006).

Two agricultural industries that have potential for growth would appear to be in the coffee and wood products sectors. The country has tried to promote coffee growing in an attempt to repeat the success found in Vietnam. However, the industry faces problems due to a lack of manpower and technical expertise. The industry's productivity as measured by tons per hectare is only about a third of what is seen in neighboring Vietnam. The wood industry in the country consists mostly of logging and other low-value-added activities. Although officially logging is controlled, the reality is there is widespread smuggling, which is rapidly diminishing the forest coverage found in the country. However, with better control of the cutting and replanting of forests, and efforts to produce higher value-added activities, there are opportunities for firms within the country to grow and prosper (Bonaglia 2006).

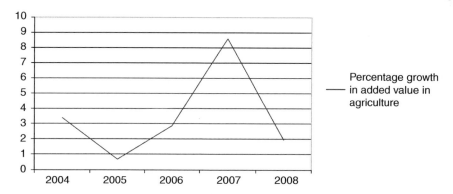

Figure 4.3 Laos' annual added value in agriculture growth (%).

Case studies

Sengdara Fitness Center

In the Laotian capitol of Vientiane can be seen the stylish building housing the Sengdara Fitness Center. The layout, atmosphere, and work practices of the business are in many ways a reflection of the young managing director of the company, Mr. Viroun Leng, who is a native of Laos but grew up in Los Angeles. The decor and ambience of the exercise areas and the offices of the company have a very "Californian" feel to them. The Sengdara Fitness Center is a place for the upscale fitness-minded residents of Vientiane, both foreign and local, to hang out in an environment that would not be considered dramatically different from what is found in modern cities in more developed countries. Founded in 2003, the Sengdara Fitness Center offers a full range of services similar to those found in fitness centers around the world. Besides being a good place to get a healthy workout, the Sengdara Fitness Center is also a place to see, be seen, and socialize.

The modern, trendy, and Western aspects of the business are not a facade, they are real, but in other aspects the company is very identifiably Asian. The company is part of a family-owned conglomerate of unrelated business endeavors. Sengdara Enterprises also consists of a communication company, an English learning center, and a private kindergarten. The patriarch of the family, Mr. Viroun Leng's father, has supplied most of the capital and the land on which the firm has been built. Although the energetic and young Mr. Viroun Leng is responsible for the Sendara Fitness Center, before making major decisions he consults with both his father and his older brother, who is more directly involved in other branches of the family business.

The basic strategy of the company is to bring in business concepts that are new to Laos. This strategy is inline with De Valk's (2003) advice that Laotian companies should focus on transferring into the country existing know-how developed elsewhere as opposed to focusing on innovation. This idea of bringing in concepts that are new to Laos is also found in Sengdara's communication company that began the trend toward producing modern-styled magazines and is now producing the very first Laotian Music Awards. Mr. Viroun Leng's bicultural and ambitious nature makes him uniquely qualified to introduce many Western concepts into Laos. Rehbein (2007a) expressed the idea that individuals who have gained an understanding of market economics while working or studying abroad will have an advantage in business as the country becomes more economically connected with the rest of the world.

Although the Sengdara Fitness Center is marketed to appeal to the upper classes of Laotian society, Mr. Viroun Leng realizes because of the small size of the population of the country, one has to be concerned with volume and therefore it is not wise to attempt to appeal to a very small segmented niche of the market. This concept is also seen in the company's communication branch which produces a bi-weekly magazine that contains a wide variety of articles to appeal to many interests in order to attract interest in a large enough segment of the population to be feasible to produce.

As the Sengdara Fitness Center is the only full-service fitness center to be found in Vientiane there are no real direct competitors; however, some of the hotels do provide some indirect competition as they provide limited fitness equipment for both their guests and the general public. Even without intensive direct competition, the Sengdara Fitness Center has to maintain its prices at a level that makes membership possible for a large enough section of the population to turn a profit. The company's long-term plans include the possibility of opening another fitness center with somewhat more limited services geared more toward middle-class office workers. Sengdara Enterprises is also looking to expand its communication business; however, the competition in this sector is quite intense and the company, in the manner of many family-owned businesses in Asia, is always on the lookout for new business opportunities, whether they are related or unrelated to existing business operations. Alongside the normal constraints found in business expansion around the world, it is felt the capability of the human resources that are available to the company are limited, which is to be expected in a developing economy, and this prevents the company from extremely rapid expansion.

In fitting with its image, most of the staff members of the Sengdara Fitness Center are young, urban, and athletic. This brings both advantages and challenges. Many of the staff members have high expectations but low levels of experience. It has also been reported the work effort expectations of the Western-raised owner/manager and the staff members who have grown up in Laos have not always been identical.

There are approximately 75 employees of the Sengdara Fitness Center and around 150 employees in all of the Sengdara businesses. Within the Fitness Center, most of the recruitment and selection of personnel has been delegated to the five department heads. These department heads use a combination of informal and formal HR practices. At times, recruitment is through word of mouth and other times more formal practices are used, such as placing ads in public. The company primarily uses on-the-job training as opposed to having a formal training program. As well as a salary, the company follows a common paternalistic practice in Asia of providing the employees with a meal while at work.

For large purchases, such as buying exercise equipment, the company must buy from Thailand as there are no local suppliers, and these purchases are strictly market-based transactions with price being the driving factor in selection. For frequently purchased supplies from local vendors, the company attempts to develop longer-term relationships with its local suppliers.

Top-of-the-line exercise equipment can be very expensive and Laos is not a rich country, therefore, the Sengdara Fitness Center needs to ensure it gets good value for money with each purchase of equipment. The Sengdara Fitness Center does not feel it is possible in the environment it operates in to supply its customers with the latest and most trendy pieces of equipment with all the bells and whistles one might find in an upscale fitness center in London, Los Angeles, or Melbourne; therefore, the company often purchases equipment second hand.

However, the company prides itself on its service. Coming to the Sengdara Fitness Center one can get a good healthy workout on quality equipment with the expectation of world-class service from the staff members. The Sengdara Fitness Center is definitely considered modern, trendy, and cutting edge for Laos, but it may be seen as a few years behind the times when compared to the most upscale fitness clubs in the most developed countries.

The entrepreneurial spirit and energy found at the Sengdara Fitness Center may not fit well into the stereotypical image of a company in a developing socialist country. The Sengdara Fitness Center is both an international and a Laotian company, but in the Laos of today, and in the future, being international and Laotian might not be mutually exclusive. While foreigners, NGO workers, foreign embassy employees, and foreign managers of businesses make up about 40 percent of the fitness center's customers, the majority of customers are Laotian. Seeking out similar services to those available internationally does not automatically make Laotian customers any less Laotian.

Cultural Production Company

The Cultural Production Company was a state-owned enterprise that was privatized in 1994. Initially, the company was purchased by a partnership of five individuals; however, one of those five has since passed away and now the company is owned by the remaining four partners. The company has five divisions of products: wood carving, furniture, document supply and printing, traditional Lao musical instruments, and sculpture and moldings. The focus of the company is on making products with a Lao cultural theme and, as Lao culture and Theravada Buddhism are inseparable, many of the products are intended for religious purposes. The company's primary customers include *wats* (temples), government offices (the furniture in the Prime Minister's office was made by the company), and public spaces, for example, the company has built many of the statues found in the nation's public parks. Approximately 90 percent of the firm's products are for the domestic market with the remainder mostly being sold to members of ethnic Lao communities living abroad.

Although not a family-owned business, the company shares the practice of not having a separation between ownership and management found in many businesses in Southeast Asia. Mr. Bounleung Veunvilaong, with 50 percent ownership of the company, is the managing director. The other three owners work for the company full time as departmental managers.

The company is one of a kind in Laos and, therefore, there is no real direct competition for some of the branches of the company. One branch, printing, has many competitors and there is some competition in both the wood carving and furniture branches of the company. Although the company does make some small brass Buddha images for the homes of ordinary Lao citizens, the majority of its work is made to order and specialized. For example, the wooden doors made for a specific temple will be unique and hand-made and unlike those made for any other application.

Mostly the company purchases supplies locally, but it does make some special purchases of equipment from companies in Thailand and Indonesia. Since most of the company's supplies are commodities, in general, the company relies on market-based transactions with its suppliers instead of developing long-term buyer-seller relationships. A unique feature of the company is that it is not uncommon for customers to supply the raw materials needed to make the finished products and, therefore, some supply purchasing decisions are taken out of the company's hands.

In addition to being managers of the company, the managers also spend time as teaching staff at the local college of arts. It is in this capacity much of the recruitment and selection of new staff members is conducted. The managers/ teachers learn about the artistic talent and work ethics of the students and the best students are then offered positions with the company. It was reported that it is always very difficult to find employees with the artistic skills needed to produce the types of products the company is known for. However, as turnover is quite low (only one employee out of a workforce of 33 full-time employees and six part-time workers has left in the last five years), the need to recruit new staff members is not a frequent task.

In general, the company makes traditional products using traditional techniques. The company does not use any type of cutting-edge technology to produce its products; instead most are hand-made pieces of art. As pieces of art, the price of most of the company's products puts the products out of reach of most individual Laotian citizens, although occasionally a wealthy member of society will commission a work to be displayed at his or her home.

For the owners of the company, their daily work is about more than just making profits. The owners take great pride in their contribution to maintaining Laos' cultural and religious identity and heritage. Spending their time and effort in creating beautiful works of art that can assist individuals in their spiritual advancement has brought more than just a paycheck to the owners and workers of the Cultural Production Company.

SMP Enterprises

SMP Enterprises is a truly innovative company using environmentally friendly methods to produce a wide range of unique and beautiful decorative products out of the hard woods found in Southeast Asia. The company began as a company that exported lumber from Laos in 1999, but shortly after the company's founding, the government of Laos placed severe restrictions on the export of lumber to protect the natural resources of the country. The company soon found its business model was not sustainable in the new environment. Therefore, the sole owner of the company, Mr. Souphout Manikong, used this challenge to rethink his business approach and came up with the idea to use the scrap wood that could not be used in construction or furniture manufacturing to create uniquely designed wood sculptures. The designs are quite modern in nature and are not all easily identifiable as Laotian. Mr. Souphout Manikong and his staff often use the imperfections of the scrap wood, which makes its unfit for other uses, to produce unique one-of-a-kind works of art. The company's work is not just quaint modern reproductions of ancient designs made for tourists, but internationally recognized modern works of art that have won many prizes at contests and exhibitions around the world.

SMP Enterprises has much in common with successful entrepreneurial firms around the world. Mr. Souphout Manikong's passion for his work, as well as his energy, business intuition, and salesmanship, are the driving factors behind the firm's success. Nearly all of the products are exported and many are then resold in fashionable outlets in the United States, Europe, and throughout Asia.

However, the company also has some features that are common throughout Southeast Asia. The firm is an entrepreneurial firm, not a corporation, and the owner is the managing director, chief designer, and the firm's number one sales person. Also, the firm uses its family connections as Mr. Souphout Manikong's brother, who is living in the United States, has been very active in creating an export market for the company's products. The firm relies on government support and Mr. Souphout Manikong is very active in civic organizations for altruistic reasons, as well as to build up the relationships with local government and business leaders that are necessary for sustainable success in the country.

The firm started off with very low levels of capital; in fact, it used advance money from its first sale to build the small factory needed to produce the products for that sale. However, the firm has taken off rapidly. Due to the firm's success, a number of companies have sprung up in and around Vientiane that are making similar products, but Mr. Souphout Manikong believes he can keep his company ahead of the competition by continuing to come up with innovative designs and by perfecting the firm's manufacturing processes. This new competition has made it difficult to hold onto employees as the competition is looking to acquire the talent that many of the employees have gained from working at SMP Enterprises.

The company has around 60 full-time employees and uses some temporary workers for special jobs. The company prefers to hire inexperienced workers and then informally train them and allow them to gain the needed skills while on the job. Therefore, there is no shortage of potential employees wishing to work for the company. The primary criterion for selecting new employees is not experience or education, but the desire to do artistic work. The company does not use much formal training, but new employees learn from the more experienced workers while on the job. Like many of companies in the region, the relationship between the owner and the workers is more than just that of an employer and his employees. Mr. Souphout Manikong tries to act more or less like an elder brother to the employees, giving the employees professional opportunities, as well as personal advice and assistance, but he tries not to be too heavy handed or focus too much on the hierarchical aspect of the relationships.

The products are hand made, but the company should not be thought of as low-tech. The production techniques the company uses were developed in-house; in fact, the company has even designed some of its own tools to use in making its unique designs. The products made by SMP Enterprises are neither mass produced nor inexpensive but compete at the top end of the international market.

The company and its owner are not content to sit on their laurels, so the company has plans to expand their number of designs, improve the quality of the products, and experiment with using less exotic forms of wood as raw materials. Also, the company hopes to expand its showroom in Vientiane, not only to attract sales but also as an attraction for people visiting the country.

5 Thailand

History

The exact origin of the "Tai" people, which the Thais are a branch of, is continually debated by professional historians; however, traditionally it has been taught the ancestors of the Thais moved from inland China, possibly coming from two kingdoms to the north of the modern province of Sichuan called the Kingdom of Lung and the Kingdom of Pa, and then settled and created a kingdom in Nan Chao, in the present-day Yunnan province of southern China. It had long been assumed the Tai people spread out throughout Southeast Asia after the Mongol rulers of China overran Nan Chao in the thirteenth century. However, currently it appears most specialists do not believe Nan Chao was a Tai kingdom, at least Tai languages were not dominant in the kingdom. Instead, a newer theory that the Tai people had been gradually spreading across regions of Southeast Asia centuries before the collapse of Nan Chao is emerging. Nevertheless, it is generally accepted the Thais and the Laotians, as well as the Shans and other "Tai" ethnic groups, share a common ancestry (Jumsai 2000: 8, 16; Pholsena 2004: 237; Syamananda 1993: 6–14; Wyatt 2003: 7–16).

One of the first "Thai" kingdoms was the kingdom that became known as Lannathai, which means "land of one million rice fields." The early rulers of Lannathai traced their origin to the Kingdom of Chiengsen (Chiang Saen). The kingdom first changed its capital to Chiang Rai and then later to the city it is most identified with, Chiang Mai. The Lannathai Kingdom in Chiang Mai was founded by King Mangrai who spent most of his time fighting off the Mongol led forces of China. Although Lannathai has been considered a "Thai" kingdom, it would appear in reality it was a kingdom filled, at least at first, with a highly ethnically diverse population that included Mons, Lawas, different types of Tai peoples, as well as leftover Khmers from the Khmer Empire of Angkor that had ruled the region previously (Jumsai 2000: 31; Wyatt 2003: 33–9).

At around the same time, another "Thai" kingdom was coming into existence to the south of Lannathai. Sukhothai had been an outpost of the Khmer Empire of Angkor; however, as the power of Angkor was in decline, Tai people living in the area took over the city and it became a "Thai" kingdom. One of the most famous kings in Thai history, King Ramkhamheang, came to power in the then small Kingdom of Sukhothai around 1279. Under the leadership of King Ram-khamhaeng, forces from Sukhothai joined with those from Lannathai to repeal the attempts of invasion by the Mongol-led Chinese forces. It has been reported that Ramkhamhaeng sent four embassies to meet with Kublai Khan, the power-ful emperor of China, in 1281, 1291, 1295, and 1297, and even personally visited China twice, in 1294 and 1300. King Ramkhamhaeng ruled until 1317 (other sources claim he died in 1298) and after his death the Kingdom of Sukhothai began a slow decline. The Kingdom of Sukhotai was eventually incorporated into the growing power of the Thai Kingdom of Ayutthaya in the early fifteenth century (Jumsai 2000: 81–3; Jumsai 2001: 26; Syamananda 1993: 20–33; Wyatt 2003: 39–49).

It is often stated the Kingdom of Ayutthaya (Ayudhya) was founded in 1350 by King Ramathibodi I in 1350 in the location of a Khmer outpost. During the time of Angkor rule, Ayutthaya was located in the Lopburi region and it seems likely Ramathibodi, also known by his given name of U Thong, did not start a new kingdom, but rather took over as ruler of an existing center of population that gained independence and became more "Thai" from the decline of the power of the Angkor Empire. By the fifteenth and sixteenth centuries, international trade had made Ayutthaya one of the strongest kingdoms of Southeast Asia (Jumsai 2001: 28; Syamananda 1993: 32, Wyatt 2003: 50–85).

By the middle of the Ayutthaya period, the main competitor for power in central mainland Southeast Asia shifted westward and conflicts between Ayut-thaya and the Burmese became a long-lasting part of the history of the region. In 1548 and 1549, Burmese troops led by King Tabinshwehti, stormed into Ayut-thaya, but were eventually forced to retreat. However, Burmese forces regrouped and sacked all of the major Thai capitals between 1558 and 1569. Within a few decades, Ayutthaya regrouped and under the military leadership of Naresuan regained its position of prominence. Ayutthaya controlled a cosmopolitan kingdom that created amazing religious monuments and a highly effective eco-nomic system. However the kingdom's main weakness was the lack of smooth transitions of political power and the frequent political splitting of the kingdom during battles for succession. Burma's invasion of 1760 was on the verge of success when the troops retreated due to the injury and eventual death of King Alaunghpaya. However, the Burmese were soon back and devastated the city and killed off all the royal family of Ayutthaya in 1767 (Wyatt 2003: 52–121).

An argument could be made that the history of Thailand, as opposed to the history of a multitude of Thai states, can be traced to the aftermath of the sacking of Ayutthaya. The Manchu dynasty's invasion of northern Burma in 1769 resulted in the Burmese presence in and control over Ayutthaya's former terri-tory diminishing as Burmese energies went from conquest to successfully defending its own territory. This left a power vacuum that was taken up by the former Sino-Thai governor of Tak province, named Sin, who became known as Taksin. Taksin's military forces began taking control of the area of present-day Thailand, which included the areas previous controlled by the Lannathai Kingdom. Instead of rebuilding Ayutthaya, Taksin decided to install his capital in Thonburi. However, it has been reported that Taksin soon became an intolerable despot and went insane. Although it appears there is independent confirmation of this behavior, this fact also was important in establishing the founder of the current royal family as national savior as opposed to being a usurper (Myint-U 2006: 104; Syamananda 1993: 93–9; Wyatt 2003: 122–8; Young 1900: 2).

The Chakri dynasty began in 1782 when the former Chaophraya Chakri accepted the invitation to take over the throne after the imprisonment and execution of Taksin. While ruling he took on the name of King Ramithibodi (Ramathibodi), and he was given the post-humous title of Phra Phuttahayofa Chulalok (Pra Buddha Yodfachulaloke), but he is most often referred to as King Rama I. Under King Rama I, the capital was moved to Bangkok and this began the building of the modern country of Thailand (Syamananda 1993; Wyatt 2003: 128–44; Young 1900: 3–4).

The country continued to grow through the reigns of Rama II and III. Perhaps the most important aspect of the reign of Phra Phutthaloetla Naphalai (Rama II) was the smoothness of the transition of power, unlike the conflicts that invariably seemed to happen during the Ayutthaya period. Rama II is remembered as one of the great Thai poets and patrons of the arts; additionally, during his reign, the "nation" continued to take form and a renewal of international trade brought increased wealth to the nation. There was considerable controversy over the succession of Prince Chetsadabodin, who ruled as Phrao Nangklao but is mostly known as Rama III. During his reign, Thailand fought a war with Laos in which many Laotian prisoners were brought to populate the Khorat plateau. Also in this era, much like in the current time, conflicts between the government of Bangkok and the Muslim populations in the south were frequent and violent (Evans 2002; Wyatt 2003: 144–65).

King Mongkut, Rama IV, is one of the most revered figures in history among the Thais. King Mongkut was 47 upon taking the throne, after having had a distinguished 27-year career as a Buddhist monk and scholar. During his reign, Thailand (Siam) began to experience pressures from the colonial powers, the British to the west and south, and the French to the east. The country began opening up to trade with the West to a greater extent and the beginning of a more decentralized and modern form of government began to take shape. As trade with the West increased, King Mongkut took a long-term view and instead of making radical changes during this era of globalization, he chose to take a gradual approach to reforms (Wyatt 2003: 166–74). At the same time, trade with China greatly decreased as the political influence of the Manchu dynasty was in decline and, therefore, King Mongkut stopped the tradition of sending tribute to the emperors of China (Stuart-Fox 2003: 119).

King Mongkut was succeeded by his son, normally referred to as King Chulalongkorn (Rama V), another of the most beloved figures in Thai history. During his reign, pressures for concessions from the colonial powers increased. King Chulalongkorn's skill at diplomacy is often credited with allowing the kingdom to remain the only major nation of Southeast Asia that was not colonized by a European power. In 1897, King Chulalongkorn visited Europe and,

while impressed by many of the aspects of modernization he saw, he also realized the European way of life had not eliminated poverty and hardships for all
citizens and so decided to continue on a program of modernization for his
country, but not to attempt to turn his country into a replica of a European
model. He felt the country should selectively choose what to use from the West
and what not to use. King Chulalongkorn placed high value on education reform,
ended the practice of slavery in the country, and was known for his hard work
and being personally involved in many aspects of government. He reigned for 42
years, in which time the country met many challenges and retained its independence (Wyatt 2003: 175–209).

King Vajiravudh, Rama VI, came to the throne in 1910 and his reign has been
considered somewhat controversial. While he supported many social changes,
for example promoting sports and increasing social standing for women, he did
not support major political changes. He appeared to be somewhat flamboyant,
very interested in the arts, had little interest in female companionship, married
late in life, had only a single child, a daughter born two days prior to his death,
ran up large expenditure for royal projects, and may be best remembered for
starting the Wild Tiger Corps, a militaristic version of the Boy Scouts (Wyatt
2003: 210–21). During the reign of King Vajiravudh, Chinese immigration
greatly increased and the dominant position of ethnic Chinese merchants in the
economy was reinforced (Montesano 2005: 185).

King Prajadhipok, Rama VII, came to power upon the death of King Vajiravudh in 1925. At first, he had a major problem to handle in attempting to get the
state's budget under control as royal expenditures had been allowed to balloon
under the previous monarch. He also believed the country would eventually have
to adopt a representative political system and he thought this should be a gradual
process. However, the Great Depression hit the country in the early 1930s, creating economic and political turmoil. In 1932, a new tradition was started in Thailand, and a group, led by Pridi Phanomyong and Luang Phibunsongkhram,
called the "Promoters," staged a coup in the name of democracy and the rule of
the absolute monarchy in the country was ended. King Prajadhipok abdicated the
throne in 1935 and was replaced by the then ten-year-old Prince Mahidol (Wyatt
2003: 222–38).

The end of the absolute monarchy did not immediately bring democracy to
Thailand. For the next few decades, the government of the country was heavily
influenced by political battles between two men, the left-leaning Pridi Phanomyong, mostly referred to as Pridi, and the more conservative Luang Phibunsongkhram, usually referred to as Phibun. But through it all, the military was a
major actor in Thai politics. In 1935, a government came into existence with
Phraya Phahon as prime minister, Pridi as the minister of foreign affairs and
Phibun as minister of defense. In 1938, Phibun became prime minister and, in a
marriage of convenience, the country officially sided with Japan in World War
II, and the military control of the government tightened (Wyatt 2003: 234–50).

By 1944, it became obvious the tide of the war was turning and having a head
of the country associated with the losing side was not deemed favorable, so

Phibun's government fell. A new government with Khuang Aphaiwong as prime minister and Pridi as regent for King Mahidol was formed. Despite the change in prime minister and his own position, Pridi held the real power for this next period of Thai political life and worked to align the country with the United States, partially to avoid the initial demands of the British government, which apparently wanted to reestablish and maybe expand its colonial holdings in Southeast Asia. However, by 1948, another shift in priority happened, as the cold war began heating up, the left-leaning government of Pridi fell out of favor and Phibun's association with the Japanese during the war was forgiven. Phibun again became the head of the government in 1948 and remained there until 1957 (Wyatt 2003: 250–65).

In 1946, King Ananda Mahidol, Rama VIII, was found shot dead under very mysterious circumstances and his younger brother, King Bhumibol Adulyadej, came to the throne, where he has now reigned for over 60 years. While the royal family has always been popular with the masses, the incredible popularity of King Bhumibol Adulyadej has grown over time and has been assisted and promoted by various governments, especially the government of Sarit Thanarat that came to power through a coup in 1957.

The Thai government aligned itself with the United States during the wars in Southeast Asia against the communist forces. During this time, the military continued to hold onto control. After the death of Sarit Thanarat in 1963, a military government led by General Thanom Kittikachorn ruled for ten years until 1973. Student-led demonstrations starting at Thammasat University initially led to a violent crackdown on protesters and the removal of many civil liberties of the people. After the crackdown, many of the student leaders of the protesters joined the communist movement and fled to the northeast, but in general the Thai population supported the crackdown. International and internal pressures eventually led to the temporary end to military rule, which led to a time of chaotic democracy with a revolving door of leaders, and which was followed by further coups and military rule (Ungpakorn 2007: 83–4; Wyatt 2003: 266–304).

In 1991, General Suchinda Kraprayoon staged yet another coup bringing down the elected government of Prime Minister Chatichai Choonhawan, claiming it was to end the corruption of the government, a justification reused in 2006 to bring down the elected government of Prime Minister Thaksin. This action led to large-scale street protests that were violently suppressed by the military. King Bhumibol intervened and the violence quickly ended; however, military rule was discredited, temporarily, and it appeared democracy in Thailand was here to stay with the election of Chuan Leekpai in 1992 (Chanthanom 1998: 67–8).

In 2001, business tycoon Thaksin Shinawatra, who amassed his fortune through a government-granted monopoly in the mobile phone section of the telecom industry, and his Thai Rak Thai party came into power, and this political movement, despite name changes, coups, and the judiciary attempts to break the movement apart, has remained popular with the electorate. After overwhelmingly winning reelection, Thaksin's government was brought down by a military coup in 2006. On the other side of the conflict are those who oppose Thaksin and use the same justification for the use of non-democratic methods to seize control of the government as the leaders of other military coups and supporters of the absolute monarchy have used for over a hundred years, that is to claim the Thai people (at least those living in rural areas) are not ready for democracy. Although officially barred from politics, it is an open secret that Thaksin was the real power behind the elected governments that sprang up after the military relinquished power (Hengkietisak 2008; McCargo 2008; Phongpaichit and Baker 2008: Ungpakorn 2007).

Outside the world of royalty and politics, life in Thailand has been a combination of continuity and change. In 1900, Young (5) reported on the dominance of ethnic Chinese in the field of business and commerce, and this has continued throughout the next hundred plus years (Montesano 2005). Young (1900: 21) also noticed the abundant presence of what today are known as "soi dogs" in the city of Bangkok. However, Young's (1900: 24) statement: "In the absence of drunken men and women and the scarcity of women of ill-fame, the streets of Bangkok might well serve as a model for some of the wealthier and more handsome towns of Europe," would appear to reflect an era before some of Bangkok's current nightlife venues came into existence. Yet, the observation that "Thais believe that Thai Buddhism is a part of their way of life and a part of being Thai" (Chanthanom 1998: 178) could have been as easily made one or two hundred years in the past.

Business and economic environment

General features

Today, Thailand has the most advanced economy, and its population has the highest standard of living, of the Theravada Buddhist countries of Southeast Asia. Thailand has seen a huge improvement in life expectancy and a lowering of infant mortality over the last half a century. "Thailand's outstanding record of poverty reduction is mainly attributable to the effects of economic growth rather than the government's efforts to assist the poor" (Warr and Sarntisart 2005: 195). Also, in line with the policies of most other Asian nations, various Thai governments have not felt inclined toward creating European-style welfare states (Warr and Sarntisart 2005: 194). The business environment in Thailand is primarily market-based. Although, in more recent times, the government led by the popular Thaksin Shinawatra introduced many programs designed to have the government take a more active part in assisting the rural poor in increasing income. These programs have been replicated to some extent by the current government in order to attempt to gain some of the popularity and legitimacy among the rural population that was found in the previously elected government.

During the recent past, Thailand's economy has been held back by political uncertainties. This continued political uncertainty, added to the global economic crisis of 2009, will likely restrict Thailand's economic performance for the near future. The manufacturing sector has held its own over the last few years, but the service sector's contribution to the economy has weakened due to a decrease in tourist arrivals. Inflation has been on the rise, but the official unemployment rate remains low. A long-term concern is the aging of the population, which is likely to restrict long-term growth (Asian Development Bank 2008b). Thailand's success in economic development and poverty reduction has been impressive; however, further gains may be slower and more difficult.

Economic conditions

Over recent decades, Thailand has experienced substantial economic growth and has received many benefits from this growth. However, not everyone has benefited equally. The percentage of individuals living in absolute poverty has been greatly reduced by long-term economic growth; however, the disparities in income between urban and rural, and coastal and inland have greatly increased (Warr 2007: Nopkhun 2005; Warr and Sarntisart 2005).

In 1945, Thailand was one of the world's poorest countries, but steady economic growth has resulted in considerable improvements in a number of indicators of well being, such as life expectancy, infant mortality, and literacy. From 1987 through 1996, Thailand had the fastest growing economy in the world; however, the financial crisis of 1997 had a major short-term impact and growth since the recovery from that crisis has been quite a bit lower than prior to it. Although the crisis had a major negative effect on the country's economic growth, it did not erase all the gains made in the boom years, and the average income of Thais at the depth of the crisis in 1997 was still much higher than it had been only a few years earlier (Warr 2007).

Business practices

Foreign investment has resulted in the creation of industrial clusters, mostly in the provinces surrounding Bangkok, while much of the rest of the country has

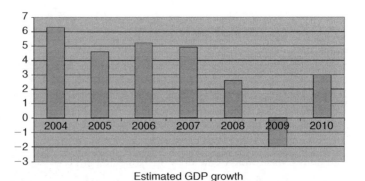

Estimated GDP growth

Figure 5.1 Thailand's estimated annual GDP growth (%).

been only lightly touched by industrialization (Sajarattanachote 2006). There is also being seen a shift in life in the villages away from the traditional subsistence farming focus toward more industrial work, and this is especially evident in the central region (Rigg *et al.* 2008).

The garment, textile, and electronics industries have been important sectors in the country's economic growth. However, the textile and garment industries now appear to be in decline. The primary reason for this decline would appear to be competition from other Asian countries. The sector also faces a shortage of expertise in design, branding, textile engineering, international marketing, and industrial design. Electronics is a major part of Thailand's manufacturing sector. There are over a thousand electronics firms employing nearly 350,000 employees in the country. However, the value added in the firms in the country is fairly low. Problems preventing the companies in the country from moving up the value chain include weak performance of supporting industries, and a lack of skills in both engineering and production staff (Bonaglia 2006).

Thailand's economy is very integrated with the regional economy and the role of the ethnic Chinese immigrants has been especially important.

> Chinese in Thailand were the prime movers in Thai economic development. They controlled modern banking and marketing systems throughout the country. This is because the Thais considered commerce ruthless and sinful acts for good Buddhists, and a lower class status job which the educated Thais are not attracted to.
>
> (Chanthanom 1998: 272)

Also, as Thailand is one of the regional economic powerhouses, it has attracted a large number of foreign workers, mostly undocumented, to work in the construction, mining, fishing, service, and other industries (Than 2005). Thailand has traditionally had a large tourism industry, and there has been a huge increase in tourists coming from within Asia and especially from China (Zhang, Huang, and Zuh 2006). However, both the images of political turmoil shown on televisions around the world and the global economic crisis appear to be having a major negative effect on recent tourist arrivals.

Entrepreneurship is alive and well in Thailand. Hatcher and Terjesen (2007) reported that Thailand is one of the most entrepreneurial focused countries in the world, and the number of women entrepreneurs is much higher than in most other countries. It was reported there are a number of factors that contributed to Thailand having such a high percentage of women entrepreneurs, such as women's entrepreneurial efforts are often aimed at supplying supplementary income to the family and most often these are small-scale business activities that can be done in conjunction with other domestic responsibilities. In addition, Thai culture does not place many restrictions on the role of women in society, allowing women many opportunities such as running a business.

Paulson and Townsend (2005) examined entrepreneurial behavior in provinces outside of Bangkok and found the majority of small-scale entrepreneurs used their own savings or other informal sources, such as borrowing from relatives, to finance the creation of a new business. The authors also found very little correlation between the amount of wealth of an individual and likelihood of starting a business, demonstrating the entrepreneur spirit in Thailand crosses social status divisions.

Thailand generally is considered to have a more competitive business environment than those found in the other Theravada Buddhist countries of Southeast Asia. Kao *et al.* (2008) ranked Thailand third amongst the ASEAN nations in economic performance, behind Singapore and Malaysia; also third in technological performance, behind the same two countries; first in human resource performance (with labor costs factored in); and third in managerial performance and in overall national competitiveness, in both cases following Singapore and Malaysia. Wang and Chien (2007) also measured Thailand's infrastructure, levels of information technology, technology management, and technology environment as inferior to Malaysia and Singapore, but it was also felt Thailand had some advantages over these two countries due to its abundance of natural resources and supply of low-cost labor.

Agriculture

Agriculture has always been an important part of the Thai identity. While that remains true today and the agricultural sector continues to be the main source of employment, the country is moving away from being a nation made up primarily of agricultural villages to a country with a more varied economy. A lack of sources of credit is making it more difficult for small farmers to continue to rely solely on farming for their livelihood (Limsombunchai, Gan, and Lee 2006), which may help explain the limited moves toward more large-scale commercial agriculture and rural households seeking a variety of sources of income.

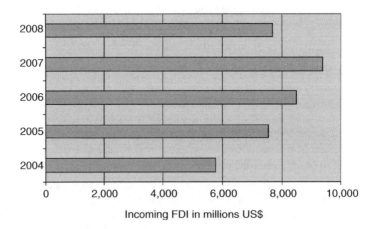

Figure 5.2 Thailand's annual incoming foreign direct investment (US$).

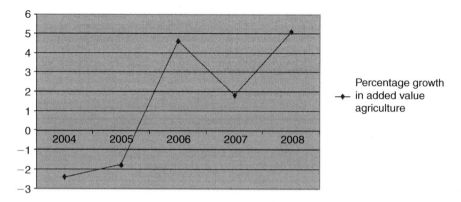

Figure 5.3 Thailand's annual added value in agriculture growth (%)

Thailand has an agricultural trade surplus, and the country is one of the world's leaders in exporting rice, poultry, and sugar. Thailand had been moving to open up its markets through various free trade agreements before the current political turmoil began, and if these trends reemerge, the agricultural sector will most likely benefit as most Thai agro-businesses are internationally competitive, although there remains room for improvement and the introduction of more scientific practices would likely improve the effectiveness of the sector (Zamroni 2006).

In Thailand, a thriving industry devoted to the relatively higher value processing of agricultural products has emerged. In particular, there are many firms involved in processing canned and frozen seafood. However, as seafood stocks off the coast of the country are becoming depleted, the firms in the industry are being forced to rely more on imported seafood or products from aquatic farming. The industry within the country has been able to hold onto existing customers but is having trouble breaking into new markets. In addition to a growing shortage of raw materials, the industry faces labor shortages, a lack of marketing research capabilities, and costly transportation (Bonaglia 2006).

Case studies

Huang Li Steel Company (Plit-Tapan Nawt Huang Li)

The Huang Li Steel Company was founded in Bangkok approximately 40 years ago. The company specializes in producing steel construction materials. Huang Li's products were used in building numerous bridges and buildings in the capital and surrounding areas during the city's period of rapid growth. The company, like so many throughout Southeast Asia, was founded and is still being run by an ethnic Chinese family.

Khun Tik Seehang founded the company after previously learning the technical side of the business as an employee in the steel industry. Khun Tik Seehang came from a humble background, had little formal education, and began his professional life as a street vendor selling noodle soup. In a typical overseas Chinese rags-to-riches story, through hard work and joining into a business network of other overseas Chinese businessmen, he was able to move from being a street vendor to being the patriarch of a successful family-owned business. Today, the head of the business is Khun Tik Seehang's daughter, Wilawan Chanajaranwit, and the operational and marketing supervisors of the business are Khun Tik Seehang's three sons. The Huang Li Steel Company follows the typical pattern of an overseas Chinese firm, founded by a technical expert with good connections, followed by the firm being taken over by a more educated and worldly second generation, as described by Chung and Yuen (2003). At the Huang Li Steel Company, management and ownership go hand in hand.

The company began with around 40 employees and there are now approximately 100 individuals working at the company. The focus of the company has changed little over its lifespan. The company has followed a fairly conservative strategy with little product diversification and without taking substantial risks after it became well established, which is a common feature of family-owned firms (Fernandez and Nieto 2005; Gallo *et al.* 2004). The company does not have any plans for major expansion, mostly due to two factors. One is location – the company is located in an area which the city has grown around so there is no room to expand in the current location and the factory is located in a convenient location for the owner-managers limiting the push for a change of location in order to expand. If there was a clear separation of ownership and management, a decision to relocate the factory to a location outside the city would be more likely. Second, as the family has moved up the social and economic ladder, members of the younger generation are less willing to work in the factory in an industry that is far from glamorous and where one will get his or her hands dirty. Hiring managers from outside the family has not been given serious consideration; therefore, growth potential is limited by the lack of new managers available. The firm has obviously had to change as the environment has changed, but the recent changes have been for the most part gradual and evolutionary.

The company operates in a competitive industry in which price is a major consideration. The firm does not rely on technical innovation nor does it use a complex marketing strategy. The firm relies to a large extent on trust and relationships with customers that were created by the founder of the firm. The firm is not the cost leader in the industry, but it creates a competitive advantage over other firms by allowing trusted companies extensive credit for purchases. In purchasing supplies, the firm has some relationships that could be described as purely market-based and others that are a mixture of relationship- and market-based. No one supplier is able to provide all of the raw steel the firm needs; therefore, the firm purchases this most important supply from a variety of vendors.

The firm's HR policies are typical of what is found in a traditional Asian family-owned business. The company takes a paternalistic approach to its employees. Employees are often provided with housing and utilities, as well as cash payments, as part of their compensation package. Employees can expect extras or bonuses in times of need, for example, family sickness or children's marriages, as opposed to bonuses based on performance. Turnover at the company has been very low, and approximately 20 percent of the existing work-force has been with the company for over 20 years. When new employees are needed, the firm recruits among the relatives of the existing employees, making this firm a family affair among the employees as well as among the owners. The firm mostly uses on-the-job training and practical work experience for employee development as opposed to formal training programs.

Huang Li Steel Company is a successful company and clearly financial con-siderations have always been a driving factor behind decisions made. However, the firm does not make much use of proactive strategic planning; instead, it gets its competitive advantage from operational efficiency and customer relations while strategically being more reactive to changing environmental conditions. The firm is not technologically innovative; instead, it has focused on exploiting a narrow product line using technologies and techniques perfected elsewhere.

The Seehang family is justifiably proud of the success of the firm and has worked hard to make the Huang Li Steel Company a success, but growth and financial rewards are not all-consuming passions. The firm does more than provide a good income to the owners. It provides financial security, employ-ment; and social status for the owners, as well as guaranteed quality employment for younger family members. The owner-managers of Huang Li Steel Company follow the middle path; success is important but does not necessarily mean unlimited growth and expansion. The company also clearly demonstrates its paternalistic and individualistic nature in its management style, while the employees in general demonstrate a low locus of control and are content to allow the owner-managers of the company to make the important decisions.

Atlanta Medicare

Atlanta Medicare is a Bangkok-based importer of pharmaceutical products that has been in business for three years. The ownership structure is that of a partner-ship in which four individuals came together to start the company. Two of the owners are directly involved in the management while the other two are strictly investors; however, these two non-managing owners are involved in the manage-ment of other companies of which they are also owners.

The firm sells a wide variety of pharmaceutical products, around 50 in total which are all imported from India. The company specifically focuses on anti-bacterial and anti-viral drugs for which the patents have run out and, therefore, there are no legal restrictions on importing these products from India for sale in Thailand. The firm's strategy is to provide inexpensive products that are as effective as higher priced products with more recognizable brand names. In the future, the company hopes to increase its market share, enter into other markets in the region (e.g., Vietnam, Cambodia, and Laos), and eventually start to manu-facture as well as sell pharmaceutical products.

Atlanta has a number of competitors; first, there are the domestic firms, with Siam Pharmaceutical being the largest. The company also has to compete with the large international companies that have well-established and trusted brand names. The company mainly competes on price. Drugs produced in India are generally lower priced than those produced in developed economies and even cheaper than those produced locally. The company mainly sells to hospitals, private clinics, and drug stores.

The majority of the 30 employees of the company are sales personnel. The company does not use a formal recruitment and selection process; instead, it relies on informal practices such as using referrals from existing employees and customers. This is consistent with the concept that personalities as well as skills are important considerations in hiring practices in the region. Also, since the company was founded, none of the staff have left. The company's project manager, Sunisa Sawasdipanich, attributes this to two main factors. First, Atlanta is a fun place to work and the owner-managers have good interpersonal skills. As noticed by Kainzbauer (2009), *sanuk*, or fun, is an important element of work life in Thailand. The second reason is the company is in its initial stages and therefore there are good opportunities for promotion and joining the partnership of the firm. Also, since the company's products and prices are attractive to customers, sales personnel currently have opportunities to gain substantial financial rewards through sales commissions.

While the company uses basically the same technological equipment as the sales forces of other companies in other parts of the world, such as cell phones and e-mail, face-to-face communication remains the primary method of acquiring sales and sharing information with customers. It was estimated sales personnel at the company spend 80 percent of their time in face-to-face communication and traveling with the use of modern IT equipment is mostly being used for follow-up communication. This example illustrates that business in Thailand is rarely conducted as an impersonal market-based transaction, most business transactions are conducted between individuals who have gained each other's trust, although market considerations such as price, quality, and service are never ignored. Atlanta's relationships with its suppliers are similar, the company has primarily relied on two main suppliers rather than constantly changing based on the latest price; however, the company keeps a constant lookout for new suppliers who can provide new products or a better mix of price, service, and quality than its current suppliers can.

When questioned about what made the company "special," project manager Sunisa Sawasdipanich responded the attributes of the owners and especially the personality and skills of the partner who is the acting managing director was where the company found its competitive advantage. At Atlanta, as in most companies in the region, companies are not normally thought of as impersonal entities in the way they are often thought of in Western societies; instead, in the vast majority of companies in the region where there is no separation between ownership and management, there is not a clear line drawn between how the company operates and the wishes, interests, skills, and personality of the owners.

Atlanta Medicare is a very modern company selling modern products to sophisticated and cost-conscious customers, and it does these tasks in accordance to norms found in the business environments in Thailand. The company is forced by its competition to supply high quality at reasonable prices, but it also needs to develop personal relationships and trust between the company's employees and its customers.

United Educational Consultants

There are a number of foreign-owned firms in Thailand; many of these are well known companies from the United States, the European Union (EU), Japan, and Korea. However, many foreign entrepreneurs have also set up shop in Thailand. Hipsher (2008a) labeled foreign firms that are start-up businesses and not extensions of existing business as "born foreign" firms. The United Educational Consultants would appear to fall into the born foreign category to some extent.

United Educational Consultants runs the TEFL Institute/United Language School. Although the company originated in 2001, it took a new direction in 2004 when Nikolaus Miche became the managing director and partner in the firm. The firm has quite a unique strategy, although located in Thailand, its primary target market is Westerners who want to come to live and teach in Thailand. The firm's primary product/service is education; the firm provides a training program in which individuals who are serious about becoming teachers can receive a teacher's certification recognized in Thailand while also earning university credits toward a masters degree in education at an accredited US university. The company is now also beginning to work to offer access to US accredited graduate level education for expatriate teachers living and working in Thailand. While there are other providers of teacher-training courses in Thailand, what makes the United Language School unique is the affiliation with and accreditation of the courses by US institutes of higher learning. The United Language School targets expats who are serious about seeking a teaching career as opposed to those who come to Asia to teach English for a few years before returning home to resume their lives. The school restricts class size to six and offers both exposure to academic educational theories as well as an opportunity to gain practical experience in classrooms round Bangkok and other parts of the country. Additionally, the firm has been active in setting up a non-profit foundation.

The ownership structure is that of a Thai–American partnership in which both owners are actively involved in the day-to-day management of the company, which would appear to be the norm within the region. Also, like so many business enterprises in the Theravada Buddhist countries of Southeast Asia, the company is relatively small with around ten full-time employees, mostly teacher trainers, and a few other part-time trainers who help out when needed.

A case could be made that United Educational Consultants is using a niche strategy in which it serves a specialized market. The company feels there are no major competitors as it supplies a unique service. It provides the only teacher preparation course in Thailand that provides university credits toward a masters degree in education. However, new teachers to Thailand do have the option of attending other training programs that are recognized by the Department of Education in Thailand, which helps meet their immediate need of obtaining a teaching position in the country. Therefore, one could argue the firm is using a differentiation strategy in which it positions itself in the high-quality/high-price quadrant.

As far as human resource management goes, the firm mostly behaves as would be expected of a small firm operating in Southeast Asia. The company prefers informal recruitment and selection procedures and relies on informal on-the-job training. As far as management style goes, since most of the employees are from Western countries, the management style could possibly be considered as being similar to that found in Western countries, but because of its size the management style might be thought of as more personalized than that expected in a larger firm, regardless of cultural context.

From an operational perspective, the firm needs to conform to US teaching standards to ensure accreditation, and as most of the students come from Western countries, this is not a problem. Theories taught, teaching techniques used, and assessments given would most likely be familiar to students majoring in education in any US university. However, the firm also tailors its courses to some extent to prepare students for working in the unique cultural environment found in Thailand.

6 Myanmar/Burma

History

Morck and Yeung (2007: 354) believed in order for foreign business practitioners to be successful in Asia they needed to understand Asia, and "Asia must be
understood on its own terms. This requires a deep respect for, and understanding
of, Asian history." This would seem to be especially important for individuals
from outside the region who are interested in the Theravada Buddhist countries
with their unique political situations and business practices. Along the same way
of thinking, Myint-U (2006: xiii–xiv) believed it is necessary to take a historical
view to understand the current complex situation in Myanmar/Burma.

The further back in time, the murkier history becomes. This is also true in the
territory that now comprises present-day Myanmar/Burma. It appears the Pyu
civilization evolved out of a pre-existing Iron Age culture in the dry areas of
central parts of Burma between 200 BC and AD 900. By the fourth or fifth century,
Buddhism had become the main religion of the Pyu, who spoke a Sino-Tibetan
language and used Indian scripts in their written language. Three major cities of
the Pyu are known, Beikthano, Sri Ksetra, and Halin, all of which were located
on tributaries to the Irrawaddy River (Higham 2001).

The legends of the origins of Burmese civilization state the history of modern-
day Myanmar/Burma began in Tagaung, north of present-day Mandalay, where
a kingdom was started by immigrants from India. While there may be little
empirical evidence to support this version of the arrival of civilization into the
country, there is considerable archeological evidence that there had been a continuously evolving culture in upper Burma from the first century BC up until the
end of the Bagan (Pagan) period in the thirteenth and fourteenth centuries AD.
Colonial scholars tended to believe the ancestors of the current residents of
Myanmar/Burma moved southward from Tibet and mixed with immigrants from
India, creating a separate ethnic identity (Dautremer 1913: 35; Myint-U 2006:
42–7; Hudson 2006).

In the early eighth century AD much of the Irrawaddy Valley was controlled
by the Kingdom of Nan Chao, who competed with the Mon for political suprem-
acy. However, around AD 849, the Burmese empire known as Bagan (Pagan) was
established. The empire slowly gained power until it was transformed by the

legendary ruler Anawrahta into a Buddhist empire (Chanthanom 1998: 38; Myint-U 2006: 48–57). "The Burmese people traditionally saw Anawrathta [Anawrahta] as the 'founder' of the first Burmese empire and the one who established Buddhism as the national religion" (Goh 2007: 1). Anawrahta was considered a ruler with non-violent Buddhist attitudes and soon Bagan was on flourishing trade routes in which the values and teachings of Buddhism as well as goods traveled. Chinese records show Bagan had frequent contacts with China in which goods, religious practices, and political support were exchanged. Buddhist monks and scholars in Bagan also kept close contact with Buddhist monks and scholars in both Sri Lanka and the newly formed kingdoms in present-day Thailand. While the spread of Buddhism and the Burmese language throughout Myanmar/Burma probably did not begin or end with the establishment of Bagan, it is generally felt by the people of the country that their culture of today is the result of an evolution that began during this period of history (Goh 2007: 19, 25, 40, 44; Myint-U 2006: 52–62).

In 1253, the armies from the Mongol Yuan dynasty were ordered by Kublai Khan to begin their campaign of conquest into Yunnan, and then the campaign expanded toward the territory controlled by the Kingdom of Bagan. When the king of Bagan refused to pay tribute to the Yuan Empire, the Mongols and their armies attacked and eventually conquered the capital at Bagan in 1287. However, by 1303, the Mongols and their armies withdrew and Bagan again became independent (Dai 2004: 149–50).

By 1330, Bagan's position as the center of the Burmese world had diminished. Throughout the Irrawaddy Valley and the rest of present-day Myanmar/Burma, a number of small kingdoms arose. The richest and most powerful of these was the Mon-speaking Kingdom of Pegu, which was located not far from present-day Yangon/Rangoon. Other kingdoms of the period located in present-day Myanmar/Burma included Ava, Prome, and Toungoo. Contact with the rest of the world slowed during this period (Goh 2007: 37; Myint-U 2006: 64–5).

Traditionally, the Kingdom of Ava had been considered a Shan kingdom and this time period was thought of as an era of disunity and warfare within the lands now comprising Myanmar/Burma. However, Aung-Thwin (1996) disagreed with this assessment and traced the origins of this myth to the assumption of the ethnicity of three brothers often thought to have been influential in the post-Bagan period. In fact, Aung-Thwin pointed out the high-level use of the Burmese language, the continuation in Ava of arts and economic activities used in Bagan, and political cooperation with Pegu, all of which provide support for the notion of Ava being a Burmese as opposed to a Shan-dominated kingdom. Therefore, the case was made that this period was not as chaotic as generally reported by historians. Aung-Thwin attributed the continuation of this myth to a bias of historians to think of periods of political consolidation as more advanced than periods of political fragmentation, and also due to colonial political considerations at the time of the British historians who initiated the study of the country's history.

The nation became again reunited under the leadership of Tabinshweti and his successor Bayinnaung in the sixteenth century. These leaders were from the

Burmese-speaking Kingdom of Toungoo. During the reign of Bayinnaung, much use was made of Portuguese mercenaries and their European weaponry to consolidate political power over territory in present-day Myanmar/Burma and also to lay waste to the Thai kingdoms of Lannathai and Ayutthaya to the east. The Shan, who had previously been constantly at war with the Burmese, were also defeated and brought into a Burmese-dominated political unit. The military victories of Tabinshweti and Bayinnaung continue to inspire the current military leadership of today as these victories show Myanmar/Burma was not always a less developed nation, but instead once was a regional power (Chanthanom 1998: 39; Myint-U 2006: 63–71).

Once again, the country's political system fragmented and was then consolidated under Alaungpaya, who founded the Konbaung dynasty in 1752. Alaungpaya conquered the city of Pegu in 1757. The Konbaung dynasty's first attack on the Thai kingdom of Ayutthaya took place in 1759 and 1760, but was prematurely abandoned due to the illness of Alaungpaya, who personally led the assault. However, in 1763, the Burmese had overrun the Kingdom of Lannathai and another attack against Ayutthaya, this time successful, was launched in 1776, bringing an end to the Thai kingdom (Dai 2004: 154; Myint-U 2006: 97–9).

However, the attention of the country's military shifted as the armies of the Qing dynasty began threatening its northern borders. The Qing dynasty of China launched numerous military expeditions into Burma, all of which were repelled by the local military forces and tropical disease. The defeat of the army led by the elite forces of the Manchu bannermen was a major blow to the rulers of the middle kingdom, and eventually both sides, weary of war, reached a peace agreement that included the sending of tribute to China, so that the Chinese could save face and claim a victory was achieved, when in reality the campaigns were military defeats for the Qing dynasty (Dai 2004).

Emboldened by the military victories over Ayutthaya and the Qing dynasty, the Burmese empire of the day launched a series of military campaigns that would eventually result in confrontation with the growing power of the British Empire in India. The Burmese became militarily involved in Arakan and Assam; these actions were seen as an approach upon British interests by the colonial rulers of South Asia. The British began to feel their position in eastern India was threatened and from 1822 to 1824 the British and the Burmese engaged in an expensive and bloody war that resulted in the loss for the Burmese of territory to the British, agreement to cease interference in Assam, Jaintia, and Cachar, and the payment of a huge indemnity. A second brief war between the two sides was conducted in 1852, which resulted in an internal split in the Burmese royal family that eventually resulted in King Mindon coming to power (Myint-U 2006: 113–34).

The political consolidation of Burma was not to last for long. The relationship between the British in India and Burma during the reign of King Mindon (1852–78), a noted patron of Buddhism, was peaceful. However, the fight over his succession, which resulted in the coming to power of King Thibaw,

weakened the state, which encouraged the thoughts of the British for further
eastward expansion. The British used as an excuse for their aggression the
immorality and ineffectiveness of the king to justify their actions. The British
also made the claim that it was necessary to invade Burma to protect British
interests in India. In a situation that in many ways resembles the more recent
US-led invasion of Iraq, removal of the "tyrant" was accomplished fairly easily,
but subduing the population proved to be much costlier and lengthier than
expected. The British arrived in Mandalay on November 28, 1885, and abducted
King Thibaw without any resistance. However, for the next three years, a fierce
insurgency continued to attack the British forces with surprisingly effective
results (Dautremer 1913).

The ethnic divisions of today have many of their roots in the era of British
domination. One example is the British policy of organizing ethnic minorities
and using these minorities to help fight the initial insurgency. The Karens, most
probably because of the significant numbers that had already converted to Christianity, became key allies of the British in maintaining British control of the
country (Smeaton 1920). To this day, the Karens for the most part have not
integrated into mainstream society in either Myanmar/Burma or Thailand and
armed conflict between some of the Karens and the government of Myanmar/
Burma continues.

Although the British thought of Burma mostly as a backwater of little importance after the initial prospects of economic gain proved to be ill-founded, the
British domination of the nation brought many changes. One was the large immigration of Indians into the country, who came to dominate government positions,
and like ethnic Chinese in other parts of Southeast Asia, many became extremely
successful in business. Another change was the increasing importance of secular
education and the diminished importance of the Buddhist monasteries in the
lives of students. The British also eliminated the monarchy and changes were
made in the legal system that deemphasized the role of the traditional authorities
(Carbine 2004: 131; Kaw 2005; Myint-U 2006: 186–7).

The British Empire in Asia was broken apart during World War II. Burma
was "sacrificed" by the British as the priority was placed on the unsuccessful
defense of Singapore, which could be used to protect the strategically important
Strait of Malacca. Aung San, Ne Win, and other Burmese nationalists ended up
in Japan, underwent training by the Japanese military, and eagerly joined in the
Japanese drive to "liberate" the country. The Japanese military replaced the
British and formal "independence" was granted in 1943 with Dr. Ba Maw being
the first prime minister. However, quickly the euphoria of being free from British
rule faded as it became obvious the Burmese had traded a European colonial
master for an Asian one (Myint-U 2006: 220–33).

However, the Japanese victory was short-lived. A massive British-led coun-
terattack coming out of India resulted in large-scale engagements in the mountainous principality of Manipur in which over 80,000 Japanese soldiers out of a
force of around 200,000 were killed. As the tide began turning, Aung San, Ne
Win, and many others began switching sides and the Anti-Fascist People's

Freedom League headed by Aung San was formed. On May 3, 1945, the British-led Twenty-Sixth Indian Division took Rangoon without any resistance (Myint-U 2006: 236–41).

Although the Japanese were eventually defeated, the initial collapse of the British Army, much like the defeat of the French in Indochina, brought to an end the aura of the invincibility of the white man. War weariness and a change in government in Britain brought to power those with less relish for colonial domination, providing an opportunity for Burmese independence. In early 1948, a Burmese delegation in London led by Aung San negotiated a deal to finalize Burmese independence. However, the joy of independence didn't last long as a communist rebellion began within months of the British withdrawal and the Karen struggle for an independent state broke out in 1949 (Min 2009: 1061; Myint-U 2006: 248–53).

Conflicts between ethnic groups have plagued Myanmar/Burma since independence. In 1947, an agreement was signed in Panglong by Aung San and leaders of a few ethnic groups, which was intended to be the foundation for an ethnically diverse political union. The agreement is often thought of as the original blueprint for a peaceful, ethnically diverse, and democratic country that somehow was pushed aside; however, this view may be more of a romanticized view of a golden past rather than an accurate reflection of the agreement. At the conference, there were delegations of Shan, Kachin, and Chin leaders, but other ethnic groups, most noticeably the Karen and Karenni, were absent. The communist rebellion, the death of Aung San, and the beginning of the Karen armed struggle for independence resulted in the promises and spirit of the Panglong conference not having the opportunities to grow into a peaceful multi-ethnic political union (Walton 2008).

In the struggle for independence, Aung San had emerged as one of the most influential political actors in the country. He had support from many sections of society and various ethnic groups. He was also viewed by many British as someone who they could work with during and after the transition to independence. However, the history of the nation took a major turn on the morning of July 19, 1947, when gunmen stormed a meeting of the interim government's executive council, killing Aung San and wounding four other council members. It was found that U Saw, a bitter rival of Aung San, and rogue elements of the British Officer Corp were behind the killings (Myint-U 2006: 254–5).

The years immediately following independence were the years of Myanmar/Burma's experiment with parliamentary democracy. The leader of democratic Burma during all but one year when he temporarily stepped aside was U Nu. U Nu was born in 1907 in the town of Wakema, approximately 50 miles from Rangoon, to a moderately wealthy family. While attending Rangoon University, where he was well liked, he developed a taste for wine, literature, women, sports, politics, and Buddhism. After leaving university, he worked at a private school in Pantanaw, where he taught English and history and was known for his anti-colonial viewpoint. He later returned to seek a graduate degree in law, which is when he met and became close friends with Aung San. U Nu became enamored with communism during his youth and remained pretty much an idealist during his time as head of the government. U Nu was prime minister and the leading political figure during Burma's days of democracy. He had a vision for the country governed by a mixture of Buddhist philosophy and socialist programs designed to aid the poor. U Nu was the first prime minister after independence and remained in that position while his Anti-Fascist People's Freedom League won numerous parliamentary elections. Although U Nu promised to retire from politics, and actually stepped down for one year, the lure of power was too great and he returned as prime minister. Over time, the League's political cohesion began to collapse, and under threat of a military coup (and to prevent his opponents from within his own party from seizing power?), U Nu appointed a caretaker military-led government led by Ne Win. In 1960, when elections were again held, U Nu's faction won overwhelmingly and he returned to the prime minister's office (Hlaing 2008; Myint-U 2006: 265–87).

Ne Win and the military apparently developed a taste for political power while in office and decided on March 2, 1962 it was time to seize power from the elected government on their own. U Nu and other leaders were arrested and the country's democratic experiment ended. U Nu was released in 1966 and later traveled abroad, attempting to garner foreign support for his return to power, but this movement quickly fizzled out. Ne Win and the government's Burmese Way to Socialism became the path the country would be destined to follow (Myint-U 2006: 290–309).

Ne Win, original name Shu Maung, was born in 1911 in the small town of Paungdale. After dropping out of university after failing his exams, Ne Win attempted to go into the coal business but was unsuccessful; he found himself working in a post office. Soon after he became swept up in the times and joined Aung San in training with the Japanese military and joined in the Japanese invasion which drove the British out of the country. He quickly rose up the ranks in the military and from independence until the coup of 1962 Ne Win was the head of the nation's armed forces (Myint-U 2006: 294–5). Under Ne Win's direction, the Burma Socialism Programme Party (BSPP) was formed. In 1974, Ne Win announced a transfer of power from the state, headed by Ne Win, to the representative of the people, also led by Ne Win. Despite a number of challenges, Ne Win remained in control of the country until 1988 (Hlaing 2008).

On July 23, 1988, the world was shocked by Ne Win's complete reversal in public attitude when he unexpectedly called for a return to multi-party elections and resigned, effective immediately. However, he also chose as his successor Sein Lwin, a military hard-liner. On August 8, 1988, student-led demonstrations calling for a return to democracy began. This led to a violent military crackdown, the sacking of Sein Lwin, and further protests. Aung San Suu Kyi, daughter of national hero Aung San, became the international face of the democracy movement. However, the military was not willing to relinquish control and brutally suppressed the calls for democracy, and a new government, calling itself the State Law and Order Restoration Council (SLORC) and led by General Saw Maung, took control of the country (Myint-U 2006: 31–6). Within a few years,

Aung San Suu Kyi was placed under house arrest, where she has for the most time remained, and other leaders of the democracy movement were jailed, killed, or driven out of the country. Although Ne Win was gone, the military remained firmly in power.

In 1992, Than Shwe took over the chairmanship of SLORC. SLORC evolved into the State Peace and Development Council (SPDC) and Than Shwe consolidated his power with the ouster of Prime Minister Khin Nyunt in 2004 (Hlaing 2008). In what seems to be a bizarre move, reportedly on advice from his personal astrologer, Than Shwe decided to move the government and capital of the country from Yangon/Rangoon to the remote area now called Naypyidaw (Seekins 2009: 173). Another uprising, often referred to as the Saffron Rebellion after the color of the robes worn by the Buddhist monks who took part, surfaced in 2007; however, the hopes of the citizens who supported democracy in the country were dashed and the military retained power.

Although to the outside world, it would appear the main struggle in the country is between the military and proponents of democracy, Hlaing (2008: 149) believed:

> In modern Burmese history, power and factional struggles were more the rule than the exception, for they were present in almost all post-independence governments. Various rival groups and factions in post-independence governments constantly sought to marginalize and undermine the role of their opponents in the governments.

In 1989, in the aftermath of the bloody crackdown on democracy demonstrators, SLORC decided to "rename" the country from Burma to Myanmar. Since this name change is often associated with political oppression, what to call the country stirs up some controversy. The United Nations, ASEAN, China, India, and Japan have chosen to accept the change and refer to the country as Myanmar. While the United States, Canada, Britain, Australia, and Aung San Suu Kyi's National League for Democracy have chosen to use the term Burma (Dittmer 2008). The unsatisfactory compromise used by the EU in choosing Myanmar/Burma would appear to be the most politically neutral of the choices available.

Initially, relationships between independent Burma and communist China were strained, mainly due to the communist insurgency that plagued Burma during its early years of independence. However, over time, closer relationships developed. After the crackdown on democracy advocates in 1988, the government of Myanmar/Burma was ostracized by much of the world; however, China did not condemn the actions of the military dictatorship and closer political, military, and economic ties have developed (McCarthy 2008: 916; Stuart-Fox 2003: 212–13).

The year 2008 was eventful in Myanmar/Burma, as Cyclone Nargis tore through the Irrawaddy Delta leaving an estimated 84,537 dead, 53,836 missing, and 19,359 injured. A constitutional referendum was "passed" by voters in which the position of the military will remain secure during and after the country's transition to "democracy." Also, the assassination of Pado Mahn La Pan, the secretary-general of the Karen National Union (KNU), in the border town of Mae Sot, Thailand (where the author was living at the time), apparently by members of a splinter Karen group that has decided to give up the armed struggle and make peace with the government of Myanmar/Burma, brings into question the viability of a continued Karen armed struggle for independence or even a limited level of autonomy (Seekins 2009).

To achieve legitimacy in the eyes of the citizenry, the military junta attempts to identify itself with the county's Buddhist traditions and values.

> As did many Kings of Burma's pre-colonial past, the military junta attempts to legitimate its rule and also sometimes tries to atone for its moral trans-gressions through state-sponsored Buddhist ceremonies. Sometimes these ceremonies have heightened a consciousness of the Buddha among ordinary citizens as the symbols used are so powerful. This shared presence of the Buddha on people's minds can help to bolster the state's power, because the latter often portrays the Buddha as an auspicious protector of the state.
>
> (Kaw 2005: 10)

At the current time, military control over the country would seem to be the path the country will continue to follow. However, Buddhist philosophy teaches that all things change and, therefore, military rule over Myanmar/Burma is not a per-manent state of affairs; however, the teachings of the Buddha do not provide techniques to predict how fast change will come or how dramatic the change will be when it inevitably comes.

Business and economic environment

General features

Myanmar/Burma has been classified by the United Nations as one of the most underdeveloped nations in the world. It is difficult for the private sector to operate effectively as "The legal framework is inadequate, corruption is rife, and skill levels are low" (Holliday 2008: 1057). Seekins (2009) finds there are two separate economies in the country. The top level is fueled by foreign investment, primarily from multinational oil companies, and consists of exporting high-value raw materials such as teak, gemstones, and natural gas to neighboring countries. Around 90 percent of foreign investment into the country goes to the energy sector. This top level is controlled by the government and individuals with close ties to the government. The bottom level, where the vast majority of citizens function, consists mostly of agriculture, services, and small-scale industries. This bottom level of the economy receives very little investment, either foreign or domestic, and is not very efficient.

Many government officials are aware of the country's problem, but have had difficulties in finding politically acceptable solutions to the country's economic difficulties. Many consider the policies of Vietnam and China as models to emulate, as these countries have been able to move to a more market-based economy while retaining a one-party political structure. The military-led government would like to accomplish these objectives as well, but it would appear retaining political control outweighs economic growth as a government priority. The government has started a policy to privatize some government-owned companies; however, since the government-owned sector employs very few people and the firms being privatized do not appear to have stellar prospects, it is unlikely this privatization scheme will have the same positive effect as was seen in China and Vietnam during their phases of privatization of state-owned firms. However, the government is beginning to more firmly control more of the lands that contain majority ethnic minority populations, which has had the result of tax revenues increasing and non-recorded cross-border trade beginning to decrease (Thawnghmung 2008: 279–83).

The country's improvised state affects nearly the entire population. This even applies to the country's Buddhist religious institutions. Members of the *Sangha* rely on alms from the lay population for their survival; however, as the lay population struggles for its own economic survival, little is left over to provide to the monks. In addition, Buddhist monasteries have often provided safety nets for society by running orphanages and schools for the poor; however, the economic difficulties are making it nearly impossible to continue to provide these types of social services (Lorch 2008). The poverty of the country is also driving workers, including some skilled workers and professionals, to seek work abroad, mainly in neighboring Thailand. While the total number of individuals from Myanmar/Burma working in Thailand is a matter of conjecture as the vast majority of these are undocumented, the number is known to be significant (Mon 2005).

The current economic situation and business environment have considerable problems, but Than (2005: 54) retained a sliver of optimism and proclaimed, "Once Myanmar achieves political stability, economic relations and cooperation will improve significantly which will result in the economic development and social well being of Myanmar and its people."

Economic conditions

Myanmar/Burma continues to be one of the poorest countries in the world and the current government's policies seem to be mostly ineffective in creating economic growth and poverty reductions. "An evaluation of the government's policy reforms on subsidies reveals a continuing preoccupation with regime survival over economic efficiencies" (Thawnghmung 2008: 282). The differences between the official and black market exchange rates make most formal international trade in the private sector impractical, but these differences allow government officials to personally profit. The official rate of the kyat to the International Monetary Fund's (IMF) special drawing rights has been kept steady at 8.5085 while the market rate of the kyat to the US dollar has fluctuated between 1,000 and 1,300 in recent years. In addition, high inflation has been causing difficulties for private banks to effectively work to help develop the private sector (Thawng-hmung 2008).

Myanmar/Burma has remained very much a closed economy with extremely little connection with the global economy. Increased foreign trade has been correlated with an increase in GDP throughout the other developing economies of Southeast Asia, while a decrease in foreign trade has been correlated with a decline in GDP in Myanmar/Burma. Imports into Myanmar/Burma have steadily declined while exports, primarily natural gas, have increased. However, this increase in natural gas exports has not had much trickle down effect throughout the economy (Alamgir 2008). "Myanmar's economy, clearly has remained mostly closed to trading links with the rest of the world, going in a direction opposite that of its neighbors" (Alamgir 2008: 984).

It is difficult for economists to accurately judge the state of the economy in Myanmar/Burma. Taylor (2008: 250) speculated "no one knows for sure" the level of GDP growth found in the country, while Alamgir (2008: 985) reported, "Even government officials have admitted the overestimation of GDP figures in official statistics." "Official statistics indicate growth in excess of 10 percent since 2000, but this is not consistent with other variables closely correlated with GDP, such as energy use. Nonofficial estimates put GDP growth at less than half the official estimates" (Srivastava 2009: 246). Part of the problem stems from the use of an unrealistic and impractical official exchange rate in calculations. Regardless of the statistics used, most observers seem to agree that the citizens of the country are not having their lives improved by economic growth in the same manner as many people throughout the Asian region have in recent times.

The country faces many economic challenges. Inflation has been high and slower growth in its major trading partners, Thailand, India, and China, will likely result in the lowering of the prices received from the country's exports. Other weaknesses include an inefficient and limited banking system, a legal environment that is not business friendly, and a lack of skills in the workforce. On the other hand, there are a few bright spots. Rebuilding from Cyclone Nargis, which will be mostly financed by foreign donors, should provide a boost to the economy, foreign reserves have increased, and tax revenues have been more effectively collected as the government gains more control over areas that had previously been controlled by ethnic insurgent factions (Srivastava 2009).

Business practices

The Economic Enterprises Law passed in 1989 restricted control of key industries such as teak, petroleum, natural gas, gemstones, fish, and metals to government controlled businesses (Alamgir 2008). State-run enterprises in the country have not proven to be any more effective than state-run enterprises have in other locations. Thawnghmung (2008: 282) reported on government-run enterprises by claiming, "Some costly projects, such as building irrigation and hydroelectricity facilities have been affected by waste, corruptions at different governmental levels, and lack of technical expertise or unwillingness to take the people into consideration." The primary destination for the exports of the state-run enterprises are Thailand, China, and Singapore (Taylor 2008).

Due to economic sanctions, most international trade is carried out between Myanmar/Burma and its neighbors. Over the past two decades, there has been a considerable increase in trade between Myanmar/Burma and the Yunnan province of China. Myanmar/Burma mostly exports fish and other agricultural products into Yunnan, and imports manufactured goods, machinery, and electronics (Than 2005). However, due to the informal and unrecorded nature of so much of the cross-border trade within the region any trade statistics reported need to be approached with caution.

> In reality, since the early 1970s Chinese consumer goods have, along with Thai goods, flooded the Myanmar market through illegal trade. Every household in Myanmar relies on cheap Chinese products, such as toiletries, cloth, medicines, electronics and so on.... The volume and impact of the illegal Chinese trade with Myanmar is difficult to assess. But it was Chinese and Thai goods that helped fill the gaps created by the badly performing centrally-planned socialist economy of Myanmar.
>
> (Myoe 2007a: 2)

Foreign investment into the country in sectors not controlled by the government has not proven to be successful. Many Japanese and South Korean firms had previously invested in some small-scale operations, but many of these projects have been abandoned. For example, it has been reported 40 percent of all South Korean firms that invested in the textile sector had pulled out of the country by 2006 (Alamgir 2008: 994). However, there has been an increase in Chinese investment, primarily in relatively large-scale industries in partnership with local government-controlled firms (Myoe 2007).

There are few official studies of business practices in Myanmar/Burma on which to rely to paint an accurate picture. However, it has been reported it is the poorest country in all of Asia (Stads and Kam 2007). Limited personal observation and conversations with individuals from the country indicate many businesses that are not directly connected with government officials attempt to keep under the government's radar and therefore are mostly concerned with short-term profits and survival as opposed to growth. Also, the fact so many citizens of Myanmar/Burma have voluntarily chosen to cross the border into Thailand and work in nearly slave-like conditions in garment factories, construction, and other industries illustrates the lack of employment opportunities within the country itself.

Agriculture

Agriculture is a very important sector of the economy of Myanmar/Burma. It accounts for over 60 percent of the nation's employment, around a third of the country's export earnings, and a little under half of the country's total GDP;

however, the country's spending on research to increase the efficiency of the sector is woefully inadequate (Stads and Kam 2007).

In the past, the government's policy was to artificially keep the price of rice, the crop that makes up the country's staple diet, low. This had been done by forcing farmers to sell at below market prices. "This practice, which squeezed farmers to a bare subsistence level while banned private rice trading, led inevitably to declines in production, productivity and the quality of rice" (Thawnghmung 2008: 279). However, the country has made modest steps toward liberalizing the agricultural sector. It appears the government has stopped using production controls, for example, forcing farmers to attempt to grow rice during the dry season, and the government is now purchasing more rice at or near market prices. While this is helping farmers to increase income, the government has also had to give cash payments to civil servants in order for them to be able to afford the higher priced rice (Srivastava 2009; Thawnghmung 2008).

Economic sanctions

In September 2007, the world was shocked by the images coming out of Myanmar/Burma showing government troops violently suppressing the political demonstrations in Yangon/Rangoon, which at times seemed to be led by Buddhist monks. The crackdown by the military resulted in numerous deaths, including the killing of a Japanese journalist by the direct actions of a government soldier. Although these events brought the suffering of the Burmese people to the attention of the world, repression and violence have been at the center of the Burmese military government's policy to retain control of the country for years. Out of sight of the international media, over 3,000 villages in the ethnic minority regions of the country have been burnt to the ground in order to prevent the villages from providing support for ethnic armed resistance groups. Additionally, local villagers have often been forced to perform labor in government-controlled infrastructure projects. Many ethnic minority people have been forced to engage in road building projects that are at least partially designed to allow more military access and therefore control of these areas.

The protests against the military-led government began in mid-August 2007, initially in response to the move by the SPDC to remove subsidies on fuel and cooking oil, which was the cause of a significant surge in prices. On August 19, 2007, members of the "88 Generation" (leaders of the 1988 student protests) organized a small peaceful march. Over the next month, the number of protests increased and many members of the much revered Buddhist *Sangha* began taking a leading role. As time went on, the protests began taking on a broader and more political flavor. During the protests, there was a sense of optimism and possibility for change within segments of society that favored having a democratic system. However, as the protests grew, the decision was made by the military junta to end the protests at all costs, even by violently attacking the most respected members of society, the Buddhist monks, which caused a further distancing of the military from the majority of the Burmese population to occur (Human Rights Watch 2007a).

The response of Western governments to political repression and violence in Myanmar/Burma has traditionally been to impose sanctions of varying degrees of severity, with the United States generally imposing stricter sanctions than European governments. The response of Western governments to the 2007 crackdown on pro-democracy protesters in Myanmar/Burma has been to increase or maintain sanctions. The stated purpose of sanctions is to cause economic harm to the ruling party, forcing a change in policy or leadership. An unstated purpose of sanctions is for governments to prove they are proactively "doing something" in response to political repression to satisfy political demands from their constituencies. It should also be remembered, for Western governments, refusing to do business in Myanmar/Burma has a minuscule effect on the national economic performance as trade between Myanmar/Burma and Western countries is more or less non-existent.

Many proponents of sanctions believe complete isolation of the government of Myanmar/Burma is the key to the success of sanctions and these proponents have been extremely critical of governments, such as China, India, Thailand, Japan, and Singapore, which have followed policies of engagement with the military junta. Some proponents of sanctions even went so far as to suggest boycotting the 2008 Beijing Olympics due to China's approach to engagement in Myanmar/Burma. The countries who have not followed the path of sanctions counter that engagement is more likely to bring positive changes. To paraphrase what a Thai official in a meeting with international aid donors said, what good does it do to try to further isolate a country whose government has voluntarily chosen to isolate itself?

Alamgir (2008) believed Western sanctions have helped to prevent the emergence of an independent trading class, which would be the segment of society that would be expected to lead opposition to the government's socialistic economic policies. Therefore, it was felt Western sanctions have had the unintended effect of supporting the status quo in the country.

In the aftermath of the brutal crackdown and detention of pro-democracy activists, there was intense interest in Myanmar/Burma in the outside world resulting in numerous Internet petitions and condemnations of the military junta by world leaders. But there has been no indication that further isolating and criticizing the military regime have resulted in any change in policy within the country. Voluntarily choosing to disengage with the current government of Myanmar/Burma limits the options available to Western governments to promote change in the country and these sanctions appear to be resulting in opening the door for greater Chinese and Indian influence, not only in Myanmar/Burma but in other countries in Southeast Asia; however, so far it appears India has not been satisfied with the results of its engagement policy (Egreteau 2008). "Based on Myanmar's trade patterns, we can surmise that sanctions have pushed the country toward Asia and away from better ties with Western democracies. Human rights activism has not affected the public image of Asian investors in the same way it pressured Western multinationals" (Alamgir 2008: 994).

The public statements by the Western powers of expecting complete submission by the current military-led government to the demands of the Western countries is being used by the military junta as a propaganda tool in order to cling to power. The government of Myanmar/Burma uses the sanctions as the basis for their claims the Western countries continue to think of Myanmar/ Burma as a colony that can be ordered around. Appealing to the anti-colonial attitude of the country's population is a way to drum up nationalistic sentiments and support for the military regime. Furthermore, the hard-line stance and demands for immediate and dramatic change by the United States and other Western nations does not play as well in the neighboring countries in Southeast Asia as it does in a Western context as it smacks of cultural imperialism. This strategy of sanctions and refusal to engage can be interpreted by individuals in the region as Western nations implying they are morally superior to the Asian nations, which use different strategies to deal with the government of Myanmar/ Burma.

The affairs of Myanmar/Burma are not a major foreign policy focus for most Western nations and few top diplomats or government officials can afford to spend the time or effort to understand all the detailed complexities of the situation. However, even before the current crackdown, many specialists of affairs in Myanmar/Burma have questioned the wisdom of the continued use of sanctions (e.g., Hlaing 2005; James 2004; Roberts 2006; Steinberg 2004).

Evidence appears to support the statement: sanctions against Myanmar/Burma have not been effective. Most indications are the recent economic performance in the country has been miserable, especially in comparison with other Asian nations from the region, and going against the global trend, the standard of living in the country has actually declined in the last decade. Sanctions are not the only reason for the country's isolation from the global economy and its poor economic performance; the government of Myanmar/Burma has also implemented policies to restrict incoming investment, tourism, and the ability of the country's citizens to interact with the outside world. Sanctions give the government of Myanmar/Burma another excuse to further isolate its citizens from potential knowledge of and support for democratic reform.

Research has consistently shown a very strong correlation between international trade and economic growth; research has also shown a consistent correlation between economic growth and measurable indications of standard of living (life expectancy, infant mortality, etc.) (Agrawal 2007; Hasan *et al.* 2007; Son 2007). Therefore, a case could be made Western sanctions could be contributing to the suffering of the people living in Myanmar/Burma. If this suffering leads to a change in regime, an argument could be made the sacrifice is worthwhile; however, if sanctions do not lead to regime change, and it is difficult to find any evidence supporting the argument that sanctions are creating enough pressure for a change in regime, increasing the suffering caused by poverty of the people would seem a high price to pay for Western governments being seen as "doing something" to appease the demands of activists and the general public who support the political opposition in Myanmar/Burma.

Many individuals may believe the ideal situation in Myanmar/Burma would include the military junta to unconditionally release Aung San Suu Kyi and all other political prisoners and to allow free and fair elections in which all political parties, including the National League for Democracy (NLD), are allowed to participate. However, there is no indication that this ideal situation will become a reality in the foreseeable future. Is giving the military-led government an all-or-nothing option the only choice for Western governments? Is considering policies that would promote slower and less dramatic change possible? Although the military junta in Myanmar/Burma whips up support within its armed forces by claiming the United States or other Western powers are planning military operations to create regime change, in reality neither the United States nor any other Western country could gather the public support internally and internationally that would be needed to launch an Iraq-style military operation in Myanmar/Burma. Without the threat of military intervention and the demonstrated lack of concern over economic growth by the current leadership of the military junta, it is questionable whether Western powers can apply enough pressure on the Burmese leadership to expedite the downfall of the military dictatorship through the use of political and economic sanctions.

If the goal is humanitarian, not political, it is felt it is time for Western governments to seek other options toward improving the situation in Myanmar/Burma rather than the use of economic and political sanctions. It is easy for government officials and citizens in the West to take the moral high ground and refuse to cooperate with a government that is almost universally considered repressive and more concerned with retaining power over improving the lives of its citizens. But the Western governments should consider the costs and benefits to all parties, especially the citizens of Myanmar/Burma, of continuing a policy when there are few indications that the policy will achieve any measurable objectives. There may be options between the extremes of supporting a brutal dictatorship and attempting to completely isolate all of the people of the country from all contact with the Western world. Although Aung San Suu Kyi is rightfully highly respected in the Western world, concern over her welfare and opinions should not block out all other concerns for the welfare and opinions of the millions of other people living in the country.

The situation in Myanmar/Burma is complex, and indications would appear to show outsiders have a limited ability to promote internal change. When dramatic events in Myanmar/Burma bring the country to the world's attention for a few days or weeks, the easy option for leaders of Western democracies is to impose sanctions. There is no significant effect on Western economies and the announcement of sanctions appear to appease the demands of Western populations for a response to the brutality of the regime, but soon the spotlight shifts to other parts of the world, and therefore few people stay interested in Myanmar/Burma long enough to review whether the policies and sanctions had the desired effect or not. Although Western politicians may play a small political price for not responding to a crisis in Myanmar/Burma caused by the violent suppression of demonstrations for democracy, because focus of the world's media does not linger on events in the country, it is unlikely that Western politicians will pay much of a political price if their responses are not effective in the long term. It is suggested that if the international community wants to take a more effective approach to the situation in Myanmar/Burma, it should take a more complex look at the situation and consider both ideal and more realistic approaches in order to promote positive change. Since isolation and sanctions have not had the desired effect; it has been suggested it is time to give engagement a chance (Hipsher 2008b).

7 Business strategies in Theravada Buddhist Southeast Asia

Introduction

There are some basic principles that apply to business transactions around the world, while the practices used to carry out the business principles will vary according to context. Merchants along the Silk Road one thousand years ago would most likely have no trouble appreciating a modern business tycoon's concern over ensuring steady supplies at reasonable prices. It is probable; consumers in the Roman Empire were as concerned about receiving value for money as are modern shoppers in Beijing. The importance of building a reputation for quality was in all likelihood as important for nineteenth-century tea merchants as it is for Toyota or Mercedes Benz today. The Theravada Buddhist countries of Southeast Asia have very different business environments than is found in other locations in the world and therefore it is not surprising one will find very different business practices; however, it should also be kept in mind many of the universal principles of business are applied by businesses in the region on a daily basis.

Strategic management

The concept of strategic management in business has its roots firmly planted in a military foundation and a focus on winning and competition has shaped its study (Cummings 2007). However, strategic management in a business does not always require conquering one's enemies; in fact, organizations can often survive and thrive by seeking out ways to avoid confrontation with competitors. Strategic management is managing the big picture, and providing direction for the entire organization over a lengthy period of time. It is impossible for a single company to do everything for everyone, therefore, "Strategies are about choices" (Peng 2002: 252). When forging a company's strategy, decision makers can not avoid making trade-offs (Porter 1996: 69). Microsoft is the world's leading software maker but it does not make hamburgers, and Wal-Mart can not supply its customers with low prices while simultaneously providing individualized service to each customer and paying its employees higher than average wages.

Much of the recent study of strategic management has been influenced by Porter's (1980) framework of three generic strategies: cost-leadership, differentiation, and focus (niche). Porter believed firms should choose one strategy carefully and a purer form of a strategy would more likely produce desired results than being stuck between strategies. The applicability of this framework has been frequently tested with varying results (for examples, see Dess and Davis 1984; Murray 1986; Zajac and Shortell 1989).

A very large number of firms within Southeast Asia are family owned, or have other forms of concentrated ownership, such as government ownership. Most of the studies of strategic management assume a firm's primary mission is to maximize profits; however, firms with high levels of ownership concentration often have goals that override maximizing profits (Su, Xu and Phan 2007). Additionally, it has been found the concept of strategic management in family-owned firms can be quite different from what is seen in the corporate world, with family-owned firms often using less formalized strategic management processes. It has been noticed that family-owned firms often can have some competitive advantages in some areas over corporations, where there is a separation between ownership and management, for example, being more responsive in uncertain environments (Ibrahim *et al.* 2008). It is likely, since a corporation has a greater need to create consensus before embarking on a strategy than would a family-owned firm, corporations would more carefully and formally plan for the future while a family-owned firm has the option of being more reactive instead of being proactive as changes of strategy and implementation can happen much quicker than in a corporation. Therefore, many family-owned firms in developing economies replace long-term strategic management with flexibility. Another factor that may be limiting family-owned firms and SMEs from making extensive use of formal strategic management is the lack of expertise or experience in the use of the tools needed to carry out a formal strategic management planning process (Reynolds and Lancaster 2007).

In strategic management, location matters. Tong *et al.* (2008) provided support for the idea that the country a firm originates in, the growth rates of that country, and the industry a firm operates in all affect the strategic options available to a firm. Peng *et al.* (2008) found the institutional environment had a major effect on strategic decision making and there are identifiable differences between the strategies of firms from developing economies as opposed to developed economies. These studies support Hipsher (2007), who believed the economic environment a firm operated in was the most important factor driving strategic decisions. In more economically developed regions, companies have a wider variety of opinions to use to get customers to part with portions of their income. However, in less economically developed countries, firms have fewer strategic options due to the lower purchasing power of both consumers and businesses. When one visits a megamall in the United States, one will see a wide variety of products being strategically marketed toward an ever growing number of market segments. However, in the rural areas of the Theravada Buddhist countries of Southeast Asia, one sees a very narrow range of businesses employing a relatively narrow range of strategies. Hipsher argued that the principles of strategic management in developing regions are basically the same as in more economically developed regions; however, because of the differing levels of purchasing power of customers, the practice of strategic management will differ considerably.

Strategic management, as taught in Western universities, involves options such as building an international brand image, using mass production techniques to produce in huge quantities for huge markets in order to gain economies of scale, and investing vast sums in research and development to constantly stay ahead of the competition. These strategies are not for the most part available to firms originating for the Theravada Buddhist countries in Southeast Asia and therefore, in many cases, the strategies employed by many smaller firms in the region may not always resemble what is found in large multinational corporations.

Yeung's (2005) concept of organizational space might be useful when examining strategies used by firms from the region. Yeung claimed firms often try to avoid direct competition; instead, they seek to carve out their own "organizational space" that they solely occupy. The borders of organizational space can stretch and contract and "unlike physical space, that has definite territorial boundaries within specific countries or regions, organizational space is only bound by the organizational capabilities and reach of specific business organizations" (Yeung 2005: 225). In general, firms from the Theravada Buddhist countries can not develop or manufacture complex products in the same manner as large Western, Japanese, Korean, or Taiwanese firms. Therefore, firms within the region search out where they have a competitive advantage and can fall into the value chain created by large companies or they find "space" not occupied by other firms. For example, the Cambodian beverage company introduced in Chapter 3 does not attempt to manufacture beverages. Instead it uses its local knowledge and connections to distribute and market internationally recognized brands, therefore creating a space that is not occupied by foreign firms in which it can provide value to customers and earn a profit. Another example, as seen in Chapter 4: SMP products are high-value unique hand-made artistic products, being from Laos provides an exotic image of its products internationally, and because of the labor intensity involved in the production of these products, the company has a competitive advantage over a Western firm making similar types of products. SMP has found a unique "space" in which to operate internationally where it does not directly compete with large foreign firms using mass production processes.

It has often been overheard in conversations with expatriate business practitioners in the region that businesses in Thailand and the other countries in the region do not plan for the long term and are more reactive than proactive. Long-term strategic planning requires a belief in the stability or predictability of the future environment a business will be operating in. In Western countries or in developed Asian economies, businesses may feel fairly confident in the continuation of the basic approach to regulating business that future governments will take. In the Theravada Buddhist countries of Southeast Asia, with its history of political coups in Thailand and command and control economies with arbitrary decision making by government officials in the other countries in the region, there is far less confidence in what the future business environment will be like. Also, in developed economies, growth is both slower and steadier than is seen in Southeast Asia, as evidenced by the fast growth seen in Thailand in the early 1990s, which was then followed by the economic crash of 1997. This unstable and fast-changing environment is not conducive to the extensive use of long-term strategic management practices.

Another factor to consider, Theravada Buddhism emphasizes the impermanence of everything. It is likely this fundamental aspect of the cultural environments found in the region has an impact on the lowering of priority on planning and taking a proactive approach. Being at ease with uncertainty about the future, as taught in the region's religious tradition, may result in many business leaders in the region being more reactive and less proactive when it comes to long-term strategic planning than is advocated and practiced in Western environments or the Confucius-influenced countries of East Asia.

However, firms in the region have to make strategic management decisions, such as identifying target markets and choosing a positioning strategy, even if these decisions are made without using long-term strategic management processes. There are no universal best practices in strategic management. Wal-Mart and Mercedes Benz have both had success, even though they use very different positioning strategies. It is proposed the principles of strategic management are universal; however, the actual practices found in the Theravada Buddhist countries of Southeast Asia will be influenced by various environmental factors, with the relatively lower level of economic development being the most influential environmental factor.

Tactical business practices

Tactical business practices refer to how an organization attempts to achieve the strategic direction and objectives an organization has decided upon. Strategic decisions involve the entire organization and are long-term focused. Tactical organizational practices are usually of shorter duration and often affect only part of the organization. Examples of tactical organizational practices include the use of a particular management style, human resource practices of hiring, training, and retaining workers, and the choice of specific marketing or packaging practices.

Hipsher (2007) argued the social-cultural environment had the greatest influence on the choice of tactical business practices; the great diversity found in management practices, marketing, and human resource management around the world indicates that the tactical business practices that work best in one location may not always produce desired results in locations with different cultural values. If there were international best practices in tactical management, market forces would be forcing a convergence of tactical business practices. Research indicates this is not happening. For example, the buying patterns of consumers from different nationalities differ widely (Chui and Kwok 2008) resulting in firms having to adjust their tactical marketing practices of advertising, distribution, and packaging to fit the social-cultural environment the firm operates in. Additionally, the differing social-cultural environments may assist in explaining the lack of success in the use of Western tactical human resource management practices involving empowerment in the more collectivist cultures of Asia (Hui *et al.* 2004; Newburry and Yakova 2006).

Kaweevisultrakul and Chan (2007) have given us an example from the region as they found firms in Thailand have difficulty in implementing the tactical practices associated with "knowledge management" as advocated in the West. The authors attribute part of the problem to cultural difference and suggest to implement these types of tactical practices in Thailand a firm needs to adapt to the cultural environment found in the country.

According to Hofstede (1980, 1983), Thailand, and all of Asia for that matter, was classified as having a collectivist culture while Western cultures were generally believed to be more individualistic. It has been noticed that firms in the collectivist countries of Asia usually use far fewer formal rules and regulations; instead, they rely on informal group dynamics to control behavior (Naisbitt 1997). It has been suggested that worker satisfaction in collectivist societies is often highly dependent upon personal relationships on the job, which includes relationships with co-workers as well as superiors and subordinates (Wong and Wong 2003). It appears being part of a social network and using one's social contacts to advance one's business interests is common in firms in the region, which is supported by research in other collectivist societies (Carney 2004: 177–8; London and Hart 2004: 362; Luo 2005: 225). It would appear that in organizations in collectivist societies, informal social contacts drive many tactical business practices to a greater extent than in organizations from Western countries, which often use more formal and structured procedures.

The importance of social relationships in the business environment in the Theravada Buddhist country of Thailand has been noticed in a number of studies. Johnsen (2007: 142) in her study of the silk industry noted, "In Thailand, in particular, the contractual obligations of the relationships were seen to be less important than the goodwill between parties...." Petison and Johri (2008) found in the automotive industry in Thailand, supplier-foreign manufacturer relationships normally begin as market-exchange types of relationships and then develop into relationships based on trust and social contacts. The authors found having these deeper relationships was often beneficial to both parties as the local suppliers benefited from the technical support from the foreign manufacturers while the foreign companies benefited by less business intelligence leakage and increased understanding of local market conditions.

If, as suggested by Hipsher (2007), the social-cultural environment has the greatest effect on tactical business practices, it is to be expected the tactical level is the area where Theravada Buddhist values will have the most effect on a firm from the region's operations. One key value of Theravada Buddhism is an acceptance of ambiguity. This acceptance of ambiguity would suggest firms in the region would not place a premium on the use of formal structures, detailed planning, and the extensive use of rules and regulations.

Duong and Swierczek (2008) found both differences and similarities in managerial attitudes between Vietnamese and Thai managers. Vietnamese managers were reported to have scored higher in long-term orientation than were Thai managers, again this supports the concept that Thai managers may be more comfortable with ambiguity than other managers, even those from other developing countries.

Another key feature of Theravada Buddhism is the belief in *kamma*. The belief in *kamma* can foster the concept that individuals with higher social status and greater wealth have earned their positions in previous lives. This belief can be in direct conflict with many of the egalitarian principles taken for granted in Western societies. Therefore, it is not surprising one does not see many egalitarian tactical management practices, such as having employee involvement in management decision making, taking place in organizations in the region. It might also explain the lack of unionization in most of the region, as employees may feel more comfortable with wider gaps in income and social standing due to the influence of the concept of *kamma*. On the other hand, an almost universal feeling of business owners in the region is the idea that employees are part of the "family" (and often they literally are) and those who have higher positions in society have paternalistic responsibilities toward employees in a manner that a manager or business owner in a Western organization would not have.

Arguably the most central feature of Theravada Buddhism is the belief in taking the middle path. Employees in firms in this region are expected to work for their pay, but there is also an expectation that work should be a place where social needs are met and workers expect a less clear separation between work life and personal life than is the norm in other societies. Management styles in the region often reflect this middle path approach. Rarely will there be found a working environment in a firm in the region that is as fast paced or achievement driven as is found in many firms from other regions. Also, cut-throat competition to get ahead within a firm may be less commonly practiced in the organizations in the region in comparison to what is seen in firms from other environments. This middle path approach to management may change some of the focus from the efficiency and effectiveness of tactical practices toward social harmony and creating an enjoyable work environment. Duong and Swierczek (2008) in their comparative study of Vietnamese and Thai managers found Vietnamese managers to be more performance oriented than were Thai managers, while Thai managers expressed more job satisfaction. This would appear to indicate that it is not just the stage of development of a country that affects managerial attitudes, and the reporting of Thai managers being less performance oriented and more satisfied with their jobs may be able to be partially attributed to the concept of the middle path that is such a central feature of Theravada Buddhism.

Operational business practices

Operational business practices refer to the day-to-day operations of an organization. This is the level where the products and services are produced, reports are written, sales calls are made, and deliveries take place. Hipsher (2007) proposed the operational practices of an organization are primarily driven by the technological environment. When talk turns to globalization in the business world, it is often the operational level that is focused on. In many organizations in the region, one is likely to find people using similar technologies as found in other regions. Accountants in Vientiane are likely using the same software programs as accountants in Sydney; sales personnel in Chiang Mai make use of cellular phones about as often as do sales personnel in Sacramento; and delivery truck drivers in Siem Riep are likely to be driving trucks which would be familiar to delivery truck drivers in Osaka. The use of ATMs, bar code scanners, and other technologies associated with modern business is becoming an increasingly common feature of life in the region.

A firm using a differentiation strategy can use a supplier who has chosen to use a cost-leadership strategy. A family-owned firm which relies on personal referrals to make tactical human resource hiring decisions can do business with a corporation that uses formal objective testing to make hiring decisions. However, there needs to be some form of standardization at the operational level in order for firms to conduct business with each other. Therefore, we see pressures to internationalize and standardize accounting procedures and we see the use of standard-sized shipping containers around the world. As trade across borders increases in the region, the pressure to standardize some operational business practices will increase. To support this idea, it can be noticed that Prajogo *et al.* (2007) found no significant difference between operational manufacturing strategies of Thai and Vietnamese firms, both operating in developing Asian economies, while Duong and Swierczek (2008) found a number of differences between the tactical managerial practices of Thai and Vietnamese managers in the two developing economies that have very different cultural traditions.

Additionally, the impact of the economic environment on operational business practices in the region should not be ignored. Compared to more economically developed countries, labor in the region is inexpensive and therefore the use of technology to reduce the amount of labor required does not provide as much value as in other areas where labor is more expensive, so there is less use of machinery to replace human effort. For example, the use of vending machines to distribute items such as coffee, sodas, and cigarettes is wide-spread in countries such as Japan where the cost of labor is high, but finding a vending machine is a rare occurrence in the Theravada Buddhist countries of Southeast Asia.

De Valk (2003) studied businesses in Laos PDR and believed a key to improvements in operations could be achieved by the transfer of existing operational knowledge into the region. While there continue to be significant differences in operational business practices between what is found in the Theravada Buddhist countries of Southeast Asia and those found in developed economies, globalization is seemingly causing a limited amount of convergence of operational business practices to occur.

Case studies

Table 7.1 shows the strategic management practices found in the case studies of the nine companies explored in previous chapters. A wide variety of target markets and overall strategies are being used; however, these strategic-level practices can be classified accurately using existing global strategic management frameworks. The owner-managers of the firms reported the specific conditions found in the local environments, especially the level of economic development of each individual country, were important in making their strategic-level management choices. For example, the lack of a substantial market for top-of-the-line clothing was given by the Cambodian tailor shop as its main reason for choosing to target middle-income workers. So, while strategic management principles can often be transferred into the region, the actual choice of practices is influenced by the local context.

Table 7.2, unlike what was seen in looking at the strategic management practices of these nine companies, shows near uniformity in tactical business practices. The one outlier, United Educational Consultants, primarily has both Western customers and employees and therefore, while operating in the same

Table 7.1 Strategic business practices

Company	Country	Industry	Target market	Generic strategy
A beverage distribution company	Cambodia	Beverage wholesaler	Mass market	Differentiation
Family-owned tailor shop	Cambodia	Clothing	Professional	Focus-cost leadership
Yaklom Angkor Lodge and Sawadee Food Garden	Cambodia	Hotel and restaurant	Thai tourists	Focus
Sengdara Fitness Center	Laos PDR	Health and fitness	Upper income locals and expatriates	Focus
Cultural Production Company	Laos PDR	Arts and crafts	Large organizations	Focus
SMP Enterprises	Laos PDR	Arts and crafts	Export to high income countries	Focus-differentiation
Huang Li Steel Company	Thailand	Steel	Industrial	Differentiation
Atlanta Medicare	Thailand	Pharmaceuticals	Doctors, hospitals, pharmacies	Low-cost leadership
United Educational Consultants	Thailand	Education	Foreign teachers	Focus

Table 7.2 Tactical business practices

Company	Financing	Corporate governance	HR practices (recruitment, selection, training)	Management style
A beverage distribution company	Self	None	Informal	Paternalistic
Family-owned tailor shop	Self	None	Informal	Paternalistic
Yaklom Angkor Lodge and Sawadee Food Garden	Self	None	Informal	Paternalistic
Sengdara Fitness Center	Self	None	Informal	Paternalistic
Cultural Production Company	Self	None	Informal	Paternalistic
SMP Enterprises	Self	None	Informal	Paternalistic
Huang Li Steel Company	Self	None	Informal	Paternalistic
Atlanta Medicare	Self	None	Informal (mixed with some formal training programs)	Paternalistic
United Educational Consultants	Self	None	Informal (mixed with some formal recruitment practices)	Participatory

legal and economic environment as the other Thai firms, operates in a different cultural environment.

Theravada Buddhist cultural influences are found in the tactical business practices of the companies examined in the case studies. All of the companies are run by owner-managers and therefore operations are extensions of the ideas and resources of the owners as opposed to having corporate cultures and bureaucratic procedures. In addition, the individualistic and personal natures of these firms are also demonstrated by the self-financing feature of the firms and the lack of a need for corporate governance. Also, the preference for paternalistic management styles is aligned with the values of Theravada Buddhism. The preference for informal HR practices in hiring and training reflect the Theravada Buddhist values of flexibility, individualism, and the taking of the middle path.

The choice of operational practices is highly influenced by the industry a company operates in, and direct comparisons between the practices of firms in different industries is of limited value. The beverage company in Cambodia used some similar operational practices (e.g., use of delivery trucks) to what is used in other locations and some unique practices found only in Cambodia (e.g., use of beer girls as a marketing tool and the more frequent use of human muscle as

Table 7.3 Core technologies

Company	Core technology
A beverage distribution company	Transportation logistics
Family-owned tailor shop	Customized production
Yaklom Angkor Lodge and Sawadee Food Garden	Service
Sengdara Fitness Center	Service
Cultural Production Company	Hand-made production
SMP Enterprises	Hand-made production
Huang Li Steel Company	Small-batch production
Atlanta Medicare	Sales
United Educational Consultants	Education/training

opposed to machinery in moving the products within the warehouse). The tailor shop in Cambodia uses designs, tools, and techniques adapted from studying international best practices. The Yaklom Angkor Lodge & Sawadee Food Garden and the Sengdara Fitness Center are continuously working to achieve an "international standard" of service. The Cultural Production Company and SMP Enterprises in Laos PDR use a combination of local, international, and self-created technologies and tools in producing their hand-made products. The Huang Li Steel Company attempts to use international best practices in its operational manufacturing processes while Atlanta Medicare's operational sales practices make extensive use of information technology, showing an internationalization of business practices while retaining a close interpersonal relationship with customers, which is aligned with the value of personal contact that is so common in the region as opposed to the use of more bureaucratic procedures, which is more common in some other locations. The United Educational Consultants need to maintain international standards to maintain US accreditation, but also make some adjustments to their curriculum to prepare students to teach in the specific environment found in Thailand.

All the companies' operational business practices in the study have been influenced by global forces to some degree; however, local conditions were also taken into consideration when decisions were made in choosing operational business practices. In non-core operational business practices (e.g., accounting, billing, and shipping), an even higher level of convergence with international best practices may be found. While there does appear to be some convergence of core operational business practices in the region with practices used in more advanced economies, total convergence has not happened and probably will not happen in the foreseeable future.

8 Tactical management
Human resources, management style, and leadership

Human resource management

Few scholars in organizational studies or practicing managers would argue with the statement that people are the most important factor in the success of an organization. Therefore, human resource (HR) management is considered a vital part of an organization's strategy. However, there are a variety of factors that influence the HR management strategies and practices a firm will use.

There appears to be substantial evidence to support the proposition different HR practices are used in different cultural environments. For example, Bjorkman, Fey, and Park (2007) found multinationals used different HR practices in their different subsidiaries in the United States, Russia, and Finland. Likewise, a number of studies have shown HR practices in Asia remain distinctly different from practices found in the United States and other locations despite the influence of "globalization" (e.g., Beer and Katz 2003; Chen and Wilson 2003; Chew and Goh 1997; McGrath-Champ and Carter 2001). Wei and Lau (2008) found the use of "Strategic Human Resource Management" practices did not always have a positive effect in the developing market of China, and this was partially attributed to differing ownership structure and the amount of autonomy of managers.

In many racially heterogeneous societies, such as the United States, Britain, and Australia, HR management is greatly concerned with the concept of equal opportunity for members of all racial segments of societies. Also, the concept of equality of the sexes has a huge impact on the practices of HR management in Western societies (Ng and Wiesner 2007). These cultural values are reflected in the legal systems of most Western countries, and are especially important in the United States. Therefore, in US organizations, HR managers spend considerable amounts of time dealing with a variety of issues to ensure legal compliance with anti-discrimination legislation (Dessler 2003, 25–58). The complexity of the legal system in the United States in regards to equal opportunity makes it important for US corporations to ensure HR personnel work with line and staff managers closely to ensure compliance and firms having individuals holding positions such as equal employment opportunity coordinator or affirmative action officer are not uncommon (Dalton 2007). The concept of equal opportunity based on race or ethnic background plays a much less influential factor in HR management practices in more racially homogeneous societies, such as those found in the Theravada Buddhist countries of Southeast Asia.

There is significant evidence that HR management practices used in developing countries are far from identical to what is found in more developed economies. Cowell (2007) reported that in Jamaica, firms used much less systematic and formal HR systems than is normally found in Western societies. While Ghebregiorgis and Karstan (2007) found both employee job satisfaction and productivity were correlated with the use of formal HR practices in Eritrea, the authors did not find employee training to be a key feature in firms in the country. Therefore, it could be speculated that the lack of formalized HR programs in many firms in developing countries may be due to both cultural factors as well as other factors, which may include the lack of resources, knowledge of modern HR management systems, or the need to comply with equal opportunity legislation.

As seen in the case studies presented in earlier chapters, and from personal experience, it does not appear that most firms in the Theravada Buddhist countries in Southeast Asia use sophisticated and formal HR systems or practices. The relatively smaller size of firms in the region, the prevalence of owner-managed firms and the lack of a need to comply with equal opportunity regulations would all appear to be factors limiting the use of formal HR practices. Furthermore, it is likely cultural aspects of these societies also influence HR practices. Collectivist societies often use less formal HR practices than do societies with individualist cultures, and the Theravada Buddhist values of acknowledging the impermanence of all things and the emphasis on the middle path likely have significant influences on decisions made by firms in regards to recruitment and selection, training, performance management, and compensation.

Recruitment and selection

In Western societies, a wide variety of sophisticated techniques, such as the use of a tend analysis, computerized forecast, qualification inventory, and recruiting yield pyramid are advocated as methods to improve the recruitment process (Dessler 2003: 90–8). Dessler (2003: 160–83) also reported companies commonly used objective measures of interviews to take away some of the arbitrary nature of this common tool used in the selection process. Pride, Hughes, and Kapoor (2008: 313–24) reported many scholars advocate the use of very detailed and formal HR planning, recruitment, and selection practices in US firms. Tipper (2004) highlighted the importance of seeking diversity in the ethnic and gender composition of new employees during the recruitment and selection processes as there are legal, social, and financial reasons to recruit a more diverse workforce. Kniveton (2008) stressed the need for European firms to deemphasize some typically male traits when recruiting managers to ensure gender balance in new hires. Simola, Taggar, and Smith (2007) reported on the importance of Canadian firms in following practices prescribed by The Canadian Human Rights Tribunal to ensure fairness in hiring, but the authors also reported that many Canadian firms do not fully comply with the recommendations. Therefore, it is apparent that in Western countries, formalized HR recruitment and selection processes are generally advocated as methods to select the most qualified personnel as well as being the best way to comply with both the legal and social requirements to be fair to all prospective employees and to ensure ethnic and gender diversity in the workplace.

However, recruitment and selection objectives in developing economies, especially those with more ethnically homogeneous populations and collectivist cultures, may be somewhat different, which is reflected in the choice of HR practices. Research by Okpara and Wynn (2008) indicated that instead of formal recruitment procedures, it may be more common to find recruitment being done informally and information about job openings is usually passed by word of mouth from existing employees to friends and relatives in developing economies. El-Kot and Leat (2008) found in Egypt the recruitment and selection processes for managers were somewhat similar to practices found in Europe; however, they also reported the hiring of non-managerial positions was normally completed using much less formal processes than those normally found in a Western context. Hooi (2008) found despite the official government policy of promoting the use of Japanese-style HR management practices, neither locally-owned firms nor Japanese joint ventures have actually adopted many of the features associated with Japanese recruitment practices in Malaysia. As job hopping is common among Malaysian workers, a high emphasis in recruitment and selection is placed on experience and, unlike in Japan, new employees receive relatively little training.

Recruitment and selection processes in the Theravada Buddhist countries of Southeast Asia would appear to be closer aligned to what is seen in other developing economies than to what is advocated in Western countries. Similar to the findings of Hooi (2008), it was reported that job hopping of employees was very common in Cambodia (Hawks 2005). For highly skilled workers in the region, such as engineers working in the automotive industry in Thailand, demand exceeds supply, which can result in difficulties for local firms in attracting talent as the draw of working for a large world-famous multinational can be quite strong. This can result in job hopping and the fairly extensive use of imported managerial and technical specialists (Sajarattanachote 2006).

Failure to seek ethnic diversity and gender neutrality in the workplace is not necessarily considered socially unacceptable or illegal in most of the region. Wu *et al.* (2008) examined posted job advertisements in Thailand and found a large percentage of these limited applications to a specific gender, more often male but a significant number also were restricted to females. Wu *et al.* (2008) also reported formal job postings were mostly used for white collar positions and personnel for most blue collar jobs were recruited and selected by informal practices. However, this openness in gender preference in the selection process does not necessarily mean women are downtrodden; in fact, women have traditionally played an active role in economic activities in the region with Thailand having one of the highest ratios of women entrepreneurs in the world (Hatcher and Terjesen 2007). While in Laos females are often more sought out as employees in certain types of organizations than are men, as women are generally believed to have more of the traits needed for working in modern organizations than do males (Southiseng and Walsh 2008: 16).

There are many environmental factors resulting in firms in the Theravada Buddhist countries of Southeast Asia using recruitment and selection practices that diverge from what are advocated as best practices in a Western context. These nations are more homogeneous racially than Western nations, resulting in less emphasis placed on equal opportunity based on skin color or religious background. That is not to say that there are no discriminated-against groups, quite the opposite is often true. For example, individuals coming from *Isarn* (the Northeast region), migrant workers from Myanmar/Burma, members of various "hill tribes," and Muslims from the southern part of the country often have difficulties in finding professional positions in companies within Thailand. However, with the exception of the Muslims from southern Thailand, in general, the other oppressed ethnic groups seem to be less militant in calling for equality than might be the norm in some other parts of the world. The belief in *kamma*, where one's position in this life is based on past merit, may be a contributing factor to more acceptance of inequality than is the norm in the United States or other Western societies. Also, the prevalence of family ownership of firms often results in top managerial positions being reserved for family members; therefore, there is less of a need for formalized recruitment and selection processes for managers. Furthermore, in most of the region, there is no tradition of local newspapers and even the use of the Internet is limited within the working class, making the traditional Western practices of placing ads for low-skilled workers ineffective.

Training

There is quite a lot of emphasis on the use of formal training in organizations in Western organizations (Dessler 2003: 184–210). There are many types of formal training used in US and other Western companies, including training on technical skills, interpersonal skills, and ethics (Robbins 2003). It has been reported that in Western countries the systematic analysis of training needs and the implementation of training programs are integral parts of comprehensive HR programs and are believed to be useful in unleashing the potential productivity of employees (Endres and Mancheno-Smoak 2008). Schmidt and Akdere (2007) felt formal orientation training helped new employees understand a firm's vision and leadership philosophy. However, there appears to be a trend away from the extensive use of some of these structured and formal training programs run by employers, as more and more employees are being encouraged to take control of their own training and development by creating their own individualized programs, which may allow employees more flexibility in future employment options (Zaleska and Menezes 2007).

It would appear firms in developing economies make less use of formal training programs than is advocated in Western textbooks. For example, Cowell (2007) found in Jamaica that firms did not normally integrate formal training programs into their operations. While it is tempting to come to the conclusion that the main reason for this lack of use of formal training is due to the deficiencies of knowledge and skills of the local owners/managers of companies in developing economies and these companies would be well served by imitating practices used in developed economies, this simplistic conclusion may not be entirely accurate. While it is true managers and business owners in developing economies often have less formal education than managers from developed economies, the managers from developing economies also operate in very different environments.

It may be wrong to solely equate the existence of formal training programs with a high level of training. For formal training programs to be cost effective, they require a certain amount of economy of scale, and naturally larger companies, where a larger percentage of the workforce can be found in developed economies as opposed to developing ones, will be more likely to use formal training programs. However, in smaller companies, more training may take the form of on-the-job training where more experienced employers or the owner/manager works one-on-one or with informal groups in supplying training. Also, reporting and appearance requirements may be different for bureaucratic corporations than for owner-operated firms. Most people believe 'training" is valuable for an organization's continued success and a manager of a corporation must demonstrate how the workforce's skills are being improved to other stakeholders, such as investors and labor unions, which requires the need for documentation of training. But, in family-owned firms, there is less need to have written documentation and proof of training and therefore informal and unrecorded training may often be more practical and cost efficient. In family-owned firms there is often a more distinct separation between management and employees with managerial positions mostly being reserved for family members. Therefore, as most employees have limited advancement opportunities, there may be a less pressing need for training of a more conceptual nature for most employees. Also, it should be kept in mind that a significant portion of formal training in developed economies is in areas such as sexual harassment, safety, and the use of non-discriminatory work practices, which are often driven by legal concerns that are not present to the same extent in most developing economies.

Firms in the Theravada Buddhist regions of Southeast Asia do not appear to use formal training programs to the same extent as do firms from developed countries. Southiseng and Walsh (2008: 19) found in Laos most firms primarily used informal on-the-job training as opposed to more formal training; we also saw in the case studies presented previously that undocumented informal training is quite common in firms from the region. However, at least in Bangkok, many multinational firms working in the region do appear to make considerable use of a variety of formal training programs as directed by corporate headquarters abroad. Many of the same factors limiting the use of formal training programs that apply to other developing economies would appear to apply equally to firms in the region. Additionally, some of the features of Theravada Buddhism may contribute to the preference for more informal types of training. As noted in Chapter 2, acceptance of the impermanence of all things is a key feature of Theravada Buddhism and if one holds an expectation that business conditions will be constantly changing, one may be less willing to invest in the development of specific skills in employees that may or may not be needed in the future. Also, with the belief in *kamma*, organizations may place less emphasis on employees working their way up from the bottom. Instead higher level positions in a company will often be reserved for family members or individuals with higher levels of social status and, therefore, as there is little expectation of employees rising from the ranks, there is less need for some forms of advanced formal training. Also, Theravada Buddhism teaches the path to religious success is primarily a matter of individual effort and there is not a single standardized method for spiritual enlightenment that fits everyone. Although the countries of Theravada Buddhist Southeast Asia are considered collectivist societies, a strong strain of individualism is easily identified which may be at least partially attributed to this individualistic nature found in the philosophy of Theravada Buddhism. Formal training normally requires standardization and a one-size-fits-all approach to some extent, while informal training through mentorship relationships may be considered more in tune with the individualistic essence of the teachings of Theravada Buddhism.

Compensation

Formal and standardized compensation systems are common in the United States as US companies have numerous legal considerations to take into account when deciding on how to pay their employees to ensure there is no appearance of discrimination based on age, gender, or other factors (Dessler 2003: 302–7). Also, in relative terms, wages are high in developed economies and are a substantial portion of a firms operating expense; therefore, they are a more vital aspect of business to be managed. However, in general, it would appear that market forces and a company's positioning strategy primarily determine a firm's approach to paying its employees, whether that firm is located in a developed or developing economy. Although wages in the Theravada Buddhist countries are relatively low when compared to international standards, it appears the approaches taken to determining wages in the region are driven primarily by market forces and are based on similar principles, minus most legal compliance issues, that are found in other regions of the world.

Career development and performance appraisal systems

The key features of HR management in many companies are career development and the use of performance appraisal systems. US companies focus heavily on the use of formal appraisal systems and well-communicated career paths for employees (Dessler 2003: 241–300). Examples of formal appraisal systems include the use of critical incident analysis reports, graphic rating scales, behaviorally anchored ratings scales (BARS), and team performance evaluations (Robbins 2003: 502–7). Formal performance appraisal systems perform many functions, including being a motivational tool, to provide feedback, identify top performers for promotion opportunities, identify poor performers, identify training needs, and to create a paper trail in order to have justification for promotional or dismissal decisions in case there is a legal challenge to any of these decisions. Although promoted as a useful tool to manage employee performance, the use of formal performance appraisal systems may be more valuable in individualist societies and it has been documented these systems where individuals are given a formal grade or ranking for their work performance are not as frequently used in collectivist societies (Robbins 2003: 509–10). Furthermore, Longo and Mura (2008) reported that white collar and blue collar workers had different perspectives on career development initiatives and had different responses to these types of policies. Career development would appear to have a vastly different meaning for young managers as opposed to a member of the cleaning staff, reminding us that career development has a substantial contextual component in all cultures.

Formal career development programs may to some extent be more accepted in individualistic societies with low tolerance for power distance, such as those found in Western societies. Formal career development programs appeal to the egalitarian ideals of fairness and equal opportunities. Furthermore, to ensure continuity in a bureaucratic organization where managers come and go, formal recording of an individual's career progress, skills acquisitions, and past performance may be essential. However, in a smaller firm in a developing country where there is no separation between ownership and management, there is less of a need for formal documentation of past performance as the owner-manager has developed detailed knowledge and opinions of the past performance of key employees and will normally make promotional and other career decisions for employees in an "informal" manner but with the use of knowledge and opinion gained from daily contact with the employees over time. Moreover, unlike in many developed economies, managers in developing economies rarely have worries about having to defend the "fairness" of their personnel decisions in a court of law.

Mohrman (2008) felt consideration of future growth should be a key feature of career development programs and, in the corporate world and with new entrepreneurial firms, growth is normally a major objective. However, in established family-owned firms in Southeast Asia, wealth preservation is often a more common strategy than growth and wealth creation (Carney and Gedailovic 2003). Therefore, career development with an eye on growth may be a less common practice in the Theravada Buddhist countries of Southeast Asia than in other regions. The case studies examined earlier support the observations of Hawks (2005) in Cambodia in that formal career development programs are fairly rare in the region. Size is of course a factor; smaller firms naturally feel less of a need to have formal career development programs and performance appraisal systems than larger firms. Also, in family-owned firms, there are limited paths for career progression for non-family members lessening the need of the majority of firms in the region to install formal programs of these types. Also, there are fewer social and legal pressures to prove the fairness of promotional and retention decisions, making the need for formal systems less pressing.

There might be some cultural features that are influenced by Theravada Buddhism which also contribute to the lack of use of formal career development programs and performance appraisal systems within firms from the region. The use of career development programs assumes having an ability to be able to predict the future to a significant degree of accuracy; however, Theravada Buddhism emphasizes the impermanence of all things. If the only certainty one has about the future is of its uncertainty, how much time, effort, and money would one spend on developing formal career development programs to prepare for a specific version of the future? In addition, in Western societies being proactive is highly prized and solving problems is what, it is believed, managers should do. One of the key features of using a formal performance appraisal system is to identify problems so they can be fixed. However, what is considered a deficiency in an employee within a firm in the Theravada Buddhist countries of Southeast Asia may be seen as only temporary and the problem will work itself out either without the manager's influence or with a less confrontational approach.

In Theravada Buddhism, the middle path and the avoidance of conflict are also important elements. One reason formal performance appraisal systems are often used is to ensure managers do not avoid the unpleasant task of confronting a poorly performing worker. There might be managers out there who enjoy confronting an employee over poor performance, but the author's personal experience has been the opposite. Normally, individual performance appraisals are used to remove as much ambiguity over an employee's performance as possible. Therefore, it is not surprising Western managers coming from an individualistic culture where being proactive is prized are more likely to use formal performance appraisal systems than are managers whose values have been shaped by the teachings of Theravada Buddhism.

The concept of saving "face" is an often cited feature of life in Asia. However, it is believed that concept is in fact quite universal although maybe a little more pronounced in Asia than in other locations. The old management adage, praise in public, punish in private, recognizes the importance of saving face in all contexts. Performance appraisals are only effective when they create a separation between top performers and low performers. And while confidentiality is expected, it is not uncommon for the performance appraisal "scores" of others to become known. Those with higher scores will gain face while those who score lower will lose face. This is expected and considered part of life in individualistic societies that are especially competitive, such as those with Anglo-American roots. However, in collectivist and less competitive societies, this loss of face of a large portion of the workforce may not be so easily accepted. However, because firms in the Theravada Buddhist countries of Southeast Asia do not usually have formal performance appraisal systems it should not be thought that differences in performance are not recognized. Owners and managers track the performance of their employees and have strong opinions on who will be considered for promotion and who will not, but by keeping the tracking of employee performance informal it allows for the avoidance of open conflict, all employees save face among their colleagues and problems are allowed to work themselves out. While a strong case could be made that a more formal and proactive approach to issues of employee performance leads to a better bottom line, an equally strong case could be made the informal approach leads to more workplace harmony, and in searching for the middle path, Theravada Buddhist managers may willingly sacrifice some profitability to increase workplace harmony.

> Many companies have found it very difficult to institute a system of performance-review based on western models because of the essentially "confrontative quality" of the exercise. In the Thai tradition, the giving of criticism, even constructive criticism, has never been done directly except by a very senior to a very junior person.
>
> (Holmes *et al.* 1996: 48)

Walking through a factory floor, loading dock or office in a company in the Theravada Buddhist areas of Southeast Asia, a foreign visitor would not likely feel out of place. Generally, one will see similar techniques and technologies being used in these operational areas as are seen in other areas of the world. However, when a foreigner finds him or herself directly involved in working in or with a company in the region, the differences in managerial style and approaches to HR management become evident quite quickly. One of the principal factors driving these different practices is the different approaches to "fairness." In Western countries, social and legal requirements drive companies to attempt to create ethnically diverse and gender-balanced workforces, and firms are required to provide proof of these efforts, which requires the use of formal systems. Without these pressures, it is not surprising that firms in the region have not used costly formal systems to the same extent. Also, the need for objective measurement of performance is more expected in individualistic societies that are naturally more competitive, while the more informal systems used in the Theravada Buddhist countries of Southeast Asia would appear to be better suited to an environment where the culture is more collectivist and prizes cooperation to a higher extent.

Management and leadership styles

Leadership and management are practiced in organizations around the world; however, how these concepts are practiced varies considerably across national boundaries. National culture has been found to have a strong impact on managerial values (Ralston *et al.* 1997; Ralston 2008) and these differing values lead to differing practices. Attitudes and practices of both leadership and management vary greatly from culture to culture (e.g., Chong and Thomas 1997; Kanungo and Wright 1983; Neelankavil *et al.* 2000; Suutari *et al.* 2002). It should be noted that the Anglo-American cultural score is at the extreme end of the scale of individualism and therefore concepts of management and leadership from these cultures may be quite different from what is expected in other locations in the world (Hofstede 1980).

Leadership is a concept that is often advocated as a cure-all for whatever ails an organization. Alvesson and Sveningson (2003: 1435) proclaimed, "Leadership is conceptualized as the extra ordinarization of the mundane." Ahmad (2001: 83) wrote that leadership "is instilling in each employee a sense of belonging and commitment toward the achievement of the goals and objectives of the organization. . . ." Bass and Avolio (1993) and Bass and Steidlmeier (1999) advocated the use of "authentic transformational leadership," which has four general components: idealized influence, inspirational motivation, intellectual stimulation, and individualized consideration. There does not appear to be much in the way of specifics when it comes to defining actual leadership traits and practices, but there is general agreement that good leadership is good, and good leadership is proactive. However, the concept of leadership as advocated in Western textbooks may be based on assuming everyone shares values that are common in societies where egalitarianism, individualism, and achievement-orientations are given high priorities, such as those cultures found in Western societies.

Pounder (2001) reported there is not any particular leadership style that has been found to be consistently more effective than others. This would appear to indicate that management or leadership style is extremely contextual in nature, and the cultural environment one works in would appear to have a major influence on the context. Giampetro-Meyer *et al.* (1998) argued the term "leadership" is an ambiguous and abstract concept that is often used as a unifier as people can agree what is needed is leadership without agreeing on specifics. Leadership can have vastly different meanings to different people, but it is always "good" and everyone can agree that "good" decisions are needed. Hipsher (2005) made the case that leadership, much like beauty, can not be defined to everyone's satisfaction and is mostly in the eye of the beholder. Can one be a good leader without the consent of the followers? It was argued that leadership traits are not necessarily possessed by the leader; instead, these traits are attributed to the leader by others. Furthermore, a case was made it is nearly impossible to separate leadership from results. Good leaders are those who have accomplished goals, and therefore Hipsher stated the opinion the substance of leadership, good decision making, is far more important to success than the use of a particular leadership style.

Management and leadership style and decision making in developing economies can be significantly different than is normally seen in more developed economies. Southiseng and Walsh (2008) found in Laos the level of education, lack of exposure to the use of more sophisticated and modern management techniques, and lack of access to knowledge about the business environment were obstacles managers had to overcome in order to be effective. Peng *et al.* (2008) found the institutional environment had a major effect on the decision making of managers from developing economies. For example, Peng *et al.* (2008: 928) reported the concept of dispersed ownership of firms, which is often an under-lying assumption in US textbooks, is in fact an exception and, in most of the world, including most of the developing world, concentrated ownership is the norm. Therefore, corporate governance, which is a main concern for a manager of a corporation, can be quite different from the concerns over controls for man-agers in firms with concentrated ownership. The leadership style of an owner-manager of a firm may be quite different from that of a hired leader in a corporate setting as the level of autonomy of each is usually considerably different.

The cultural environment found in the region appears to have an effect on the style and management practices used. Acceptance of ambiguity and the imper-manence of all things may affect management practices. Hawks (2005) noticed many experts working in Cambodia reported on the short-term mindset of Cam-bodian managers. Hawks also found that keeping records and reviewing past performance was not a high priority in Cambodian businesses. Southiseng and Walsh (2008) also reported on the short-term orientation of small business owners in Laos, which was partially attributed to the changing nature of the busi-ness environment and the arbitrary enforcement of regulations by government officials. Additionally, short-term orientation would be expected in cultural environment where the acceptance of impermanence is commonplace and there-fore flexibility often replaces long-term planning.

Theravada Buddhism, with its emphasis on *kamma* being an important factor in explaining differences in social and economic status, can be thought of as a factor encouraging hierarchical structures and authoritarian styles of manage-ment in the region. "Most Thais are reasonably comfortable with the notion that some individuals in society 'deserve' to have more power" (Holmes *et al.* 1996: 62). However this acceptance of unequal power may be softened to a considera-ble extent by the concept of the middle path found in the teachings of Theravada Buddhism. "Thais have grown to expect a leader to demonstrate a blend of authoritarianism and benevolence" (Holmes *et al.* 1996: 62).

This paternalistic form of leadership may have deep roots in the region. In Western societies, slavery is often thought of as being one of the cruelest institu-tions ever conceived by man. However, in Thailand, slavery, which was only abolished in the twentieth century, may have had both hierarchical and paternal-istic characteristics. In 1900, Young (127) wrote the following about slavery in Thailand:

> There is nothing cruel or revolting in the treatment of the serfs, and many of them are sincerely attached to their masters, and have been known voluntar-ily to afford them any assistance they could when misfortunes have over-taken them. They are fed, clothed, and housed at the expense of their owners, and rarely experience in their dependent condition any real

hardships. Away in the country the majority of the people prefer to live as the bondservants of some powerful person, who in return for their labour provides both them and their families with protection and support.

This paternalistic attitude is still common today, as demonstrated in the previously presented case studies where workers were referred to as family members, but this usually indicates the owners of a company will treat employees more like children who need protection rather than as siblings of equal stature.

In Thailand there are two norms that can confidently be said to exist:

- that Thais work hard to build and maintain relationships among a wide and complex network of people; and
- that Thais' interactions are more or less controlled within the context of a strong hierarchical system.

(Holmes *et al.* 1996: 17)

Another key aspect of management is communication style. A common method of classification of communication styles is to use the high-context low-context framework originally described by the anthropologist Edward Hall. Low-context cultures, such as found in most of the societies located in North America and Europe, are associated with direct communication; while high-context cultures, such as those found in the Theravada Buddhist countries of Southeast Asia, use a more indirect communication style (Moran *et al.* 2007: 49–53). "Verbally, Thais can be disarmingly indirect. Non-verbally, they can be even more subtle, and most confusing to outsiders who may not be able to read aii the signs" (Holmes *et al.* 1996: 22). The indirect or high-context communication style helps to avoid direct confrontations and allows all parties to have a better chance of saving face as displeasure over disagreements is hinted at as opposed to directly stated.

The concept of the middle path is often associated with a lack of questioning of authority and the need for harmony. Chanthanom (1998: 103) reflected on this aspect of culture found in Thailand.

Confrontations and challenges from people of different backgrounds and professions is almost unheard of because according to the norms Thai people, confrontation and arguments are unacceptable and should be avoid[ed]. To argue with someone is unacceptable, a sign of hostility and disrespect. Much of the knowledge provided by teachers, experts, or professors easily become a belief system when the public internalize the issue and believe that it is the truth.

Swierczek and Onishi (2003: 202) reported:

- There is no custom in Thailand to scold subordinates for training purposes of socialization. Criticism is only for a major mistake.
- Thai managers seldom criticize subordinates. It is a virtue of the Thai manager to show generosity to his/her subordinates for their mistakes.

- Thai managers try to explain how serious the impact of mistakes is to others because it disturbs the harmony of society (workplace), which is negative in Thai society.

Therefore, this middle path concept of avoiding confrontation reinforces the existing hierarchy and authority within an organization, but it also can limit abuse of authority as misusing the power coming from one's position is likely to lead to confrontation, which is to be avoided.

> Thailand is a hierarchical society.... Each Thai person who is trained to be a functioning member of society learns, early in life, what rank he or she holds and how he is supposed to treat others according to that rank."
>
> (Holmes *et al.* 1996)

The concept of the middle path is also sometimes associated with the work ethic of the people from the Theravada Buddhist countries of Southeast Asia. While it would be unfair to label the people of the region as lazy, obsession with work and work for work's sake are not common attitudes in the region. Being too serious at work is not in accordance with the concept of the middle path; therefore, both achieving organizational goals and enjoying the social aspects of work often take on nearly equal importance. And this is not necessarily a new phenomenon, Young (1900: 207–8) reported that harvest time in the villages of Thailand was both a time for hard work and great merry-making. Work and play are not considered mutually exclusive. This attitude obviously affects managerial and leadership styles, as managers need to consider the organization's goals alongside the desire of the workforce for entertaining social interactions.

> For the Thais, good interpersonal relationships and a high level of fun are regarded as crucial factors for staying in a job. When these are missing, people will very likely seek alternative employment even if other extrinsic or intrinsic needs are fulfilled. What foreigners often view as a lack of "seriousness" in work attitudes are often an integral part of personal and group motivation and cohesion. Unlike in Western cultures, having fun is a legitimate and worthy aspect of work life. It is somewhat perplexing to the Western manager that having fun is a predominant feature of the Thai workplace.
>
> (Kainzbauer 2009: 9)

In Western societies, there is a lot of emphasis placed on rational and "scientific" decision making, but the actual method of executive decision making is often less rational than is advocated by academics (George and Jones 2008). Kainzbauer (2009) found in Thailand a less analytical and a more holistic approach to decision making was common. Kainzbauer also found Thais generally took a more intuitive approach to decision making and placed less emphasis on rational and scientific approaches to decision making.

An extremely important concept in understanding leadership in Asia in general is the concept of "face." While face is normally considered a feature of Asian societies, a case can easily be made that face is equally, or nearly equally, important in Western societies as well. However, the concept of face in Asian societies may take on slightly different characteristics from the Western concepts of reputation, honor, and fame.

Persons (2008: 142) wrote, "It seems reasonable to hypothesize that to understand Thai leaders one must understand their rules of face." Persons (2008: 2) explained:

> Face is initiated by a person's claims to worth, but it is consummated as valid only after society, not just one social exchange partner, awards actual value for that person's claims and performance. At its core, face is about human desires for *acceptance* and *significance*.

The concept of face is nuanced and there are many different types of face. Five components of face have been identified, which can be loosely and imprecisely translated as: reputation, honor, fame, virtue, and dignity. While theoretically virtue is the highest level of attaining face, it has been found in modern Thai society, wealth is often the key determinate of face. Therefore, leaders often spend beyond their means in order to gain and maintain face. Face is something to be protected at all costs and also something a leader is constantly working to obtain. Rehbein (2007a: 45) believed in Laos PDR making economic gains was not an end in itself, but wealth was used to increase personal capital, which increases an individual's face and standing in society.

In the client-patron system so common in the region, a leader-patron needs to be able to provide both tangible and intangible benefits to one's clients in order to retain their respect and loyalty. With face comes power, and this power is often used to acquire more wealth and more face. However, use of this power is often tempered by the fear of loss of face. If a patron abuses power, face is lost, which results in loss of power and clients. Of course, not all types of face come from wealth and power; however, the moves away from village life to a modern life where the mass media plays such a major role in shaping public opinion, face based on honor and "goodness" is becoming less common and face based on wealth and fame is becoming more common (Persons 2008).

Although face is commonly thought to be bestowed upon one by society at large, there is also a strong internal element to an individual's feeling of self-worth, called *saksii* in Thai. "*Saksii* seems to be an independent, individualistic force with a Thai person that stands in contrast to the strong collectivist sanctions and pressures to conform" (Persons 2008: 86). This suggests the concept of face in the Theravada Buddhist countries of Southeast Asia share many similarities with the concept in other collectivist Asian societies, but the concept in the region may also have slightly more individualistic elements that, it can be speculated, are due to the focus on the individualistic nature of Theravada Buddhist teachings.

I wish to float the idea that face may be the broadest and most inclusive generalized medium in Thai society – encompassing money, threat power, influence, and morality. The man who amasses wealth often controls others not just because of what he is willing to share with them, but simply because his considerable wealth is visible or known and gives him "the appearance of being honorable." The man who gains a titled position often controls others not just because he has jurisdiction to harm people, but because his position itself lends face to him. The man who persuades others on the basis of what is best for them is successful not just because he is eloquent, but because using power for the sake of others is face-giving behavior that earns him face in the eyes of others.

(Persons 2008: 329)

Face is extremely important in the business environments in the Theravada Buddhist countries. Business relationships, including those between employer and employee, are often quite personal in nature. Instead of working for an impersonal company represented by an individual's boss who has authority primarily due to his or her position, not his or her status in society, employees in the region are clients who have personal relationships with their bosses, who are also often their patrons. Furthermore, in the hierarchical societies of the Theravada Buddhist countries of Southeast Asia, face is used to distinguish where on the hierarchical ladder one belongs. Of course, the components of face, reputation, honor, fame, virtue, and dignity, are important in all societies, but these components often take on more egalitarian characteristics in Western societies. When working in this area of the world, avoidance of harming the face of others or oneself should take on added importance.

In general, tactical work practices in the Theravada Buddhist countries of Southeast Asia are more personalized and relationship oriented and less bureaucratic than the tactical business work practices found in more developed regions of the world. In an oversimplification, these informal tactical business practices may lead to some organizational inefficiency, but they are also likely to lead to a more pleasant work atmosphere, a trade-off managers in the region may be more willing to make than managers in more "competitive" societies.

9 Marketing, finance, labor relations, operational management, and internationalization

Marketing

The components of what constitutes "marketing" appear to be growing and at times appear to encompass the entirety of business practices. Pride, Hughes, and Kapoor (2008: 414) include buying, selling, transporting, financing, standardizing, grading, risk taking, and gathering market information as some of the business functions conducted under the term "marketing." However, a more limited definition may be more useful. For our purposes, the definition of "marketing" will be restricted to sales, positioning, and promotional strategies.

Consumer purchasing habits and preferences differ along cultural lines, and therefore universal marketing practices are rarely seen. Suh and Kwon (2002) found local differences in many consumer tastes and spending patterns were not swayed to any great extent by the marketing efforts of large multinationals. Therefore, tactical marketing decisions have to take into account the variation of languages and cultural values found in different locations. This is aligned with Hipsher's (2007) contention that tactical marketing business practices, such as promotional practices, will be mostly influenced by the social-cultural environment, while the positioning strategies would be considered strategic decisions; and while the principles of positioning are more or less universal, the actual practices will differ considerably from location to location primarily based on economic conditions. For example, McDonalds is positioned as a low-cost "fast-food" in the United States where purchasing power is high; however, in Thailand and other developing areas of the world, McDonalds is positioned to appeal to the higher income portions of the population and going to McDonalds is often thought of as a special treat to be savored over a considerable period of time. Same product but different positioning strategies based on the different local economic conditions.

It would appear there are substantial differences between marketing practices in developing countries as opposed to more economically developed economies. There are fewer large corporations in developing economies and more SMEs. Sengupta and Chattopadhyay (2006) reported that SMEs, regardless of environment, can not follow conventional marketing practices as advocated in textbooks due to limitations caused by the lack of availability of resources. The authors also found the majority of the promotional activities of the bakery chains found in Kolkata, India took place at the shops as opposed to firms doing media advertising. This may be explained by firms in developing economies having fewer opportunities to establish impersonal exchanges with potential customers through the media and other sources than would be possible in more developed economies, as suggested by Bang and Joshi (2008). Abimbola (2006) found branding was used to only a very limited extent by African firms, and firms from developing economies have generally not been able to generate value through the use of branding, at least not to the same extent as large multinationals headquartered in developed economies.

However, large multinationals do conduct more or less conventional marketing campaigns in Thailand. Fam and Grohs (2007) found young Thai adults had very similar reactions to different types of advertisements as did young adults in other Asian countries from both South and East Asia. This may suggest that shared Asian cultural features, such as collectivism and high tolerance for power distances using Hofstede's (1980, 1983) dimensions, may best explain responses to advertising in the Theravada Buddhist countries of Southeast Asia. It has often been noticed that consumers in the region are very much influenced by belonging to a group and prefer to stick with "popular," which are often foreign, brands; Venkatraman and Nelson (2008) found a similar phenomenon in China, where young people would go to Starbucks due to a variety of reasons, including being part of the fusion of Eastern and Western cultures found in the local branches and the overall "special" atmosphere, even through many of the customers did not especially enjoy drinking coffee. Group dynamics seem to play a large part in brand selection. The collectivist nature of Asian society along with the hierarchical nature of society may often result in a "follow the leader" mentality making it difficult for firms to find brand niches that appeal to a minority of the population. Vallaster and Hasenohrl (2006) found urban consumers in Thailand were fairly open to purchasing new products or brands, especially when the products had already been proven to be successful in more economically developed regions. Sangkhawasi and Johri (2007) also reported on the strong pull that status brands had in Thailand. Therefore, it appears the trendsetters in Thailand often take their cue from the international environment, while the rest of the population takes its cues from the local trendsetters.

However, outside of the large urban areas, the informal and small scale nature of much of the businesses in the region often makes marketing more of a personal affair with face-to-face interactions with customers being more important than impersonal advertising in attracting and retaining business. It is common to see many restaurants and other small businesses operating throughout the region without any signs indicating the actual name of the business. Instead of relying on name recognition, these small businesses rely on personal interactions with customers as their primary marketing tool. Also, when selling in the business-to-business market, a lot of the marketing that takes place is done by creating personal connections and trust between buyers and sellers, which is illustrated by the report of Petison and Johri (2008) of the supplier–manufacturer relationships in the automotive industry in Thailand. Johnsen (2007: 142) found developing and maintaining relationships were important in business-to-business marketing in her study of the silk industry and noted that in Thailand personal relationships were often more important in a contractual relationship than the words written in a legal contract.

Finance

Financial strategies and practices stretch across the strategic, tactical, and operational levels. Hipsher (2007) argued strategic financial decisions would primarily be affected by the economic environment. There is a fairly well-developed financial system in urban areas of Thailand and it would appear the principles and practices of finance followed by large Thai companies closely resemble those found in economically developed areas of the world. However, in Cambodia, Laos, Myanmar/Burma, and rural areas of Thailand, economic development is much lower and therefore one sees very different financing strategies. For example, Hawks (2005: 120–1) found in the cases of SMEs in Cambodia, bank borrowing to finance the start-up of a new business was extremely rare. Instead, most small business owners used personal savings, borrowing from family members, and other informal methods to finance the launching of a new business. Southiseng and Walsh (2008: 13) reported similar findings in Laos PDR and found the lack of access to capital prevented small businesses from any form of rapid growth. This would appear to be consistent with findings in other developing economies (Claessens 2006). Aribarg, R. (2005: 16) reported on how traders on both sides of the Thai–Myanmar/Burma border used informal "open accounts" rather than formal letters of credit due to the lack of banking facilities on the Myanmar/Burma side of the border, which reflects both the economic development of the area as well as the preference for informal arrangements as opposed to formal contracts that is common in the region. There would appear to be some convergence with more developed economies on the operational aspects of finance as the use of ATMs, internet banking, and bank transfers is increasing in the region, but the use of these technologies is still far from universal.

Accounting procedures would be considered to be part of the operational-level of finance. Constable and Kuasirikun (2007) provided a detailed account of the history of accounting systems in Thailand and claimed the creation of a detailed accounting system was an important prerequisite in building Thailand into a modern nation-state. The authors made the point that the accounting system in Thailand evolved from an indigenous system based on principles found in Buddhist cosmological texts in the mid-nineteenth century into the modern international system in use today. It was felt international forces caused by Western colonial powers moving into Southeast Asia and the increased trade between Thailand and its colonized neighbors in the nineteenth and twentieth centuries were the driving force behind this convergence of operational accounting practices.

Labor relations

The existence of labor unions and collective bargaining is widespread through-out individualistic Western societies. Also, labor unions are common in some Asian countries, such as Japan; however, in Japan labor unions have a tendency to act more as business partners than the confrontational nature of most management-labor relationships seen in Western countries. Yet, the existence of labor unions or collective action by workers is quite rare within the Theravada Buddhist countries of Southeast Asia. Hadiz (2002) believes the lack of labor unions in Southeast Asia can be partially attributed to the countries of the region being latecomers to industrial development and pressures from international competition make the formation of labor unions less feasible today than in the past. Hadiz also believed the Asian economic crisis of 1997 left labor unions in a weaker position than before the crisis.

The existence of a large percentage of foreign workers without legal rights makes it difficult for labor unions to operate in some industries in Thailand, as outlined by Arnold and Hewison (2005) in their study of workers from Myanmar/Burma in Mae Sot which is located near the Thai–Myanmar/Burma border. However, in Cambodia, primarily due to pressure from international donors, on whose aid money the economy of Cambodia is dependent, there have been some moves toward ensuring treatment of workers that is more in line with international standards while some form of employee representation is also becoming more common (Polaski 2006).

A case could be made that the lack of labor unions and labor militancy is aligned with values found in the teachings of Theravada Buddhism. The belief in *kamma* may lead workers to more readily accept differences in power and wealth. Also, the non-confrontational aspects of the teachings of Theravada Buddhism could play a part in the limited use of collective bargaining mechanisms as there is such a clear distinction between labor and management. Furthermore, the concept of the middle path may at times limit the excesses of management, which often drives employees to seek power in numbers within an organization.

Foreign managers in the region may find they hold some values that are different from the local staff, which can be sources of conflict in labor relations. Swierczek and Onishi (2003) found some major differences in values and work attitudes of Japanese managers and Thai subordinates in Japanese-owned companies in Thailand. However, they also found through long-term contact these differences lessened over time. It was found Japanese managers, when they initially arrive in the country, had more egalitarian approaches and considered members of the same company to be part of a large family; while Thais were more hierarchical in nature and expected more respect paid to individuals based on standing in the organization and community at large. Additionally, the Japanese placed a high value on consensual decision making, while the Thais showed more individualist traits and preferred decision making by individuals without the hierarchical structure. It was also found Japanese managers were much more focused on achievement and working long hours, while Thai workers placed less importance on work in their lives and preferred a more balanced approach to life. Also:

> Japanese management prefers specific company rules over flexible rules. Thai subordinates prefer flexibility. Thai employees feel that Japanese managers are too serious in decision making. Japanese managers feel very uncomfortable in the frequent decision changes of Thai subordinates who believe that a decision should be adjusted as the environment changes.
>
> (Swierczek and Onishi 2003: 198)

In Western countries, individuals generally have a single source of income and this often causes employees to have a high dependency on their employers. But,

> unlike people in the west who generally have just one income source, people in Southeast Asia may have many income sources – a bit of rice growing, some fishing to supply protein, a few months work on a construction site, washing dishes in a restaurant, hawking hand-woven cloth on city streets, even sitting quietly at home for a time and living from children's earnings.
>
> (Hill 2002: 186)

This lack of dependency on a single source of income is a two-edged sword for workers in the region. One the one hand, having the ability to walk off a job at any time prevents employers from exploiting the workers; on the other hand, the temporary nature of much of the employment in the region prevents employers from investing resources in improving the skills of the workers.

Logistics

The field of logistics would primary fall into the category of operational management. Hipsher (2007) proposed that operational business practices are heavily influenced by the technological environment and there can be found worldwide best practices and global convergence of logistic practices to some degree. While geographic terrain and infrastructure have major impacts on logistic business practices, it would not appear that cultural factors have a significant impact. Transportation and logistics through much of the region is often hampered by poor infrastructure and difficult terrain. Sajarattanachote (2006: 149) showed how manufacturers, suppliers, and customers tended to be located in clusters in Thailand, which may be a reflection on the high cost of transportation in the country. Historically, logistics in the region relied on water transportation (Young 1900); however, the river systems do not lend themselves to becoming efficient transportation routes in the modern era.

Logistics plays a vital role for business in Laos; it is how companies connect with the global trading system and companies exporting out of Laos or importing into Laos are highly dependent on the infrastructure in neighboring countries (Banomyong 2004). Being the only land-locked country in the region, having low population density, and being one of the least developed countries in Asia, companies in Laos PDR have very specific logistics concerns. Roads and infrastructure in Laos are limited and often of poor quality; there is no rail system and the river system can not be used as an effective transportation system. Although 90 percent of all transport is conducted over the roads, 40 percent of the population lives more than six kilometers from the nearest road and a quarter of all district centers do not have access to roads connected to trade routes throughout the entire year (United Nations Economic and Social Commission for Asia and the Pacific 2003: 49). Some goods are transported by air and on the Mekong River but, because of costs and the limited amount of the river that is navigable, these forms of transport are used only sparingly.

Much of the cross-border transport of material within the region is done on a small scale and is often of an informal nature. Rubesch and Banomyong (2005) speculated more goods enter Vientiane, the largest market in Laos PDR, by informal channels (which are not reflected in official trade statistics) than by formal means. Rehbein (2007a) pointed out the fact that nearly all consumer goods sold in Laos were imported due to the lack of manufacturing in the country, indicating the heavy presence of international trade networks, even if all the imports into the county are not officially recorded. Aribarg (2005: 70) described the blending of modern technology, manual labor, and informal practices that occurs during some of the trade between Thailand and Myanmar/ Burma:

> Another common sight that might surprise outsiders in this otherwise developing country environment with porters so instrumental in the exchange, is the use of cell phones and the like. Quite literally, Thai traders can agree on specific riverside areas that they can ship their goods *via* porter to their Burmese counterparts. Another common sight along the river, therefore, is one individual, or a group, waiting on the other side with a lorry, pick-up truck or car. The overall impression clearly, is quite different from cross-border commercial activities that might take place in a developed country context. The formality of international trade among developed states has led to large shipments *via* lorry, or other, and this is notably different from the developing country case. "Cross-border" trade of the kind described here takes place in these kinds of "ad hoc" arrangement in smaller quantities.

Aribarg (2005: 83) went on to explain, "the most frequently traversed areas at the border are areas that are not officially designated as government checkpoints." This would appear to indicate that the actual amount of cross-border trade in the region is much higher than is reflected in official statistics.

Within each country, many firms attempt to use international best practices to most efficiently move cargo; however, due to the lack of infrastructure, the efficiency of transportation is often less than is found in more developed economies. An interesting method of transporting small amounts of goods by small businesses is through the use of motorcycles. It is not surprising while in Cambodia,

Laos, Myanmar/Burma, or rural parts of Thailand to see supplies for restaurants, auto-repair shops, and other small businesses arrive on two wheels.

Production and manufacturing business practices

Production techniques would mostly fall into the category of operational business practices and according to Hipsher's (2007) framework it would be expected to see technology being the primary driver of choice of production techniques and not cultural factors. Prajogo *et al.* (2007) found despite having substantially different cultural environments, the manufacturing strategies and practices found in firms in Vietnam and Thailand were not significantly different, which supports the concept that production techniques are not greatly affected by cultural environment.

Prajogo *et al.* (2007) also found a lack of research and development activities in firms from both Thailand and Vietnam; the authors advocated firms in the regions increase levels of research and development (R & D). However, Hawks (2005) believed while innovations were important for manufacturing firms in Cambodia, the use of cutting edge technologies was not. De Valk (2003) felt by concentrating on transferring existing production knowledge from other locations, firms in Laos could improve their efficiency and effectiveness. De Valk did not believe firms in Laos had the capabilities to create new technologies and would be better served to innovatively adapt existing technologies created in other locations for use in the local environment. Harrigan (2007: 6) wrote, "Not until quite sophisticated capabilities have already been acquired does it make sense to invest in R & D aimed at innovation on an international level." And it would appear most industries and businesses originating from the Theravada Buddhist region of Southeast Asia have not reached the stage where attempts at technological innovation on an international level make sense.

Hipsher (2007) argued it is at the operational level where much of the globalization is taking place in the business world. The use of cell phones, ATMs, standardized shipping containers, computers with software that is compatible worldwide, standardized accounting procedures, and bar codes at checkout counters can be found in locations throughout the world. Companies do not have to have compatible strategic and tactical level business practices, but often do need operational practices in common to effectively do business. Therefore, increases in international trade pressure firms to seek global convergence in operational business practices, but this increase in trade does not necessarily put pressure on the convergence of strategic and tactical business practices.

Technological advance has in the past been strongly correlated with economic growth and poverty reduction (Harrigan 2007); therefore, it has also been advocated that many operational business practices and technologies can be directly transferred from developed to developing country with only minor adaptation (Hipsher 2009). Foreign aid organizations and international business educational institutions working in the region have been encouraged to pay particular attention to transferring operational business practices when working with local organizations to improve their efficiency and not attempt to transfer HR management systems or concepts of leadership from the outside without substantial adaptation being made for local conditions.

Hawks (2005), in his study of small manufacturing firms in Cambodia, reported local business owners generally believed equipment and supplies from more economically advanced areas, such as Thailand, were superior to what was available locally; also, business owners in and around Phnom Penh felt new and better equipment was the key to improved quality as opposed to improving training of employees. Hawks also found business owners were reluctant to make major investments in modernizing their equipment due to uncertainty over market and political conditions. In addition, Hawks discovered, due to low labor costs and the unreliability of electricity, many firms used labor intensive technologies instead of using more modern equipment.

Prasertrungruang and Hadikusumo (2007) found distinct differences in Thailand between large and small firms in the management of heavy equipment used in highway construction and repair. These differences may suggest large firms in the region are adapting worldwide best operational practices, while smaller firms may often lack the capital to use the same best practices.

Internationalization strategies

Internationalization can be defined as the process of moving from being a domestic firm into an international one. Bartlett and Ghoshal (1998) proposed the concept firms operating internationally could use four basic internationalization strategies, and the authors believed these four strategies were stages a firm would often go through. The first strategy/stage is called the international strategy and is where a firm's international operations are simply added on to its existing domestic operations. For manufacturing firms, exporting is the most common feature of using an international strategy. The second strategy/stage is where firms become multi-domestic and have semi-independent operations in multiple countries of the world. In this stage, the primary focus is on being responsive to local needs. The third stage is where firms become "global" and operate as if the world is a single market and the focus is usually on achieving economies of scale. The final stage is when a company becomes a "transnational," where the company is locally responsive and globally efficient simultaneously while avoiding making the normal trade-offs associated with these two different strategies.

It is questioned how applicable Bartlett and Ghoshal's (1998) framework is for identifying internationalization strategies of firms originating from the Theravada Buddhist countries of Southeast Asia. How many firms from Myanmar/ Burma, Laos, or Cambodia have even approached the multi-domestic stage? Although economies of scale and efficiencies in production are common business practices in manufacturing firms in Thailand that have international connections, it would be a real stretch to claim most of these firms with their limited size and scale were using a "global" strategy.

Five major factors have been identified as drivers of firms from developing countries, such as those found in the Theravada Buddhist countries of Southeast Asia, to internationalize operations; these five are: access to resources, access to technologies, access to markets, diversification, and strategic value (Deng 2003). Much of the theoretical foundations of the internationalization literature comes from studying large multinationals in the United States with the product life cycle theory of Vernon (1966) and Dunning's (1973, 1980) eclectic paradigm being seminal frameworks that have influenced thinking about how firms expand abroad. But it should be kept in mind, both the product life cycle theory and Dunning's electric paradigm were conceived assuming manufactured goods were the core products of the firms that were internationalizing and the flow was primarily from more developed to less developed regions. Hitt, Ireland, and Hoskisson (2005: 235) examined the literature and, in summary, classified macro internationalization strategies into four groupings: international business level, multi-domestic, global, and transnational, all of which assume international business is being conducted by large multinational firms.

A more recent focus on internationalization strategies has been on international new ventures, or "born global firms" (for examples, see Gabrielsson, Sasi, and Darling 2004; Knight and Cavusgil 2004, 2005; Knight *et al.* 2004; Moen 2002; Moen and Servais 2002; Rasmussan *et al.* 2001). The credit for the initial identification of this phenomenon is usually given to Oviatt and McDougall (1994). Traditionally it was assumed that firms went through a predictable pattern. Firms in their infancy were only domestic in nature and after a considerable time a firm might grow and mature to the stage it would consider moving into the international arena. However, Oviatt and McDougall noticed there were a considerable number of firms that became internationally focused immediately or shortly after coming into existence. Harveston *et al.* (2000) discovered the founders and manager of these born global firms were more likely to have had extensive exposure to living, working, and traveling in foreign countries before initiating their new international enterprises.

Firms invest into foreign countries for two main purposes, either to access resources or to access markets (Zitta and Power 2003). However, while using a strategy to access resources, it would appear the resources firms from developing economies seek may at times be different from the resources firms from developed economies seek. Firms from developed economies when investing to access resources may normally be concerned with gaining access to raw materials and inexpensive labor. Research by Chandprapalert (2000) found support for the idea firms from developed countries often invested in the relatively less developed country of Thailand in order to access the country's abundant natural resources and low-cost labor.

Yang (2003: 169) found two distinct types of markets that were attractive for resource-driven foreign investment by firms from the developing economy of China. The first were countries that have large quantities of natural resources, while the second were countries with technological leadership. Thomas (2001) believed traditional theories did a poor job of explaining the internationalization activities of many firms from developing countries and thought many of the moves of firms from Latin America into a developing region, usually the United States, were not to leverage existing strengths, but instead the moves were made to gain new strengths and knowledge from competing in a competitive and advanced environment, and then these new strengths and knowledge could be used to the firm's advantage in its domestic market.

Most internationalization moves are to attempt to access new markets. When internationalizing to access markets, firms from developed economies generally tend to seek out other developed economies where markets are large and similar to the market in the home country (Zitta and Power 2003). However, firms from developing economies often seek internationalization in order to access markets in other developing economies that are in geographical proximity (Fauver *et al.* 2003). Cuervo-Cazurra and Genc (2008) found firms from developing economies often have advantages over large multinationals when operating in foreign developing economies. The authors claimed these advantages come from experience and knowledge of operating in unstable environments where legal concepts are quite different from what is found in developed economies.

Business conditions in the Theravada Buddhist countries of Southeast Asia can be very different from those found in the United States or other countries in more economically and technologically developed areas of the world. Firms in the region are generally smaller, are more likely to be family owned, and are less likely to have technological advantages over firms in other locations. On the other hand, because of labor costs in Thailand and transportation or other costs of firms in the other Theravada Buddhist countries of Southeast Asia, the firms in the region often lack the cost advantages seen in firms from China or Vietnam. While the names of Thai, Burmese, Cambodian, or Laotian firms do not automatically spring to mind when the topic of international business comes up, there is a considerable percentage of business in the region that is international in nature, although much of the cross-border trade that stays in the region goes unrecorded.

Internationalization strategies of SMEs, which make up the vast majority of firms in the region, appear to have some similarities and some differences from the internationalization strategies of large firms (Andersson *et al.* 2004). The authors did not find a relationship between size, technological level, age of the firm, or age of the CEO to be associated with increased levels of internationalization of SMEs, which contradicts predictions one would expect to find according to Vernon's (1966) product life cycle theory and intuition. What was found was the more "perceived dynamism" in the industry a firm operated in, the more likely the firm would move some activities abroad. Westhead, Ucbasaran, and Binks (2004) reported no differences between the internationalization patterns of urban or rural SMEs in Britain, which counters intuition to some extent. Kuo and Li (2003) found a negative correlation between capital intensity and internationalization levels of SMEs from Taiwan; therefore, showing firms were reducing the possible risks associated with internationalization of operations. Karadeniz and Gocer (2007) reported lower levels of growth in the domestic market, as well as possessing greater levels of intangible assets, were associated with increased internationalization with Turkish SMEs. These results of research on SMEs suggest industry and other external factors may play a greater role in driving the internationalization of smaller firms than do internal resources as was suggested by Dunning's (1973, 1980) eclectic paradigm.

Most theories of internationalization assume a firm scans the environment and then rationally makes choices that will maximize profits. However, Li *et al.* (2004), in their study of United States-based SMEs, found the internationalization process actually was normally initiated by an unplanned acquiring of knowledge of business opportunities in a foreign country. Erdilek (2008) reported the motives for SMEs to expand internationally in Turkey were "idiosyncratic and opportunistic." Ellis (2000) came to a similar conclusion in a study of firms in Hong Kong, where social connections in a foreign country usually drove international activities of firms as opposed to formal planning and selection procedures. It would appear SMEs around the globe are more likely to expand operations internationally due to chance circumstance as opposed to methodical planning and evaluation of alternatives.

Family-owned firms in Southeast Asia often have objectives other than maximizing shareholders' profits and, once established, often take more conservative strategies than do corporations where there is a separation between ownership and management. In established family-owned firms in Asia, wealth preservation is often a more primary objective than wealth creation (Carney and Gedailovic 2003). Fernandez and Nieto (2005) found a negative correlation between family ownership and the amount of internationalization of a firm, supporting the concept that family ownership is associated with more conservative strategies. However, it appears that "internationalization knowledge" can be used by family-owned firms to expand business across borders in many cases (Basly 2007). This may help explain the dominance of ethnic Chinese family-owned firms within the region, as these firms can gain knowledge about business opportunities in different regions through family and ethnic ties with those living in a different country, as suggested by Sim and Pandian (2007).

Firms in the Theravada Buddhist countries of Southeast Asia usually are not innovators of cutting edge technology; therefore, firms need to find non-technological advantages to be successful during the internationalization process (Lau 1992). The primary advantage most firms from the area have is access to raw materials or natural resources. Laos is able to export electricity to Thailand because of the availability of fast-flowing rivers. Agriculture and forestry products are also often exported from firms originating in the region. We also see relatively cheap labor in some areas, which helps explain the continuing presence of the garment industry in Cambodia and other areas of the region.

Internationalization normally refers to expanding operations outside one's domestic borders. On the other hand, Bjorkman and Kock (1997) made the case that a firm, especially within the tourism industry, can internationalize by attracting foreign customers and/or suppliers while solely operating within the confines of the domestic market. As tourism provides a substantial portion of the GDPs of Thailand and Cambodia, as well as an increasing portion in Laos, there are an increasing number of restaurants, guesthouses, hotels, and travel agencies that have "internationalized" their operations by attracting more foreign customers. Another method firms in the region use to internationalize without leaving home is to create joint ventures or partnerships with foreign companies. By creating joint ventures, firms can gain access to resources not available locally without expanding operations internationally. For example, Charoen Pokphand (CP), the Thai conglomerate that initially focused on agriculture, used joint ventures with Western companies such as Arbor Acres Farms Inc. and DeKalb Genetics Corp. in order to gain access to US technological know-how without expanding into the hyper-competitive US market (Biers *et al.* 1999).

Many firms from outside the region have internationalized their operations by expanded into these four countries. It has been reported that, in general, firms from more developed countries invest into lesser developed countries in order to access markets or obtain access to inexpensive labor; geographic proximity has also been found to be a contributing factor (Bitzenis 2003). Tahir and Larimo (2004) discovered market size and less cultural distance had a positive effect on the decisions of Finnish firms on which countries in Southeast Asia to invest in. Luo (2003) and Bitzenis (2003) found a negative correlation between foreign investment and levels of "red tape" a firm needed to go through. As a result, it is not surprising Thailand, with its larger market size and more investment friendly policies, is the recipient of far more foreign investment than are the countries of Myanmar/Burma, Cambodia, and Laos, which all have both a small market size and considerable bureaucratic obstacles for foreign investors.

As Thailand is geographically in the center of the region and also is the economic powerhouse of the Theravada Buddhist countries of Southeast Asia, it is not surprising Thailand is a major trading partner of the other three nations. Another factor in addition to geographic proximity that may be resulting in increasing trade linkages between the nations of the region is cultural similarities. Tsai and Cheng (2004) reported that firms from Taiwan were much more likely to invest in culturally similar countries, primarily mainland China, than in other locations. D'Souza and Peretiatko (2005) reported that US firms invested at a much higher rate into the culturally similar country of Australia than in Asian nations due to the comfort levels of working with those from similar cultural backgrounds. Bitzenis (2003) found a similar result for firms in Bulgaria, as they preferred to invest into countries with both geographic and cultural proximity. Ellis (2008) found both market size and cultural similarities to be factors driving investment in Asia, while Slangen and Hennart (2008) found cultural similarity influenced choice of entry with firms preferring to start a new venture in culturally distant locations while acquisition was more likely in culturally similar regions. Therefore, sharing a common religion and having somewhat similar social-cultural environments most likely has an effect on the internationalization strategies of the firms within the region, which is bringing the economies of the four nations closer together, although there is a lack of empirical evidence at this time to support if this hypothesis holds in the region.

It has been suggested that firms from less developed regions face many obstacles to internationalizing their operations, including lack of foreign market knowledge and lack of connection to international trade networks (De Valk 2003; Ibeh and Young 2001). It has also been found in the developing economy of Vietnam, product quality and logistics management can impede the internationalization of SMEs (Neupert *et al.* 2006). Yet, despite the obstacles, many firms from developing economies in Southeast Asia have successfully internationalized their operations.

Much of the academic focus on internationalization is on the issue of the manner in which countries enter foreign markets, commonly referred to as "mode of entry" (for examples, see Brothers 2002; Davis *et al.* 2000; Head and Ries 2004).

In their textbook, Hitt *et al.* (2005: 235) identified five modes of entry: exporting, non equity entry (licensing or franchising), strategic alliances, acquisitions, and establishment of a new subsidiary from the ground up (greenfield project). Many of the research frameworks and theories of mode of entry use Coase's (1937) transaction cost theory as a guiding principle where it is believed firms will internalize parts of their foreign operations when the transaction costs are lower than using market mechanisms (Sarkar and Cavusgil 1996).

The majority of internationalization strategies of firms in these four countries would appear to fit into these categories quite well, with exporting being the most common mode of entry used. However, Hipsher (2008a) studied the mode of entry decisions of Thai "firms" in Cambodia and found an interesting result. It was found that many of the Thai-owned companies in Cambodia were not extensions of existing business but totally new businesses. In some incidences it was found Thai owners started their first entrepreneurial venture in Cambodia, either for personal reasons or because the less competitive nature of the business environment in Cambodia made it easier for an entrepreneur to get a new venture off the ground. In other cases, existing Thai firms entered the Cambodian market in a totally different product area than the firms were involved in within Thailand. Hipsher labeled these firms "born foreign" as the firms were launched in a foreign environment but are distinctly different from "born global" firms.

10 Features of firms in Theravada Buddhist Southeast Asia

Entrepreneurial

One of the characteristics of the business environment of the Theravada Buddhist countries of Southeast Asia is the wide-scale existence of small entrepreneurial firms. Pride *et al.* (2008: 13) define an entrepreneur as "a person who risks time, effort, and money to start and operate a business." While this definition applies to some of the business owners in the region, there are many entrepreneurs in the Theravada Buddhist countries of Southeast Asia who have very different motivations and approaches to starting a business from those found in this definition.

Research indicates entrepreneurs have a variety of motivations for starting a new business, with financial rewards being only one of many motivators. In New Zealand, Pinfold (2001) reported entrepreneurs were motivated to achieve a variety of goals, including financial rewards, personal development, and independence. In a study conducted in Singapore, Choo and Wong (2006) found the top five motivators of entrepreneurs were: challenge, realization of dreams, taking advantage of creative talents, to be one's own boss, and to have an interesting job. These five motivators would appear to be more lifestyle motivators rather than economic motivators. Choo and Wong also discovered financial goals were important considerations when deciding to start a business, but their results suggest lifestyle factors can also be powerful motivators for entrepreneurs and stereotyping all entrepreneurs as being driven by dreams of wealth may be misleading. Research by Hatcher and Terjesen (2007) indicates lifestyle and other non-economic considerations play a critical role in the decision to start a business for entrepreneurs in Thailand as well.

It would appear the concept of entrepreneurship in developed countries has both similarities and differences with the concept of entrepreneurship in developing nations. In developed economies, there is an assumption that quality paid employment is available and entrepreneurs forsake the safety of a monthly pay check for the uncertainty and possibilities that come with having one's own business (Shahidi and Smagulova 2007). Therefore, it is not surprising that in their study conducted in the United States, Thomas and Mueller (2000) reported entrepreneurs generally had an internal locus of control, high levels of energy, and were risk takers. It is likely these traits are necessary as modern developed economies present many barriers to entry for potential entrepreneurs (Helms 2003: Imai and Kawagoe 2000). However, in developing economies, quality paid employment may not be available and entrepreneurs are often "pushed" into starting a business as opposed to be pulled into it by dreams of riches (Kalantaridis and Labrianidis 2004; Kristiansen 2002). In some cases, the primary motivator in starting a business can be survival and not the search for wealth or independence, as there is a lack of availability of any kind of paid employment in the environments found in the world's least developed economies (Pitamber 2000). Research by Paulson and Townsend (2005) suggests many small-scale entrepreneurs in Thailand are also more motivated by push than pull factors.

Entrepreneurs in the Theravada Buddhist regions of Southeast Asia share some common characteristics with entrepreneurs in other locations as well as some differences. Thomas and Mueller (2000) found some universal personality traits in entrepreneurs in different locations, but also they noticed some distinct variations of traits found in entrepreneurs coming from different cultural contexts. Entrepreneurship may be a universal phenomenon, but the exact nature of it would appear to differ to some degree from location to location.

There may be a recognizable difference between the concept of entrepreneurship in the East and in the West. Moy *et al.* (2003), in their study of attitudes of students in Hong Kong, reported students in Hong Kong with intentions of becoming entrepreneurs were more likely to have more positive and conformist views than students in Western countries with similar intentions of becoming an entrepreneur. The desire to start one's own business is often associated with having non-conformist views in Western societies. The results of this study are consistent with the observations by the author, who has found in universities in both Thailand and Vietnam the most common answer to the question of what do you want to do after you graduate is "to start my own business" (or take over my family's business). In the United States and other Western countries, starting a business is normally considered a path toward independence and is often associated with rugged individualism. However, in Asia, entrepreneurship normally means joining an interdependent business network and therefore entrepreneurship in Asia may be considered more collectivist and less individualistic than in the West (Bjerke 2000).

Owning a business in a Western context is normally considered a personal affair with relatively fewer businesses being passed down from generation to generation (Fairlie and Robb 2007). However, throughout Asia, the focus of entrepreneurship often shifts from the individual to the family (Shapiro *et al.* 2003). Thailand, like much of Asia and the other Theravada Buddhist countries of Southeast Asia, is dominated by the existence of family-owned firms (Suehiro and Wailerdsak 2004). Many business owners in Thailand and the other countries of the region are second or later-generation entrepreneurs who have taken over family businesses, and these later-generation entrepreneurs are generally better educated but less technically proficient than first-generation entrepreneurs

(Chung and Yuen 2003). In Asia, carrying on the family business is often thought of as a family obligation, while not going into the family business may be considered selfish and overly individualistic. It has been shown Asian entrepreneurs on average may have more conservative and family-oriented values than do Western entrepreneurs.

It should be kept in mind that career advancement opportunities for outsiders in family-owned firms are limited, often resulting in non-family paid employees leaving their employers in order to seek out their own entrepreneurial opportunities in order to have an opportunity for advancement and job security. There are few government-enforced workforce legal protections in the region, and therefore an employee's career is often subject to the arbitrary decision making of the owner of the firm, and becoming an entrepreneur is often a path to increased financial and professional security and not necessarily a more risky decision than working in someone else's family-owned firm with no legal protection. Entrepreneurship in different locations is shaped to a large extent by the available alternatives. Ambitious individuals in the West often have the option of starting a business or climbing the corporate ladder in seeking professional success, while the second option is often quite limited in the Theravada Buddhist countries of Southeast Asia where family ownership of companies is more common than ownership by corporation.

The institutional environments found in the Theravada Buddhist countries of Southeast Asia have a direct impact on entrepreneurship in the region. As a visitor to the region quickly discovers, a thriving informal economic sector exists and the streets are filled with people seeking financial opportunities, which Kamrava (1999: 47) reported was natural where a "mixed" economy was present, as is currently seen in Myanmar/Burma, Laos, and to some extent Cambodia and Thailand. Bowen and De Clercq (2008) found the higher the level of corruption found in a nation, the more entrepreneurial efforts will move away from more productive activities in the formal sector toward generally less productive activities in the informal sector. Therefore, as corruption is not unknown in the region, it can be speculated a large amount of entrepreneurial effort is expended within the informal sectors of the economies in order to avoid having to go through official channels.

Laos is a country where the majority of the population is rural and where subsistence agricultural and small-scale trading make up most of the economic activities undertaken in the country. This pattern has not greatly changed from pre-colonial times, through the period of French domination, and now into the present communist period (Prakoonheang 2001). However, beginning with the New Economic Mechanism policy in 1986, more private SMEs have arisen and it has been reported that family-owned SMEs make up 74 percent of the total number of businesses in the country (Southiseng and Walsh 2008). Rehbein (2007a: 60) reported, "almost all Lao households engage in some form of trading," even when individuals are officially classified as employees.

Entrepreneurs in Laos face many of the same challenges as entrepreneurs in other developing economies. Lack of capital, limited demand due to the small size of the market, a highly competitive environment, lack of access to techno-logy, and inconsistent application of government policies have all been cited as obstacles small business owners face (Southiseng and Walsh 2008: 2). Also, as noted in the case studies in Chapter 4, finding and retaining skilled and profes-sional labor has proven to be problematic for some firms. The primary workforce for many small entrepreneurial firms in Laos is family members, and this often results in family considerations taking precedence over financial considerations in the decision making of the business, but it also decreases recruiting and selec-tion costs (Southiseng and Walsh 2008: 12, 20). The competitive environment in Vientiane was found to be more intense than in other parts of the country; fur-thermore, products from Thailand, China, and Vietnam can be found in retail markets throughout the country, demonstrating that while Laos is often con-sidered isolated from the rest of the world, there are extensive international busi-ness connections throughout the nation (Southiseng and Walsh 2008: 21), even if many of these connections and business transactions are not incorporated into the official statistics.

Entrepreneurs in Laos would appear to share some similar traits with entre-preneurs in the other Theravada Buddhists countries of Southeast Asia. As expected, Southiseng and Walsh (2008: 15) found a combination of education, experience, conceptual skills, and technical abilities were associated with entre-preneurial success; however, the idea of the ambitious and driven business owners was tempered with the *bo pen yang dok* (never mind/don't worry about it) attitude that is common in the country. Southiseng and Walsh (2008: 14) found business owners enjoyed the flexibility of having their own business and often took advantage of their independence to spend time with family or in relaxation as opposed to constantly working to grow their business. In addition, business owners enjoyed being able to meet directly with customers and employ their own individual management style. Southiseng and Walsh also reported most entrepreneurial firms in Laos PDR were self-financed, short-term oriented, and had no plans to expand internationally.

The short-term orientation found in Laotian entrepreneurs is similar to find-ings in other businesses in the Theravada Buddhist countries of Southeast Asia and may be associated with the Theravada Buddhist teachings of impermanence, while the moderation of ambition would appear to be aligned with following the middle path. The teachings of Theravada Buddhism stress the individual nature of the path to enlightenment, and it would appear entrepreneurs in Laos also follow an individualistic path toward economic activities to a considerable extent.

As in Laos, there is a vibrant entrepreneurial spirit found in Cambodia. In a similar fashion to the findings of Southiseng and Walsh (2008) in Laos PDR, Hawks (2005: 110) found an individualistic and short-term strain to entrepre-neurship in Cambodia and wrote:

> An interesting point among the SME owners interviewed is the focus on the owner himself or herself as the exclusive factor in determining the future of

the company. A company's success seemed to be tied to the owner rather than putting in place an organizational structure that would last beyond the owner and that would focus on growth.

Hawks (2005) also reported on how the challenges faced by and characteristics of entrepreneurs in Cambodia were similar to those Southiseng and Walsh (2008) found in Laos PDR.

Entrepreneurship is alive and well in Thailand, in fact Hatcher and Terjesen (2007) reported Thailand has one of the highest rates of entrepreneurial participation in the world and also had an extremely high rate of participation of women in entrepreneurship. The authors felt a number of factors contributed to Thailand having such a high percentage of women entrepreneurs. These included the supplementary nature of much of the business activities conducted by women toward family income and a cultural environment that allows women to take on a variety of different roles within society.

The use of official statistics of entrepreneurs in Thailand can be very misleading. There is a considerable amount of unrecorded business activity in the country and only comparatively large-scale businesses are officially registered. Paulson and Townsend (2005) studied entrepreneurial behavior within provinces outside of Bangkok and discovered most small-scale entrepreneurs used their own savings or other informal sources to fund the creation of new businesses. The authors also reported many of the new businesses required extremely low amounts of start-up capital, very rarely employed non-family members, and it was quite common for entrepreneurial activities to be used as a supplement to, not a substitute for, working for wages. The authors also found no correlation between wealth and the likelihood of starting a business, showing the entrepreneurship spirit in Thailand crosses social status divisions. It is likely that entrepreneurs starting larger scale businesses in Thailand are primarily motivated by pull factors and have some of the characteristics associated with entrepreneurship in more developed Asian countries. On the other hand, it is likely most small-scale entrepreneurs (especially in rural areas) are mostly driven by push factors and share many characteristics with entrepreneurs in the other developing areas of the region.

Most small-scale entrepreneurs in Thailand are domestically focused. The Thai government has made some efforts to promote the internationalization of Thai SMEs. Some examples of these efforts include the creation of the Department of Export Promotion and the One Tambun (Village) One Product (OTOP) Project. There have been limited moves by some Thai SMEs to enter foreign markets; however, the size of the Thai economy in relation to most of Thailand's neighbors provides limited incentives to seek new markets within the region. Andersson *et al.* (2004) discovered small firms in more dynamic industries were more likely than SMEs in less dynamic industries to internationalize operations and, as most Thai SMEs are in more traditional industries, there appear to be limited intangible benefits to be gained from internationalizing operations. Additionally, the majority of SMEs in Thailand are family owned and it has been reported family ownership is negatively correlated with internationalization of operations (Fernandez and Nieto 2005). Moreover, family ownership of firms in Southeast Asia appears to be associated with the use of risk adverse strategies, such as those involving internationalization (Carney and Gedailovic 2003). However, as Thailand's neighbors begin to grow economically and trade barriers are lowered, Thai SMEs and entrepreneurs are beginning to seek new opportunities in neighboring countries. In studying Thai-owned SMEs in Cambodia, it was found many of these enterprises were not extensions of existing Thai SMEs but were the first businesses for the Thai entrepreneurs. These "born foreign" firms were created because of new opportunities, lower barriers to entry, and less intense competition compared to what is found in the more mature economy of Thailand (Hipsher 2008a).

Although it is difficult to find recent studies on entrepreneurship in Myanmar/ Burma, informal personal observations by the author of entrepreneurial activities by Burmese small business owners on both sides of the Thai–Myanmar/Burma border would indicate most entrepreneurial activities in the country are driven by push factors due to the lack of availability of paid employment. It appears entrepreneurs from Myanmar/Burma share some characteristics with entrepreneurs in other parts of the region; however, the institutional environment found within the country undoubtedly presents some unique challenges.

Microenterprises

Small-scale businesses, often referred to as microenterprises, are common throughout the region. In general, it has been found the less developed an economy is, the higher the percentage of individuals who are self-employed and engaged in microenterprises (Fajnzylber *et al.* 2006). Therefore, it is not surprising that a large number of individuals in the Theravada Buddhist countries of Southeast Asia are self-employed and run their own businesses. The following cases come from interviews that were conducted with owners of microenterprises.

Case 1

This case is of an individual who runs his own motorcycle repair shop in Battambang, Cambodia. He has had his own business for over 15 years. He chose to start his own business in order to earn money to support his family and himself. He feels his lack of education makes it difficult to find paid employment. He really enjoys the independence of having his own business and having the ability to set his own hours. His main concerns are over being able to sustain the level of income needed to support his family, also this type of mechanical work is dirty and messy which is not always pleasant. He doesn't have any plans for the future; instead, he takes things day to day.

Case 2

Located in Bangkok, Thailand, the individual in Case 2 works out of her home as a beautician. Her main customers are people from the neighborhood and teachers in the nearby school. By working at home, she doesn't need to travel to work and can combine working with her duties as a housewife and mother. She was interested in being a hair stylist and therefore went to a training program to learn the skills needed and then started her own business. She feels her lack of education makes her unattractive to employers. She likes the independence of having her own small business, but wishes she had more customers. On the other hand, her family is not dependent on her income, instead it is seen as a supplement to the family's income and therefore there is little pressure to hustle up new customers. She doesn't have any real plans for the future, just to continue on as is.

Case 3

Case 3 is of a lady in Bangkok who individually cooks and sells food to order. Her customers mostly come from the office building next to where she sets up her business. Her main selling points are she provides customized service along with convenience. She also claims her food is very delicious. She has been in business for about six years. She claims she is too old and does not have enough education to find work with a company. Her family is not dependent on her income, but the extra she brings in does make a difference to the standard of living for her family. She says her main plan is to win the lottery and stop working, but until that happens she will continue on. When she feels she is too old to be out working everyday she will stay at home and take care of her grandchildren.

Case 4

Case 4 involves a lady in Bangkok who sets up a snack booth in front of a school when the school day ends. She mainly sells to students and parents. She sells French fries, fried chicken, and other snack food. She has been operating this business for about eight years. She feels she is too old to find work at a company, she enjoys the freedom that comes from being her own boss, and she does not have to worry about being laid off. The main problems she faces are the low profit margins and the lack of opportunities during the rainy season. She doesn't have any plans to change the way she does business or to expand. She says if she wasn't running a snack business, she would probably be babysitting.

Case 5

Case 5 involves the owner of a small convenience store, also in Bangkok. The owner keeps a wide variety of items for sale and her main customers are students and housewives. She has been in business for 22 years and one of the key elements of her success is her location. She prefers to have her own business for both personal and professional reasons. She enjoys the freedom and status of having her own business and she is quite satisfied with the income she makes. Although being a community-based business, she finds herself often selling on credit and occasionally some items sold are never paid for. Her plans are to continue with her existing business plan and to save money for the future.

Case 6

Case 6 involves a seller of cotton candy. He normally sells in the local market. As there are few sellers of cotton candy in Bangkok, he finds a steady demand for his product. He mentioned that because of his lack of a higher education qualification, he feels he can make more money working on his own than he would as an employee of a company. He likes the fact he gets paid daily for his work; however, his income is somewhat dependent on the weather and on rainy days he is unable to earn any income. He doesn't have any plans for the future, just to keep running his business without any major changes.

As illustrated in these cases, owning and operating a microenterprise in a developing economy does not perfectly conform to the vision of being an ambitious and risk-taking business owner found in most of the entrepreneurial literature. None of the interviewed microenterprise owner-operators had any thoughts of growing into a larger size business. Instead, it appears these individuals were creating jobs for themselves as opposed to starting a "business."

Personal, not bureaucratic

In the study of organizations in Western contexts, an underlying assumption one normally begins with is that the organization will have a bureaucratic structure and be more or less an impersonal entity. The organization structure and designs of bureaucracies use positions or jobs as their fundamental building blocks. Individuals are normally hired and promoted based on "objective" criteria, often found in detailed job descriptions that were created using an objective and impersonal job analysis. Individuals are most often encouraged to avoid taking into account personal connections with individuals while hiring and the terms favoritism and nepotism have negative connotations. In general, a clear separation between the position and the individual working in the position is encouraged.

It is speculated that this emphasis on the separation between an individual and the position found in Western organizations can be partially attributed to a need to accept the natural hierarchical nature of organizations while maintaining societal egalitarian values and legal frameworks where "all men are created equal." Keeping a fairly clear separation between person and position may allow people to come to terms with the hierarchical reality of organizational life while holding on to egalitarian personal values. Positions within an organization can be unequal, but the people holding the different positions are "equal," at least when outside of the workplace and outside of work hours. Additionally, it can be speculated that this need to come to an acceptance of a reality that conflicts with societies' ideals may result in placing more emphasis on the voluntary and equal nature of an employment contract while downplaying the necessary difference in power and authority of people within an organization.

Having no need to come to terms with these conflicting values may help explain why in societies with higher acceptance of power distances, such as the societies found in the Theravada Buddhist countries of Southeast Asia, there is less emphasis on maintaining a clear separation between a person and a position. Maintaining a separation between person and position requires the extensive use of "impersonal" rules, regulations, and business frameworks, which added to the dispersed ownership environment and large size found in many Western organizations, especially those found in the United States, results in relatively more bureaucratic structures and impersonal business practices.

In collectivist societies, workplace interactions may be more of a combination of personal and profession relationships than is considered the norm in other societies. Chen and Peng (2008) believed there were significant differences between co-worker relationships between cultures and they found in China both job-relevant and non job-relevant behavior had an impact on the closeness and trust developed between co-workers. Quality of relationships with co-workers is important to people around the world, but it may take on added importance in cultures where the separation of work and personal life is less distinct.

Not only are business relationships within organizations in the region more personal than bureaucratic, this is also true of relationships between organizations. Although there has been more emphasis recently on creating relationships within a value chain, Western companies are still more likely to use arms-length relationships where price and market forces are the prime determinates to be used in the selection of business partners. This is not necessarily the case within the Theravada Buddhist countries of Southeast Asia and other areas where there is less likely to be a separation between ownership and management.

> Quality of product is important. Price is important. But most important of all, a Thai wants to know if you are his or her "kind of person." If he or she feels comfortable with you, he might be inclined to do business with you. And more importantly, he may introduce you to some of his friends.
>
> (Holmes *et al.* 1996: 18)

Aribarg (2005) found choice of business partner in cross-border trade was primarily based on trust and personal relationships, and it was observed that most of the traders on both sides of the Thai–Myanmar/Burma border were of ethnic Chinese origin. This is consistent with the findings of many other scholars who have noted the use of trust and personal relationships within ethnic Chinese business networks throughout East and Southeast Asia (Carney and Gedailovic 2003; Keller and Kronstedt 2005; Suehiro and Wailerdsak 2004; Tsang 2001; Yan and Sorenson 2004). Aribarg believed the lack of formal systems left business operators no choice but to rely on trust in conducting this cross-border trade, which is aligned with the findings of Luk *et al.* (2008), who found social capital to be especially important in transition economies and less important where markets operated more efficiently.

Both importers and exporters from Thailand found having positive relationships with business partners in Australia to be important factors in making decisions about which companies to do business with (Styles *et al.* 2008). This may suggest international companies working in the region adapt to some extent to the local conditions by placing additional emphasis on gaining and maintaining personal relationships.

Personal relationships are also important for business operators in the region in their dealings with government officials. In the West, governments are thought of as primarily being bureaucracies and decisions are mostly made according to objective criteria. That is not necessarily the case in many other parts of the world, including the Theravada Buddhist countries of Southeast Asia, where enforcement of rules and regulations is mostly carried out according to the arbitrary decision making of individual government officials. About business in the region Aribarg (2005: 126) wrote, "People find personal relations and social networks more efficient than interacting with formal institutions, since laws and regulations are susceptible to authority's discretion." Hawks (2005: 111) found small businesses in Cambodia often attempted "to stay under the radar so as to avoid attention from the government." Nevertheless, it was reported having personal connections with government officials is often considered a competitive advantage for local business owners and managers.

Of course, this lack of bureaucratic institutions and having government officials with high levels of arbitrary decision making abilities leads to what is referred to as "oil for the machine," "tea money," or just plain corruption. It is rarely questioned how most senior government officials have lifestyles that would be impossible if one was solely dependent on a government salary. However, corruption is not always seen as strictly a black and white affair; instead, there may be many acceptable and unacceptable shades of gray. For example, many people in the region may not see anything particularly wrong with a police officer accepting a reasonable paid-on-the-spot fine instead of writing out an official ticket for a traffic violation. However, a police officer stopping traffic and demanding payment where no traffic violation occurred would almost always be considered as unacceptable behavior. Aribarg (2005: 127), in writing about Thai businesses operating alongside the Thai–Myanmar/Burma border and their relationship with government officials, explained:

> It was common for elite traders to openly present gifts to local officials of higher authority. They often invited them for sumptuous banquets. They also participated in social events and made donations to charity events organized by provincial authorities to demonstrate that they support the government's activities. The provincial authorities often need traders' financial contributions to their social events since the central government-supported funding usually does not cover all the expenses.

The author's personal experience showed international NGOs working in the same area also openly contributed to government agencies to help ensure cooperation. These payments were not made directly to an individual under the table; instead, contributions were made to specific government projects in the open to build personal relationships and promote cooperation. Whether or not this practice is considered corruption is open to interpretation. Hawks (2005: 112) also found unofficial payments to government officials were a major expense for businesses in Cambodia.

One would be hard pressed to make a case that the governments of the Theravada Buddhist countries of Southeast Asia have made significant moves toward the creation of a Western-style impersonal bureaucracy. Prakoonheang (2001) in Laos PDR felt government bureaucrats see themselves as following the tradition of government officials, being direct representatives of royalty and therefore are elite members of society who are entitled to "rule" over the people as opposed to having the Western idea of government service being where one subverts one's own interest for the good of the "people." Most organizations in both the private and public sectors in the region have resisted moves toward becoming impersonal bureaucracies on Western models, and it would appear that due to the social-cultural environments found in the region, organizations in these countries are unlikely to become replicas of organizations found in nations with different social-cultural environments and traditions. Instead of attempting to create impersonal government bureaucracies based on Western models within the region, inter-government agencies such as the UN and Asian Development Bank may find attempts to make the existing system based on the populations' preference for personal relationships over impersonal rules and regulations more efficient.

Labor intensive

In general, labor in the region is relatively inexpensive and this obviously affects the priorities of businesses in the region. Labor-saving technologies provide fewer benefits than they would in regions with higher labor costs. For example, as seen in Chapter 3, the Cambodian beverage company studied did not use fork trucks in its warehouse; instead, the company chose to use more labor intensive techniques as these techniques were more cost efficient. In Cambodia, Hawks (2005: 137) observed labor saving machines standing idle while the same operations the machines could do were being done by hand. It was explained electricity was more expensive than labor and the machines were only used when time became a higher priority than cost.

Paternalistic

Robbins (2003: 496), on reflecting on employer-employee relationships in the United States, noted, "It has gone from paternalism – in which the organization took nearly complete responsibility for managing its employees' careers – to supporting individuals as they take personal responsibility for their future." Individuals in today's Western societies are encouraged to think of themselves as business partners, or at least as independent agents who contract their services out to an employer on a voluntary basis, thereby emphasizing the freewill of the employee while downplaying the differences in power found in hierarchical organizations.

However, this emerging view of independent agents working in hierarchies through voluntary contractual relationships may not be universal. In the Theravada Buddhist countries of Southeast Asia, working and living arrangements often take on paternalistic aspects resulting in a patrimonial relationship. In describing organizational life in Laos and Cambodia, Rehbein (2007b: 71) claimed, "A patrimonial relationship is not simple domination but something like an exchange of protection against loyalty. This often includes the exchange of labour against remuneration as well." Within the Theravada Buddhist countries of Southeast Asia, hierarchies are considered a natural part of the world and can be explained by religious principles. Schober (1989: 103) wrote:

> Burmese clearly perceive and articulate the link between social position and religious accomplishment. The greater the merit a lay person is believed to have acquired through religious exchange, the greater his influence (*oza*), the greater the respect due to him and the greater his social standing.

Although hierarchies may be considered more natural as a result of the different levels of *kamma* individuals bring with themselves into this life, lower status individuals are not powerless in these relationships. Historically, lower status members of society had the freedom to voluntarily attach themselves to different patrons from the higher levels of society; therefore, while these relationships were very hierarchical in nature they were also voluntary and it was extremely important for the members of society to not only focus on their own personal power but also to ensure the welfare of those who were located below them in the hierarchy. A patron who ignores the wishes of his clients would soon find his flock moving toward other more considerate leaders and the patron's position in society would be endangered. Curtis (1903: 120) studying the "Lao" living in northern Thailand at the turn of the twentieth century explained this relationship:

> All the peasant class are in a manner serfs, for they are attached to some *Chau* to whom they look for protection, and to whom in return they render a certain amount of labor.... Often a man may go for several years without being called out for labor. Probably the reason for this, aside from the usually clement disposition of the *Chaus*, is that a peasant can at any time he may wish change his protector without a change in residence. Thus a kind and genial *Chau* will gather about himself a large following of peasants upon whom he can exact *corvee* at any desired time, while an over-exacting and ill-tempered one will be left with only his slaves.

This feature can still be seen today and would appear to limit extreme forms of exploitation. An employer is expected to be obeyed, but an employer who is not concerned with the welfare and happiness of the workers will probably experience rapid turnover.

An employee in a Western organization is often expected to have a primary loyalty to an impersonal organization, while in the Theravada Buddhist countries of Southeast Asia loyalty is more commonly personal in nature and loyalty to abstract concepts is less common. Holmes *et al.* (1996: 34) wrote that in Thailand, "The senior is expected to provide direction, control, protection as well as emotional support, looking after the needs of his colleagues and staff, much like a prosperous father might do. This support is strongly *personal* in nature." In return, the subordinate is expected to be loyal to the senior. This is very evident in the political parties found in the region. Political parties in Thailand and Cambodia are not heavy on ideologies and platforms, instead they rely on the popularity of individual politicians to attract votes. It is not uncommon to see politicians in Thailand changing political parties without a significant change in the loyalty of their constituencies; the voters are loyal to the politician, not to an abstract concept of a political party and its ideology.

The preference for personal and paternalistic leadership is also found in the formal structure of organized religious life in the region. Schober (1989: 234) found the position of the abbot of a temple in Myanmar/Burma

> is comparable to that of the head of a household in the lay domain. He presides over the monastic compound and its residents in the same authoritarian manner. All decisions affecting the monastery are ultimately his prerogative. Hence, an abbot is a teacher and spiritual superior, who also enforces discipline. He assigns numerous tasks, like sweeping and cleaning the compound, schedules the daily routine of study, meditation and/or leisure. He decided which monks may reside in the monastery, who may attend rituals sponsored by lay donors and gives permission for resident monks to go on journeys. His decisions cannot be questioned by any of his juniors. In return for obedience, he must show his disciples kindness, compassion and concern for their spiritual and physical welfare.

While paternalistic leadership and preference of personal loyalty over loyalty to intangible entities is not necessarily totally unique to this region, these features do appear to be quite compatible with the teachings and practices of Theravada Buddhism.

Flexibility

It is tempting to come to the simplistic conclusion that business practices developed in more developed countries are superior to those found in developing countries such as the Theravada Buddhist countries of Southeast Asia. However, recent rapid growth in Asia, as well as the phenomenal success of many small IT firms in the United States and other Western countries in the 1980s and 1990s, has demonstrated the viability of organizations with primarily non-bureaucratic features. Large bureaucratic corporations are able to gather and leverage the use of resources to a great extent giving them in many ways a competitive advantage over smaller organizations. However, the impersonal and decentralized nature of large corporations also creates an incredible amount of inertia that often results in change happening at a slow pace. For example, looking at the big three auto-makers in the United States, a consensus on the need for and types of reforms had been reached years ago; however, actually changing the culture and direction of these corporate giants has proven illusive.

Dewett *et al.* (2007: 15) believed low levels of formalization (e.g., lack of formal job descriptions and few rules and regulations) created a fuzzier environment, which often facilitates the implementation of change. Naisbitt (1997) felt the overall flexibility that came from the informal and personal nature of businesses in Asia would give Asian companies competitive advantages in the twenty-first century over companies originating from Western environments, which have more bureaucratic features and need to follow strict government regulation. Western companies have limitations placed on their ability to respond rapidly to change due to factors such as government-mandated hiring and pay practices. Firms in Asia often have more structural flexibility due to the lack of separation between ownership and management; but actually the flexibility of most organizations depends on the flexibility of the organization's leadership.

Firms in the Theravada Buddhist areas of Southeast Asia share many business practices with firms from more developed areas of Asia, which are distinctly different from the most common business practices in Western countries. It would create a false impression to automatically assume business practices used by firms in the region are inferior to business practices found in other locations. After all, most of the firms in the region have to respond to market forces. Therefore, if Western business practices consistently worked better than indigenous ones, the market would drive out all local variations. While there is considerable global convergence in some areas of business practice, in other areas there remain distinct local differences.

11 Politics and democracy

Theravada Buddhism and democracy

It has often been astutely stated that democracy is interpreted as having different meanings by different people in different contexts. However, the term democracy is seen as a label of legitimacy and good governance and often the most undemocratic countries add the phrase "democracy" to their nation's official title. Generally, in the West, non-democracies are considered a threat to world peace and need to be dealt with (Buger and Villumsen 2007). For example, US foreign policy seems to be far more concerned with North Korea, Iran, and Cuba than with Switzerland, New Zealand, and Canada. In the modern world, "democracy" is normally associated with having a good government and is something every country should strive for.

However, democracy has had a very difficult time taking firm root in the Theravada Buddhist nations of Southeast Asia. Kamrava (1999: 87) stated, "Developing a democratic culture takes time; it is a matter of cultural change, and not every change does a democratic culture make." While the region has seen dramatic changes in political and economic systems over the past hundred years, those changes have not necessarily led toward democratically elected governments. Does having a culture strongly influenced by Theravada Buddhism deter moves toward democracy? Jackson (2003: 245) made the claim, "doctrinal Buddhism provides a weak basis for democratic principles." This statement could lay the foundation for a hypothesis why multi-party democracy with free and fair elections is not the form of government that has evolved in these four countries.

While democracy is generally promoted as the best system of government yet created by mankind, democracy does not automatically result in good governance. Johannen and Gomez (2001) prophesized that in Southeast Asia, "There is a danger in the region that the democratic process will be blamed for bringing corrupt leaders into office. This underlines the fact that a trend toward democracy is by no means irreversible." This has come true to a considerable extent in Thailand. Despite overwhelming popular support in elections and presiding over a government that oversaw rising economic growth, Thaksin Shinawatra was removed from office, with the justification his government was corrupt, by a military coup and subsequent elected governments and prime ministers have been forced out of office by non-elected forces that have openly promoted abolishing governments selected by the one-vote-one-person method (Phongpaichit and Baker 2008; Ungpakorn 2007). While referring to the situation in Indonesia, Darusman's comments (2001: 47) would equally apply in Thailand, "If we are to have democracy, we have to accept that we may be defeated politically in the political process by the majority; that we may have to pay taxes for the benefit of others."

However, acceptance of defeat at the ballot box has not become a universal value in the region. As of this writing, the transfer of power through an electoral process is the exception rather than the rule in the region as politicians in Cambodia, Myanmar/Burma, and Thailand who have lost at the polls have all refused to accept the results, while in Laos PDR there are no openly contested elections to select national leaders.

Most consider a well-informed population and a free press to be integral parts of the foundation that is required for an efficient democracy to grow; however, throughout Southeast Asia, collusion between reporters and leaders of both public and private institutions is fairly common, limiting the quality of information available to voters on which to make decisions (Mangahas 2001). Although in the past Thailand was considered the most politically advanced of the nations in the region, bribery and the threat of going to jail for insulting the royal family, which is often used to stifle debate, are common, and thus limits the effectiveness of the media in playing its informational role in a democracy (Vatikiotis 2001). Both Laos PDR and Myanmar/Burma have some of the world's most restrictive rules under which the media has to operate, while in Cambodia at the present, it would appear the press for the most part is allowed to openly criticize the existing government to a limited extent; however, this is a fairly recent development and is in no way an entrenched aspect of Khmer society.

While it is hard to argue with the notion that culture has an influence on the political system found in a country, it is probably a good idea to refrain from attributing in whole the lack of democratic institutions in the region to a cultural context heavily influenced by Theravada Buddhism. Kamrava (1999: 23) explained:

> The precise connection between culture and politics is even more complicated. Culture helps articulate personal and societal identity – itself a task of tremendous complexity – but it alone does not articulate politics. In fact, it is at best only one of the elements that go into constructing politics. Political leaders, themselves coming from specific cultural backgrounds, operate within and seek to further particular sets of values and cultural agendas. But to maintain that the larger framework within which they operate is informed overwhelmingly (or even largely) by culture is to overlook other potentially important forces such as economics, domestic and international politics, personal ambitions, and other similar dynamics with little or no cultural content.

Nevertheless, democracy, or at least democracy as defined in individualist countries in the West, has not taken root in any of the Theravada Buddhist countries
of Southeast Asia. It could be argued that much of the ideology of Theravada
Buddhism conflicts with values associated with democracies. In a democracy,
the ideal is of equality and of one-person-one-vote. However, belief in *kamma* is
non-egalitarian in nature and therefore it appears there is often general acceptance of the legitimacy of a non-elected ruler as it is assumed the individual could
not reach that position without having earned a significant amount of *kamma* in
previous lives. Moreover, elections are competitive and confrontational in
nature, which is often at odds with the middle path values of compromise and
avoidance of confrontation found in the teachings of Theravada Buddhism.

It should be kept in mind that it is not only the Theravada Buddhist countries
in Asia that have not adopted democracy as it is known in the West. It has often
been argued that the "Asian values" of cooperation and collectivism are incom-
patible with Western-style democracies that rely on competitive and confrontational elections; also, it has been argued the economic success of many Asian
economies is proof that an alternative and non-democratic method of government can be a successful form of government in Asia (Kraft 2001; Thompson
2001). While debate continues on, there does appear to be a relationship between
democracy and economic growth in Asia, as all of the larger more developed
countries in Asia (Japan, South Korea, and Taiwan) hold competitive elections
and therefore the concept of a modern developed economy in Asia led by non-
elected leaders is still only theoretical.

A common feature found in non-democratic societies is a feeling of political
apathy where many people go about their daily business the best they can while
avoiding and ignoring the government as best they can (Kamrava 1999: 78).
This behavior of avoiding and ignoring the government has also been noticed by
the author while living in Vietnam. In developed democracies, one is considered
a citizen and is allowed and expected to be a participant in the process of policy
formulation. On the other hand, people living in monarchies or in other non-
democratic systems often feel more like subjects who are to follow their leaders'
direction, or not, depending on the power of the leaders to enforce their wishes
and the alignment of the leaders' wishes with that of the subjects. But subjects
do not feel they have much of an opportunity or obligation to be involved in
political policy formulation.

It would appear most residents of the Theravada Buddhist countries of Southeast Asia take more of a subject as opposed to a citizen approach to political
identification. For example, one would expect the replacing of a democratically
elected government with a military dictatorship to be a major event that would
affect everyone in a country. However, on the evening of September 19, 2007,
the day the latest coup in Thailand occurred, the author had dinner with his
family at a restaurant in suburban Bangkok and everyone observed appeared to
be going about their normal lives and there was little to no talk of politics in the
air. Unless one had watched television, listened to the radio or read the news on
the Internet, one would not have guessed from the behavior of the majority of

the population of the city that there had been not only a change in political leadership of the country but also a complete change in system of government from being a democracy to a dictatorship. It appeared most people kept their political thoughts to themselves and went on with their normal lives with the assumption that not much would actually change.

Politics in Cambodia

Whether or not Cambodia has a functioning democracy is highly debatable, with supporters of the government most likely to believe so while supporters of opposition parties more likely to point out the undemocratic elements found in the Cambodian political scene. However, despite all the complaints and bad press in the West for the existing government, it does appear Hun Sen's Cambodian People's Party (CPP) is the choice of a significant number of Cambodian citizens. While there are plenty of reasons to be dissatisfied with the openness of the political process in the country, considering the complete lack of a tradition of democratic values, having a less than "perfect" democratic system is not all that surprising. The Khmer people have been ruled by absolute monarchies, a foreign colonial power, one of the most brutal authoritarian regimes in history, the Khmer Rouge, and a government imposed upon the country by the communist government of Vietnam. Using the country's past as a benchmark, one has reason for optimism from looking at the ongoing trends as well as dissatisfaction with the current situation.

The nation-state of Cambodia is the descendent of the Khmer Empire, which had a traditional political organization that included absolute monarchies and slavery. After the fall of the Khmer Empire, various monarchs continued to lay claim to various parts of modern-day Cambodia; however, how tightly these monarchs controlled the land varied from time to time and place to place. Nevertheless, while the rule of various monarchs was often challenged, the idea of rule by monarchy was never seriously challenged. The monarchy was kept in place during the era of French colonial rule and, for the most part, the ideals of the French Revolution were not among the exports from the homeland that were ordered by the colonial government centered in Phnom Penh.

Following the achievement of independence, the country's politics were dominated by one man, the sometimes monarch, sometimes abdicated monarch, Sihanouk. Sihanouk's system was described as "Buddhist socialism," which was hierarchical in nature and did not allow for dissent (Chandler 2000: 199). There were democratic features in the early post-independent governments, but it would be a real stretch to refer to Cambodia as a democracy at that time. Chandler (2000: 197) described this period:

> The two most consistent aspects of Sihanouk's domestic policy were his intolerance of dissent and his tendency to identify his opponents with foreign powers. To be a Cambodian, in his view, meant being pro-Sihanouk, just as Sihanouk himself, the father of the Cambodian family was pro-

Cambodian. There was no real tradition of pluralist politics in the country, and throughout the Sihanouk era, dissent was viewed as a mixture of treason and *lese majeste.*

For the most part, Cambodian affairs rarely make the news headlines in North America or Europe these days. However, the period of the rule by the Khmer Rouge has been largely explored and analyzed by the outside world. Why the socialist movement in Cambodia turned into an economic disaster and with so much bloodshed is a hotly debated topic. Writers, especially those associated with the anti-Vietnamese war movement, such as Noam Chomsky, place the blame squarely on the US policy of bombing the countryside to slow the advance of the Khmer Rouge troops. Others see a more complex situation that included jealously of the rural leaders of the Khmer Rouge of the urban population, and the extreme belief in socialism in a simplistic form. Raszelenberg (1999) attributed much of the violence to the Khmer Rouge's attitudes and policies toward Vietnam. Whatever the contributing causes, rule by the Khmer Rouge was not democratic in nature and the Khmer Rouge government abolished ownership of private property, guaranteed no human rights, outlawed organized religion, and attempted to forcefully move all agricultural production into collectivist systems despite naming itself Democratic Kampuchea (Chandler 2000: 214).

The worst fears of the Khmer Rouge came true in 1979 and the Vietnamese Army invaded and quickly overran the country, ending the genocidal rule of the Khmer Rouge. While a Vietnamese-dominated government slowly improved the lives of most normal Khmers, it did not lead to rapid economic progress, nor could it be seen as a real step toward democratic rule. The Vietnamese found what the French had found previously, attempting to run the Cambodian government had much higher financial costs than returns. After the fall of the Soviet Union and the withdrawal of all financial aid to Vietnam, the Vietnamese Government decided it could no longer afford to support an occupying army in Cambodia and withdrew (Chandler 2000: 235), leaving the UN to sort out the country's political future.

The UN Mission (UNTAC) to Cambodia has often been criticized as being a huge waste of money in which the unstated main mission was in fact to ensure large salaries for a large number of individuals associated with the UN mission rather than help Cambodia's transition to a functioning democracy. In the end, elections were held and, in a bizarre turn of events, the government was to be co-ruled by the winning political party, FUNCINPEC (a French acronym), led by Prince Ranariddh, and the existing government, which controlled the military and had collected the second most votes and ran under the banner of the Cambodian People's Party (CPP) (Jeldres 1993). Around 90 percent of the Cambodian population voted in these UN-sponsored elections in 1993 (Jeldres 1993), but in the end the UN did not ensure the will of the people was reflected in the new government; instead, a decision was made to allow both major political forces to rule jointly while the UN withdrew from the country and allowed the opposing sides to fight it out among themselves. Not surprisingly, the CPP, which controlled the military, was able to become the dominant political force after the UN pullout as opposed to the party that had gathered the most votes in the UN-sponsored elections.

Hun Sen and the CPP have continued to rule the country. In the election of 2003, the CPP captured nearly 50 percent of the popular vote and over 50 percent of the seats in parliament. The two main opposition parties, FUNCIN-PEC and the Sam Rainsy Party (SRP), named after its founder and leader, each won less than half the popular vote and parliamentary representation that the CPP did. The CPP relies heavily on the rural vote and relies on a patronage system where personal loyalties and rewards for loyalty are commonplace. FUNCINPEC traditionally has been the party of the urban elites while being popular in some rural areas, and the SRP has long relied on its status as the main opposition to the government and on the charisma of the leader it is named after (McCargo 2005).

The elections of 2007 were not marked by the scale of violence seen in the run-up to previous elections; however, concerns remained about the CCP's control of the media, the police, and the military. Also, the CPP has developed "vast political networks extending deep and wide into communes and villages" (Um 2008: 107), which resulted in little doubt about the outcome of the election. One of the factors leading to a more stable political environment has been the loss of popularity of FUNCINPEC while the SRP has moved into the position of second most popular party in the country and has mostly shed its founding values and now is quite willing to work as part of a coalition government headed by Hun Sen and the CPP (Sokheng 2008; Um 2008: 109). Hun Sen appears to have every intention of holding on to power and using the power of the state to crush all political opposition while retaining the appearance of Cambodia being a democracy (Sokheng 2008).

One of the key features of functioning democracies, the protection of human rights, is glaringly absent in Cambodia. Assassinations and intimidations of rights workers as well as the banning and expelling of international human rights organizations have been known to happen (Um 2008: 115). However, many Cambodians appreciate the stability and progress the country has enjoyed during the reign of Hun Sen and the CPP. Political power in Cambodia seems to take on an "all or nothing" quality.

> Cambodian history since World War II, and probably for a much longer period, can be characterized in part as a chronic failure of contending groups of patrons and their clients to compromise, cooperate, or share power. These hegemonic tendencies, familiar in other Southeast Asian countries, have deep roots in Cambodia's past.
>
> (Chandler 2000: 245)

In the decades following the Cambodian civil war and the subsequent Khmer Rouge era, peace, stability, and the end of extreme poverty and starvation have been the primary political concerns of the Cambodian people; concerns over democracy and political freedoms were mostly limited to the small group of educated urban elites. However, times may be changing. Economic expectations of average Cambodians may be increasing faster than the current government can deliver (Rehbein 2007b).

Politics play an important role in the life of most urban Cambodians. In fact, government connections are important while doing business and are also a source of social status. The Cambodian government, despite the relatively small population, has the largest cabinet in the world, which in 2003 consisted of 15 senior ministers, 28 ministers, over 100 secretaries of state, and another 100 plus under-secretaries of state. Add to this an extensive parliament and the bestowing of the official title, *Oknha*, which is highly sought after by business practitioners and connects wealthy individuals with state controlled privileges, and the huge number of government "advisors," and the percentage of the population connected to the state is huge, although real power remains in the hands of only a few (Ear 2009).

Although the current government did not initially come to power through a democratic process, it does appear to currently have more popular support than any of the opposition parties. The authoritarian nature of the government is not questioned, but is it possible that Cambodia is moving toward becoming a democracy controlled by a single party for decades, such as has been the case in Singapore and Japan? Or is it more accurate to label Hun Sen and the CPP's rule as a dictatorship? It is difficult to imagine Hum Sen and his political cronies peacefully transferring power in the aftermath of an election defeat, a reality most Cambodians most likely realize, and therefore it is likely many Cambodians want stability above all else and are willing to live with being ruled by a corrupt and authoritarian government rather than a return to the divisions and chaos that tore the country apart in its recent past.

Politics in Laos PDR

There was no division in 2007 from the policy directions set down by the Eighth Congress of the ruling Lao People's Revolutionary Party (LPRP) in March 2006. The Lao People's Democratic Republic will remain a one-party state with old-style, Soviet-era political institutions, while encouraging free enterprise and foreign investment.

(Linter 2008: 171)

Laos does not have a tradition of democratic rule nor is there any intense internal or international pressure to move the country toward becoming more democratic. Instead, it appears the Communist Party is evolving and becoming more market-orientated to solidify and extend its rule over the country. Prakoonheang (2001: 5) claimed that the traditions found in the country, where the majority of the people are living in villages, practicing subsistence farming, and being isolated from the political centers, goes back to the Nan Chao period, and as this tradition continues for much of the population of today, there has been little popular participation in government and the political apathy of the people allows for authoritarian, but loose, rule. Also, as it has been estimated that up to 90 percent of the educated class left the country after the communist takeover (Stuart-Fox 2002), it is unlikely a large disgruntled middle class will emerge any time soon; which is often thought of as a prerequisite for moving toward democratic rule.

Authoritarian rule has a long history in the lands in and around present-day Laos. As mentioned in Chapter 4, consolidated Laotian rule in the area can be traced back to the Lan Xang Kingdom, which was apparently splintered from the Khmer Empire around 1352. From that time up until the colonizing of the country by the French in the nineteenth century, Laos was ruled, or at least aligned with, various monarchs (Jumsai 2000; Phothisane 2002). French rule over the country did not lead toward the implementation of democratic institutions; instead, the country's affairs were primarily administered to by Vietnamese civil servants under orders from a handful of French officials (Evans 2002).

After the end of French rule, the political arena continued to be dominated by members of the royal family, with factions being led by Prince Souvanna Phouma and his brother Souphanouvong (Evans 2002: 105–6). Before and after being caught up in the cold war struggles, Laos was unable to develop a functioning democracy and the methods used in the transfer of power were decidedly undemocratic. In August 1958, Souvanna Phouma was forced out of power due to the US suspending financial aid, which brought Phoui Sananikhone to the position of prime minister. In August 1960, a coup led by Captain Kong Le brought down the existing government, which was quickly followed by a neutralist government made up of members aligned with the United States, North Vietnam, and "neutral politicians" (Evans 2002: 111–21). Attempts at creating a democracy were not embraced by the general population; in fact, "The ideals of liberal democratic politics were best understood in the cities, and least understood in the countryside, where the response to excessive authoritarianism was the old one of moving away rather than standing up and demanding one's rights" (Evans 2002: 129). This led to an urban dominated political arena.

Soon Laos found itself directly involved in the Indochina war with the United States and its allies on one side and communist forces on the other. This eventually led to a takeover of the country by communist forces, an end to attempts at democracy, an abdication of the monarch, and a political environment dominated by individuals with roots in the countryside as opposed to the elites from the cities (Evans 2002). Of this period, Kurlantzick (2005: 115) wrote:

> But Laos was no idyll. No opposition to the new Lao government was allowed. Religious freedom was severely limited. Foreign Media were essentially banned, and the local press consisted of a thin gruel of state propaganda delivered by bored-sounding announcers. The few Westerners who visited Vientiane in the early 1980s remember it as one of the sleepiest capitals in the world, a place where water buffaloes still grazed a few hundred yards from the "downtown." Living standards continued to fall,

though top communist leaders, who lived in extravagant villas such as the enormous, bright yellow presidential palace, prospered – in part because of corruption.

In a similar manner to what was seen in Vietnam and Cambodia with the incoming of communist regimes, the officials and supporters of the previous government did not fare well. It has been estimated between 10,000 to 40,000 people were sent to "reeducation camps" and many of these ended up having very lengthy terms in the camps and some individuals who went into the camps were never seen again (Evans 2002: 180–1).

The new leaders of the country attempted to use a Soviet-styled economic model in the country, but because of the lack of success of the programs, the increasing fleeing of farmers to Thailand, and the drying up of aid due to the collapse of the Soviet block, the country's leadership soon realized there was a need for a new direction. Imitating the path China took, the country adopted what was called the New Economic Mechanism (NEM) in 1986 which was a step toward reverting back to a capitalist economy while the Communist Party continued to monopolize political power (Evans 2002: 97; Prakoonheang 2001). Kurlantzick (2005: 116) analyzed the changes and found:

> The changes in Laos in the late 1980s and 1990s were more cosmetic – and subject to greater resistance by the leadership – than in China and Vietnam. The Lao government, still run by pre-1975 hard-liners, refused to liberalize many sectors of the economy, forcing businesspeople to wade through tangles of red tape to start companies. Western diplomats and business-people complained about a lack of consistent policy direction from the government. Most bureaucrats were divorced from policy making at the top. The government also continued to subsidize money-losing state projects, which often wound up enriching top leaders.

Economic liberalization in the country has not resulted in political liberalization. "The launch of NEM in 1986 marked the abandonment of the centrally planned economy. It was the change of socio-economic development model but not the regime" (Prakoonheang 2001: 147). Laos PDR appears to be following the lead of both Vietnam and China in mixing private ownership with authoritarian rule by a "communist" party. Laos has relied very heavily on political and financial support from Vietnam and, in 1977, signed a 20-year Treaty of Friendship and Cooperation with Vietnam (Evans 2002: 188). This was a continuation of the relationship between the communist parties of the two countries and Prakoon-heang (2001: 108) wrote, "The Pathet Lao [Lao communist movement] was always under the direction of the Vietnamese dominated Lao Regional Committee of the ICP [Indochinese Communist Party]." Evans (2002: 189) found that a case could be made that Laos swapped being part of the French colonial system to being more or less a colony of the Soviet Union and Vietnam. Many Lao nationalists, including Dr. Khamsengkeo Senesathit, have had reservations about the Vietnamese dominance of the communist movement in Laos (Prakoonheang 2001: 63), and in a striking similarity to the French colonial system, the administration and leadership of the communist movement in Laos was dominated by Vietnamese and Laotians with strong connections to Vietnam. Although, in recent times, Chinese business practitioners are becoming increasingly numerous in the country (Linter 2008: 176), and although publically the Laotian government maintains its loyalty to Vietnam, it is entirely possible that a shift in alliance toward China is evolving.

"The leadership of the 1950s continued as the leadership of the 1990s" (Prakoonheang 2001: 119). Laos PDR was led and dominated by Kaysone Phomvihan, from inception until his death in 1992 (Prakoonheang 2001: 151). There were attempts to create a cult of personality, in much the way Ho Chi Minh has been depicted in Vietnam, but the attempts can be considered a failure (Evans 2002: 208–9); which may demonstrate that the people of Laos have accepted the reality of communist rule of their country, but do not find any real reason to celebrate it.

One of the factors that may have contributed to retarding the development of democratic institutions and values is the isolation of the country. The country more or less sealed itself off from the rest of the world after the communist takeover of the country and foreign tourists and capital only began to come into the country in any significant amount in 1994 (Rehbein 2007b). Prakoonheang (2001: 191) stated, "For more than half a century after the end of World War II Laos was not a member of any particular regional or world trading organization." Gunn (2008: 68) cautioned against taking the view that increasing integration with the outside world would result in weakening of state control, as the dynamics involved in this type of situation are poorly understood. Rehbein (2007b: 76) found that in the urban population of Laos, increased contact with the outside world was having an effect on expectations, which may over time increase pressure on the government to consider further reforms. Linter (2008: 172) proposed:

> With the urban population becoming wealthier, new social trends can also be discerned, which do not necessarily conform with the authoritarian ideals of the LPRP [Lao People's Revolutionary Party]. Laos has no political opposition as such, but in the capital Vientiane and other urban centres, a new middle class is emerging, which sooner or later may be asking for participation or a higher degree of political pluralism than is the case today.

With the collapse of aid from the Soviet block and the inability to create a dynamic economy, the country now relies heavily on foreign aid and one of the government's main concerns is the influence of foreign NGOs and programs aimed at empowering various communities; also, due to the similarity in languages, the Thai media is having a powerful effect on the expectations and values of many of the people of Laos (Linter 2008). The effects of the work of the NGOs may be most felt in the villages, as the government has for the most part ignored the rural areas and has never allocated any specific budget for village-level development (Prakoonheang 2001), therefore opening up opportunities for Western NGOs, which often have fairly egalitarian values.

There have been some formal changes, most likely brought upon due to pressure from international donors. Although strictly controlled by the communist party, national elections began in 1989, but candidates who opposed the regime were not allowed to take part (Evans 2002: 199). In 1991, a constitution where monopolization of power by the party was a centerpiece was approved (Evans 2002: 201). However, within the party, the day-to-day decision making and real power have traditionally been held by the politburo and party president (Prakoonheang 2001: 13). At the time, many were skeptical that the reforms of the 1990s would lead toward a more open and democratic society (Prakoonheang 2001: 159) and results seem to have proven the skeptics right.

Choummaly Sayasone, aged 70, has recently replaced the even older Khamtay Siphandone as president, while Bouasone Bouphavanh, a member of the younger generation, has replaced Bounnyang Vorachit, born in 1937, as prime minister (Gunn 2008; Linter 2008). There have been considerable moves in recent years to include ethnic minorities into higher levels of the government and there continues to be a close connection between the military and the civilian government (Linter 2008).

There are four levels to the current government: national, provincial, district, and village, with the village level being mostly unchanged since the colonial era and mostly neglected by the national government (Prakoonheang 2001: 221–2). Therefore, the national government is almost entirely urban in nature and focus while "85 percent of Laotians still survive by subsistence agriculture and know little of national politics" (Kurlantzick 2005: 117).

Communism as an economic and political ideology has lost what little appeal it ever had for the majority of the Laotian population, resulting in the government attempting to change its image and beginning to attempt to identify itself as a promoter and defender of Buddhism (Evans 2002: 203). Nevertheless, the communist party of Laos appears to have no intention of relinquishing its power and has passed laws, possibly punishable by capital punishment, against attempts to promote democracy or the changing of form of government within the country (Prakoonheang 2001: 217).

While on the surface Laos PDR has a stable political system, there is considerable dissatisfaction with the government's performance (Rehbein 2007b: 81); however, it does not appear a change to a democratic form of government is just around the corner in Laos, instead, "It would seem that Laos is condemned to the long march through authoritarian rule of the kind some politicians and thinkers believe is necessary, if not inevitable, for developing countries" (Evans 2002: 223).

Politics in Thailand

To the casual observer, Thai politics in recent times have been a mixture of fascinating characters, unexpected twists and turns, and unexplainable legal rulings.

Recent years have seen the prime minister being forced out of office for hosting a cooking show, a bloodless military coup occurring, the country's courts system constantly making legal rulings against the country's most popular political movement, and a host of shifting coalitions attempting to gain power, while all the time the figure of Thaksin Shinawatra, the controversial ex-prime minister whose party won two straight national elections by landslides, has been looming in the background. Currently the Democratic Party is leading a shaky coalition, although the Democratic Party has received far fewer votes than the various "Thaksin" parties have in all recent elections. However, the Democratic Party is the preferred party of the Bangkok elites, while Thaksin's Thai Rak Thai Party and its descendants have been the preferred parties for the majority of the people living in the highly populated north and northeast parts of the country. It is likely that there will have been some new twists and turns in this fascinating story by the time this is being read.

Thailand is a kingdom and the monarchy has remained at the heart of the Thai identity despite the ending of absolute rule of the monarchy in 1932. Although Thailand formally became a democracy in 1932, it has been more a democracy in name than function since then. The country has been through a staggering number of military coups and for most of that time there has been no independent electoral commission or press freedom and vote buying during elections has been common (Chirakiti 2001). Although officially the monarch, the beloved King Bhumibol Adulyadej who has reigned for over 60 years, is above politics, there is speculation by some he may have had a hand at times in shaping the direction Thai politics has gone (Economist 2008a; Economist 2008b).

Following the end of World War II, Thailand became a staunch ally of the United States and lent substantial support to the US war effort in Vietnam. However, with the withdrawal of the US military forces from Southeast Asia in the 1970s, Thai politics became polarized between conservatives and left-leaning sectors and there were serious worries about the domino effect taking place, with Thailand being the next country to be incorporated into the communist sphere of influence, resulting in a bloody coup by the military that replaced the democratically elected government in 1972 (Aribarg 2005: 6; Chanthanom 1998: 252; Ungpakorn 2007: 71). In the 1980s, as the country become one of the growing Asian economic tigers, the influence of big business on politics increased, but always within a coalition with a significant number of the military forces (Aribarg 2005: 8). In 1991, the Thai tradition of changing governments through military coup as opposed to the ballot box continued, with the overthrow of a government headed by Chaticahi Choonhaven by military forces. After General Suchinda reneged on his promise not to seek political power, demonstrations broke out in Bangkok; the government responded by violently cracking down on the demonstrators resulting in the deaths of a considerable number of people (Wyatt 2003: 304–5). After being publically chastised by the king, Suchinda resigned and made way for a democratically elected government. For the next decade and a half it appeared that Thailand was on its way to becoming a democracy.

The most recent chapter of the drama that is Thai politics began in the aftermath of the 1997 economic crisis. Thaksin Shinawatra, a wealthy businessman who used his political connections to secure a monopoly in the booming mobile phone telecommunications networks industry, started a political party called Thai Rak Thai (Thais Love Thailand or TRT). The TRT came to power with a sweeping mandate from the electorate in 2001. At first, the TRT was very much a pro-business party and had its base of support in Bangkok and among the business community; however, as the majority of people in Thailand live in the countryside and the key to electoral victory lies in the rural areas, the party began transforming into a populist party, focusing on winning the loyalty of the rural poor (Phongpaichit and Baker 2008: 18–19). The TRT used a dual track method of being a capitalist pro-business party as evidenced by its endorsement of the acceptance of a number of free trade agreements while simultaneously using more socialistic policies of using government funds to stimulate the economies at the village level (Ungpakorn 2007: 16). Soon Thaksin became an extremely divisive figure and he lost substantial support from Thailand's growing urban middle class and other entrenched interests. However, as Thaksin consolidated his support with the rural segments of society, the TRT's margin of victory increased in the next election. Thaksin became the first Thai prime minister to be reelected in a general election.

Thaksin's detractors mainly pointed to his abuse of public position for personal gain as the reason for wanting to remove him from office. "The *Thai Rak Thai* government was corrupt, but this was little different from previous elected governments and little different from every single military government" (Ungpakorn 2007: 18). Phongpaichit and Baker (2008) believed the TRT's policy of bringing the rural poor into the political process had as much or more to do with the extreme opposition to TRT rule than did Thaksin's questionable business practices. McCargo (2008: 334) pointed out that Thaksin's supporters are not all rural and poor; he had also attracted "elements of the middle classes and business community who applauded his criticisms of the bureaucracy and the country's traditional institutions." Nelson (2007) reported that in the election of February 6, 2005, Thaksin's Thai Rak Thai Party received 61.2 percent of the party list vote, compared to only 23.2 percent received by the second-place Democrat Party, and the Thai Rak Thai won a majority of votes in both the rural and urban areas.

By 2006, the opponents of Thaksin were becoming more militant, and protests in Bangkok led by a group calling itself the People's Alliance for Democracy (PAD) were a continuous occurrence. Thaksin called a snap election to let the people decide whether he should stay or go. Opposition political parties refused to contest the election as all polls showed the TRT would win in a landslide. The PAD "protests seem to have been a highly personalized affair focused on Sondi Limthongkul's conflict with Thaksin Shinawatra, rather than a principled and broad based people's movement" (Nelson 2007: 8). Nelson (2007: 8) also reported, "It would be a mistake to assume that the 'people's sector' represents the 'people.' Rather, it comprises interest groups that deem themselves more democratically advanced than the supposedly passive and ignorant majority."

On September 19, 2006, the old pattern repeated itself and once again tanks were on the street of Bangkok and the military took control of the government to prevent the election from taking place. After the coup, the PAD did not organize any demonstrations but considered their mission complete (Nelson 2007: 33).

> At the very core of the protests was not a broad-based and country-wide "democracy movement," unified against an unquestionable evil and grossly abusive head of government. Rather, we encounter a very limited group of quasi-professional socio-political activists focused on an individual leader, Sondi Limthongkul, who tried to hold the political system hostage due largely to personal motives. Some sectors of the citizenry and their dissatisfaction with the prime minister, which should be nothing unusual in any democratic system, were used as tools in the endeavor to overthrow a government that had been convincingly elected not even a year earlier. At the same time, the citizen's political sovereignty was principally undermined by the strong inclination of the protest leaders towards using extra-democratic and extra-constitutional power ascribed to the supposedly constitutional monarch, and, when this failed, to the military.
>
> (Nelson 2007: 34)

The coup was bloodless and nominally led by General Sonti Boonyaratgalin, although few believe he was able to so easily and successfully remove the democratically elected government without support from many more influential people. The rule by the military-installed unelected government was benign in comparison to most other dictatorships seen around the world; however, it was also very ineffective. Economic growth was lower than during the years of Thaksin's rule, there were no noticeable advancements in ending the insurgency in the south of the country by Muslim militants, and the political divisions remained. The TRT was disbanded and most of its leadership was banned from politics by judges appointed by the military-installed government and new elections were called. The remains of the TRT regrouped under the banner of the People's Power Party (PPP) and selected controversial ex-Bangkok governor Samak Sundaravej as its leader (McCargo 2008: 356). It was an open secret that Thaksin was calling the shots for the PPP from behind the scenes.

Elections were held, the voters once again favored Thaksin, or his proxy, over his opponents and the PPP won a resounding victory. Soon, though, the country was back to square one and the PAD once again took to the streets, this time occupying the prime minister's offices, demanding Samak be removed from office. He was, not through the ballot box but by the courts in a bizarre ruling where his hosting of a cooking show was deemed a conflict of interest. Samak was replaced by Somchai Wongsawat, which did not appease the protestors, who were emboldened by their victory and took over the country's main airport causing a major crisis. Once again the courts stepped in and removed the leader of the country. To break the stalemate, a faction of Thaksin's supporters switched sides and gave the Democrat Party what it has long desired but could not earn through the ballot box, political control of the country. Wealthy and handsome Abhisit Vejjajiva was elevated to the position of prime minister and so far has refused to call for elections.

It is obvious that the court system in Thailand supports the anti-Thaksin political movement and, instead of removing elected governments through military coups, Thailand has moved to removing elected governments through a biased court system. The military coup was obviously illegal, and yet the courts have not tried or convicted anyone for their actions. Occupying government offices and stopping operations at the country's airports was obviously illegal, and yet the government is not making any moves to prosecute anyone for these actions. There has been a move by the anti-Thaksin movement to believe "complex political problems could not be solved through electoral politics or by elected officials, but were best left to knowledgeable and highly moral judges" (McCargo 2008: 335–6).

Thailand's current government has won its position through a military coup and through a biased legal system, not through the ballot box. Thailand, once the shining beacon of democracy of the region, is now being used by other non-elected leaders in neighboring countries as an example of the chaos that elections bring and an excuse to not make democratic reforms.

Although using the term "democracy" in its name, the PAD has advocated moves away from a one-person-one-vote system.

> The PAD argued that the rural mass was poor, uneducated, politically naïve, and thus easily bought by Thaksin and his political followers. They proposed a lower house with 70% appointed, then backed out to electoral constituencies based on occupation. Their analysis ignored the increased prosperity and sophistication of rural society over the past 20 years, and the way that Thaksin's popularity had diminished the need for vote-buying. But the analysis perfectly captured the urban middle class fear of their vulnerability as a minority, and gained widespread urban support, including among former democratic activists.
>
> (Phongpaichit and Baker 2008: 21)

Thailand's political system seems torn between the traditional hierarchical structure of society and more modern and egalitarian values. It is also split between urban and rural. Will the current government be able to bridge these huge gaps? Will change in government again be accomplished through elections? Or will the current trends of coming to power through non-democratic methods continue?

Recently, the sight of the yellow-shirted PAD protestors has been replaced by the red-shirted protestors from the United Front for Democracy against Dictatorship (UDD), which are normally thought of as a pro-Thaksin movement. Unlike during the yellow-shirted protests, the police used force to disrupt the UDD protests, which had turned violent in a few cases. The recent attack on the PAD leader, Sondi Limthongkul, in which he surprisingly survived, has led to rumors there is a faction of the army that supports Thaksin and the red-shirted protesters.

Eldridge (2008) wrote:

> The cultural values of Thailand offer an interesting avenue for understanding the Thai thought patterns underlying these recent political events. They also explain why Westerners might need to accept that they may never appreciate the Thai logic that has led to the current political mess.

Politics in Myanmar

Unlike in Thailand, political observation in Myanmar/Burma can not be described as entertaining. The military government of Myanmar/Burma is one of the most criticized governments in the world, and it is also a government that has proven as resilient as it is repressive. The country, like the rest of the region, had been dominated by authoritarian monarchies prior to the arrival of the European powers. Burma became part of the British colonial system and after independence "Burma's experiment with parliamentary democracy was short-lived" (Ismail 2001: 52). Since 1962, the country has been ruled by various juntas controlled by the nation's military. As the country is of little strategic or economic importance to the Western world, the plight of the country is mostly ignored internationally with the occasion tightening of economic sanctions imposed as a show of opposition to the country's military dictatorship. "The modern politic of Burma, within the last two and half decades, has been nothing but ongoing insurgencies, conflict between totalitarian government and the pro-democratic party, and economic turmoil" (Chanthanom 1998: 65).

Burma was granted its independence at 4:20 a.m., a time chosen by astrology advisors, on January 4, 1948. The leader of the newly independent country was U Nu. U Nu's political philosophy was a blend of socialism and Buddhism, and therefore market-based economics was not a cornerstone of the early years of Burma's independence. U Nu, unlike the majority of leader's with socialistic leanings, actually lived the simplistic life he advocated. Consensus would appear to indicate that U Nu was a well-intended, although naïve, man who tried his best to create a peaceful state built upon Theravada Buddhist values and politics that were neither aligned with the United States nor the Soviet Union during the cold war era. However, the cohesiveness of the government could not last and because of bickering factions within the government, U Nu asked the military, led by Ne Win, in 1958 to install a caretaker government. In 1960, new elections were held which U Nu won in a landslide. On March 2, 1962, democracy in Burma came to an end when the military seized power and began "The Burmese Way to Socialism," which has been such an economic and political disaster for the country (Chanthanom 1998: 241; Myint-U 2006: 257–91).

Thawnghmung (2008: 277) described military rule under Ne Win:

General Ne Win's twenty-six-year rule of the country from 1962 until 1988 transformed the economy with a promising future into perhaps one of the least developed countries in the world. Its self-imposed mismanagement, isolationist policies, and distrust of foreigners all deprived the country of necessary skills, technology, and revenues.

The first major threat to military rule came in 1988 when student-led demonstrations brought major pressure on the government; however, in the end the uprising failed, the military retained power, and the country continued its economic decline. The face of the democracy movement in Myanmar/Burma to the world is Aung San Suu Kyi, daughter of one of the heroes of Myanmar/Burma's drive for independence, Aung San. Aung San Suu Kyi has continuously advocated peaceful change as opposed to armed rebellion (Kaw 2005). In 1990, the Burmese military government allowed elections in an attempt to legitimize its rule; however, the people of Myanmar/Burma rejected military rule and the majority voted for members of the National League for Democracy (NLD) which was led by Dr. U Tin Oo and Aung San Suu Kyi; instead of accepting the will of the people, the military led government ignored the results and imprisoned the leaders of the party chosen by the electorate, and in 1997 the government changed its name to the State Peace and Development Council (SPDC) without significant change in policies (Chanthanom 1998: 66).

Ne Win's grip as leader of the country began faltering after the 1988 uprising, and although he resigned as head of the government, most observers believed he still was the power behind the scenes for a number of years after officially departing; however, even after his death in 2002, the iron grip of the military junta did not lessen to any considerable extent (Myint-U 2006: 339–40). The SPDC announced that elections would be held and there were elections in 1990 in which the NLD won the majority of votes. However, after winning the elections, the NLD took a very confrontational approach toward the military-led government and even hinted the then-current government leaders would be held accountable for their previous actions. In light of this attitude, it was not surprising the SPDC refused to transfer power until a constitution could be agreed upon, a process that continues to this day, approximately 20 years after the elections were held (Myoe 2007b).

The Myanmar National Convention, which was officially designed to move the country toward democracy, was convened in January 1993 and finally ended in 2006, but there are still no elections, at least those that would meet the minimum requirements to be labeled democratic, in sight and the principle of military dominance of the government has not been officially challenged (Taylor 2008).

In 2007, the world was watching as protestors once again took to the streets of Yangon/Rangoon, and when Buddhist monks joined the protests, there was real hope that a major turning point in the country's history was possible. At the time, the author was living in Mae Sot, a town on the Thai side of the Thai–Myanmar/Burma border with a significant population of people from Myanmar/Burma. There was a substantial amount of anticipation and optimism in the air.

The protests have been called the Saffron Revolution due to the color of the robes of the monks who partook in the protests, which lent the protests a high level of legitimacy among the primarily Buddhist population (Lorch 2008: 33).

The spark that set off the protests was the lowering of government subsidies for fuel, but quickly the protests took on a political flavor. The protests grew, and when the number of protesters reached in the neighborhood of 25,000, the government violently cracked down and eliminated the public outcries for regime change (Taylor 2008; Thawnghmung 2008). The sense of optimism in the supporters of a democratic Myanmar/Burma quickly dissolved into deep despair and disappointment.

The international community is mostly united in the desire for change within Myanmar/Burma but is split on how to encourage constructive change to take place. Western countries have mostly followed the path of economic sanctions and isolation of the country, as promoted by Win (2001); while China, India, and ASEAN have followed a path of engagement. So far, economic sanctions and isolation do not seem to have moved the country closer to democracy but have cost the people of the country "foreign aid, investment, revenues, jobs, and technical know-how" (Thawnghmung 2008: 278). The costly building of the new capital, Naypyitaw, in an isolated location, apparently for security purposes, is an indication that the government continues to place a priority onto holding onto power over economic growth and the welfare of the citizens of the country.

Since independence, the country's military has been involved in a number of armed conflicts against armed ethnic minority groups that are seeking independence/autonomy. Both the military of Myanmar/Burma and many of the armed resistance groups have been charged with using child soldiers in the fighting (Human Rights Watch 2007b). One of the justifications for continued military rule is the need for the military to have a free hand in order to maintain the country's territorial integrity (Hudson-Rodd and Hunt 2005). The longest lasting and most intense of these conflicts is with the Karen National Union (KNU). This conflict has its roots in the colonial era when Karen and other ethnic minorities made up a considerable portion of the British colonial military forces in the country, which led to mistrust between the majority population and the minority Karens after the country achieved independence (Roberts 2006). This conflict has resulted in approximately half a million people being displaced around the conflict zone (Brees 2008). However, the intensity of fighting has been lessening in recent years as the nation's army has taken control of all but the most remote areas of the country and most of the fight in the insurgents appears to be dying out (Taylor 2008: 252–3).

The international community continues to condemn the actions of the military junta in Myanmar/Burma while the military junta continues to promise to move the country toward democracy in its own way and in its own time. At this point it does not appear the country has made any significant moves toward becoming a member of the community of democratic states since the military takeover in 1962. However, Lorch (2008) feels the weakness of the state has allowed for the emergence of civil society, which may be just a stopgap measure or could be the foundation from which political change can grow.

The idea of continuous military rule from 1962 up to the present may be an oversimplification of reality. Thinking of the military of Myanmar/Burma as an organization filled with factions under the client-patron system, which is common throughout organizations in the Theravada Buddhist countries of Southeast Asia, may be a better reflection of reality than the concept of rule by a single dictator riding atop an organization that follows all orders in lockstep. Traditionally there has been a split and tensions between officers in the intelligence services and those in infantry (combat) positions (Min 2009: 1020). There have been a number of purges and struggles for power within the military structure itself. There were purges in the 1970s, including the ouster of General Tin Oo from the inner circle; a different General Tin Oo was removed from his position in 1983; in the 1990s more purges occurred which helped consolidate the position of Than Shwe; later while much of the world thought Khin Nyunt was the leading general of the junta, this in fact was not the case and he was arrested by the other generals in 2004 and sentenced to 44 years in prison; and thereafter Than Shwe's position as the successor to Ne Win has been firmly established (Min 2009). As the current crop of military leaders reach old age, there is speculation over the future leadership and political direction the military junta will take.

The face most associated with the democracy movement in Myanmar/Burma belongs to Daw Aung San Suu Kyi, also called "the lady" or Daw Suu by her followers. Aung San Suu Kyi won the 1991 Nobel Peace Prize and is the daughter of the almost universally respected national hero, Aung San. She is often thought of internationally and by her followers as being near perfect and treated almost like a semi-divine goddess, although it can not be said that Aung San Suu Kyi has actively promoted this image of herself. Aung San Suu Kyi's celebrity helps keep the issue of democracy in Myanmar/Burma alive in the Western media; however, she is not without her critics. She has been criticized as being too soft to be able to effectively deal with the political realities of life in Myanmar/Burma (Lychack 2008). There are other activists who have questioned the effectiveness of her continued insistence on non-violent political activities after the brutal government repression of both the 1998 and 2007 political protests (Hlaing 2007). Furthermore, as the regime has spent decades demonizing Aung San Suu Kyi, any compromise with her would result in a huge loss of face for the leaders of the military junta that is unlikely to happen as "face" is an extremely important part of life in the region (Persons 2008).

Despite nearly fifty years of non-democratic rule, there is little indication the proposed government-controlled elections in 2010 will bring the country significantly nearer to democracy in any way but in name.

> It seems unlikely under any future leadership to retreat from a position that runs so deep in its culture. Top generals also have extensive economic interests at stake. In addition, they see little reason to change course when on the one hand they believe themselves to be winning, and on the other they fear oblivion should they relinquish control.
>
> (Holliday 2009: 1052)

12 Trends and the future

Ethnic and religious minorities

Not all of the residents of these four countries are followers of Theravada Buddhism. While Theravada Buddhism is often thought of as a religion that tolerates diversity and its adherents can coexist peacefully alongside followers of other faiths, conflicts between the ethnic majority populations and ethnic minority populations continue to plague the region. This situation is illustrated by the Islamic insurgency in southern Thailand, as well as the long running civil war between the Theravada Buddhist-dominated government of Myanmar/Burma and the Christian-dominated Karen National Union (KNU).

Ethnic division and ethnic identity in Southeast Asia, as elsewhere, rarely remain unchanged throughout time, and boundaries separating one group of people from another are not always absolute. Therefore, it is acknowledged that commonly used classifications of ethnic groups have limitations.

All of these four countries have traditions of ethnic diversity. The first ethnic group in the region in which its members became followers of Theravada Buddhism was the Mon, and from this ethnic group Theravada Buddhism spread to the Tai, Burmans, and Khmer. Today there are approximately 3 million ethnic Mons living in Thailand and Myanmar/Burma who are in danger of having their culture lost through assimilation (Weng 2008). While in Thailand and Cambodia the dominant ethnic group represents an overwhelming majority, this is not the case in Laos PDR where only approximately 40 to 50 percent of the population belong to the Lao ethnic classification, most others are classified as members of "hill-tribes" (Evans 2002: 134), which is a generic classification used to lump together various diverse minority ethnic groups, who usually live in higher elevations throughout the region and use different agricultural practices than those living in the lowlands.

Myanmar/Burma is also much less ethnically homogeneous than Cambodia and Thailand. One of the largest ethnic minority groups in the region is referred to as the Karen. Although it is difficult to estimate the actual population of Karen people, Petry (1993: 14) estimated the number as 5 million with, at that time, approximately 90 percent living in Myanmar/Burma and most of the rest living in Thailand. The term Karen is a modern construction in which a number of loosely affiliated groups of people were lumped together by foreigners, and this classification has assisted in the creation of a Karen identity (South 2007). Rajah (2008: 13) found the Karens living in northern Thailand saw themselves as having a separate cultural identity from the Thai-speaking residents of the area; they did not think of themselves as Thai whether or not they held Thai citizenship.

Adoniram Judson, an American Baptist missionary, is the individual most credited with bringing Christianity to the Karen people. After spending an unsuccessful decade attempting to convert the Burmese to Christianity, Adoniram Judson turned his efforts toward the Karen people. Most of those who converted to Christianity were members of the Sgaw Karen community and this Christian segment of society, with their access to writing and financial support from Western Christian organizations, have come to dominate the leadership of the Karen people (Petry 1993). After independence, some segments, primarily Christians, of the Karen community have been engaged in an armed struggle for independence, although recently the official objective has been lessened to being allowed some form of autonomy within a union controlled by the military government of Myanmar/Burma.

Out of sight of most of the world, armed conflicts have had a devastating effect on ethnic minority communities inside of Myanmar/Burma. Brees (2008: 4) claimed, "close to half a million people have been displaced internally over the last decade on the eastern border alone." The strategy of the military government includes the cutting of food, funds, recruits, and information which is often carried out by destroying villages believed to be sources of these four valuable resources (Shukla 2008). This strategy has resulted in significant numbers of individuals fleeing toward Thailand where they are forced to live in refugee camps (Alexander 2008). As this is a protracted situation with no political solution in sight, many of the refugees are being resettled to countries outside the region (Banki and Lang 2008).

There are a number of other ethnic groups living in areas that span the borders of Thailand and Myanmar/Burma. The Shan are an ethnic group whose language and culture are closely related to the Thais and Laotians. The Shan call themselves "Tai," practice Theravada Buddhism, are physically indistinguishable from the northern Thais, and speak a related but recognizably different language to the Thais; it is estimated there are between 4 and 5 million Shan currently living in the Shan State in northeastern Myanmar/Burma and approximately another half million living in Thailand (Montlake 2008). The Shan may be best known for the myths and stories surrounding the ethnic group's most famous, or infamous, member, the legendary Shan warlord Khun Sa. Khun Sa was a major player in the opium trade in Southeast Asia during and after the Vietnam War. Although recently attempts have been made to curtail opium production by the Shan, it appears due to the weak control of the government and lack of economic development in the region, opium production is making a major comeback in the Shan State (Jagan 2009). Other ethnic minorities living in Myanmar/Burma include the Wa, Kachin, Chin, Mon, Arkanese, Naga, and Karenni (Walton 2008).

One of the better known ethnic groups to the outside world is the Hmong (Miao), who mostly come from Laos. Most scholars believe the Hmong culture originated in southern China before most Hmong migrated into the mountainous areas of Laos, Thailand, and Vietnam, although there are still a few Hmong living in southwestern China. The Hmong may be best known for the group's alliance with the CIA and the US government in the 1960s and 1970s in an attempt to prevent a communist takeover of Laos. Since that time, the Laotian government has not trusted the Hmong, and this ethnic group has been subjected to continuous discrimination and repression by the government. Being aligned with the losing side in the war resulted in a large number of Hmong fleeing their homeland in Laos, thus becoming refugees, and subsequently many resettled into other countries including the United States, Canada, France, and French Guyana. As with some of the other hill-tribe peoples, the Hmong have traditionally used agricultural techniques, such as fallow cultivation, that differ sharply from the techniques used by the lowland dwelling majority populations. These highland agricultural techniques are generally not considered to be environmentally friendly, which is another reason for conflict with the majority-led governments. The Hmong have traditionally been animists and in addition to growing dry rice and maize, the Hmong have also been involved in growing opium (Siriphon 2006).

Another major ongoing armed conflict in the region can be found in the southern tip of Thailand where Muslim insurgents are seeking to break the southernmost provinces free from the control of the Buddhist-dominated central government. Separatist violence in the provinces of Yala, Narrathiwat, and Pattani has a history that goes back nearly 50 years; however, the scale and brutality of the violence has increased considerably over the last decade. One of the factors attributed for causing the insurgency is the fact the Muslim descendents of the former Kingdom of Pattani have failed to accept rule by the Buddhist-led government of Bangkok. There have been three main organizations seeking independence from Bangkok: Barisan Revolusi Nasional (BRN), Pattani United Liberation Organization (PULO), and New Pulo. However, all three organizations have been harmed by internal dissention and the removal of safe havens in Malaysia; nevertheless, the violence has increased in recent years. Between the beginning of 2004 and the end of January 2007, 2566 people were reported to have been killed in separatist violence in southern Thailand (Chalk 2008). Although the policies of the government of former Prime Minister Thaksin have often been blamed for the escalation of violence, the military dictatorship that replaced the elected government did not have any substantial success in lessening the amount of violence. While many observers believe there is no concrete evidence linking the insurgency with outside militant organizations worldwide, there has been a correlation between the increased violence and brutality found in the insurgency in the region with the increase in the popularity of militant Islamic movements worldwide. Due to the continuing divisions in Thai politics, the governments of Thailand have failed to create a united policy in order to effectively combat the insurgency (McCargo 2008: 352).

In order to achieve peace in these three southern provinces, where approximately 80 percent of the population is Muslim and most speak a local Malay dialect (Pattani-Malay), Jitpiromsri and McCargo (2008) proposed a plan that includes creating a cabinet level position to deal with the situation, parallel non-elected bodies of local elites to act as special consultants, and to increase the power of the elected municipal and sub-district organizations. These increased powers would include the ability to impose some aspects of *sharia* law. The authors acknowledge that there is stiff resistance to this proposal from many factions in the Thai government and population.

Although Theravada Buddhism is normally thought of as a religion of universal peace and tolerance, the conflict in the South is producing its share of militant and nationalistic Buddhist sentiment. Although the Muslim population is increasing in the region while the Buddhist population is decreasing, there has been a concerted effort to keep Buddhist *wats* occupied even in areas without a surrounding Buddhist lay population in order to keep a Buddhist presence. Many *wats* are being used as military outposts, and there are rumors of military-monks occupying a number of *wats* to provide protection to the abbots and other monks. Buddhism is linked with Thai nationalism in the conflict and while Theravada Buddhist doctrine, like most major religions, preaches peace, some followers of Theravada Buddhism in southern Thailand have justified armed conflict as a means of protecting the religion and the state (Askew 2009; Jerryson 2009; McCargo 2009).

Minority groups in the region have often found coexistence alongside the majority Theravada Buddhist populations difficult. Armed conflict and repression have been common. In theory, Theravada Buddhism is a religion of peace, diversity, and tolerance; however, in their dealings with ethnic minorities, the practices of leaders in the region have not always lived up to the ideals of Theravada Buddhism.

Foreign firms and foreign influence

These countries are situated between two of the oldest and largest civilizations in the world, China and India. Additionally, three out of the four countries are former colonies of European powers. Therefore, it is not surprising the cultures and business practices found in the Theravada Buddhist countries of Southeast Asia have been heavily influenced by foreign ideas and practices. Foreign firms and enterprises headed by ethnic minorities have been a key feature of the business environment in the Theravada Buddhist countries of Southeast Asia for a considerable length of time. As Theravada Buddhist values can at times conflict with the values of capitalism, it is not surprising foreigners have often dominated the business environments in the region. However, even though much of the large-scale business in the region is being conducted by firms headed by individuals with ethnic origins from outside the region, the influence of Theravada Buddhism on the workers, customers, and government regulators can not be ignored.

Much of the historical foreign influence on the economies of the region came from China and ethnic Chinese business operators. Adams (1879: 175) wrote, in regards to Cambodia, "Trade and commerce are almost entirely in the hands of Chinese merchants, who, here as elsewhere, exhibit an extraordinary amount of patience, industry and thrift; and, here as elsewhere, untiringly amass large and even enormous fortunes." In referring to Laos in the 1950s, Evans (2002: 97) wrote, "As in Thailand and Cambodia, commercial activity has been largely left to the Chinese while Lao sought a career in the state." The dominance of ethnic Chinese firms in Thailand and other parts of Southeast Asia in more recent times has also been widely acknowledged by observers and scholars (Carney and Gedailovic 2003; Keller and Kronstedt 2005; Suehiro and Wailerdsak 2004; Tsang 2001; Wang 2004; Yan and Sorenson 2004).

While ethnic Chinese-owned and operated firms have played an important part in the business environments for decades, the Chinese government and firms from mainland China are only starting to become increasingly more influential on business operations in the region. Due to China's relatively weak military and economy power (compared to that of the United States and European Union), it is likely China will remain a regional power as opposed to a global power in the near future and all of the nations of ASEAN will do their best to avoid becoming pawns in a potential diplomatic struggle between the United States and China (Stuart-Fox 2003: 225–41). In Laos, while trade with Vietnam and Thailand are important for the economy, trade with China has increased substantially in recent years and therefore balancing relationships with all of its neighboring countries has become an important governmental objective (Linter 2008). The influence of Chinese firms is also growing in Myanmar/Burma, Cambodia and, to a lesser extent, Thailand.

The economy of Myanmar/Burma was dominated by ethnic Indians during the colonial era; in fact, Yangon/Rangoon at one time had a majority Indian population. However, the end of the colonial era and the military government's policy of pushing out foreign influence have greatly reduced the influence of ethnic Indians on the country's economy. Myint-U (2006) speculated that the early experience of Ne Win, the leader of the military government from 1962 until 1988, as an unsuccessful entrepreneur who was unable to compete with Indian-owned firms in the coal industry had a major influence on the country's decision to expel the majority of ethnic Indian business owners and move toward "self-reliance." In recent times, there has been an increase in Chinese and Thai investment into the country, but there has been far less influence from foreign companies and less "globalization" seen in Myanmar/Burma than in most other areas of the world.

The foreign influence that is coming into the business environment of Myanmar/Burma is mainly coming from Asia. ZTE is an example of a foreign firm that is operating in Myanmar/Burma and is having an impact on the country's business environment. ZTE is a Chinese telecommunications company that is listed on the Shenzhen Stock Exchange and has had operations in Myanmar/Burma since 2004. The company's main competitors in Myanmar/Burma are other Chinese firms. The company supplies the only two authorized internet providers, Myanmar Posts and Telecommunications and Myanmar Teleport, not surprisingly both companies are government-controlled. As internet access in the country is still not widespread, the company's operations in the country are quite small with only 47 employees and five supervisors. However, the firm uses very similar HR management practices as it uses in China and the company's main activity is to transfer its operational knowledge that has been gained in China into Myanmar/Burma.

> Chinese investment in Myanmar is driven by both geopolitical and economic factors. Official Chinese investment in Myanmar is rather small; but there are a large number of hidden Chinese investments and business ventures, most of which are in the names of their relatives who hold Myanmar citizenship. Many businesses, both large and small, in almost all major cities in Myanmar have some form of Chinese investment.
>
> (Myoe 2007: 14)

Thailand has been the recipient of considerable amounts of foreign direct investment in recent decades and the presence of these foreign firms has had a considerable impact on economic growth and business practices within the country. For instance, what is observed when visiting the factory floor of an automotive plant in Rayong is not significantly different from what one would expect to see in Detroit. Additionally, Thailand's retail sector is becoming dominated by the foreign firms Tesco and Carrefour, which have brought in a number of modern retailing business practices that are now being imitated by local firms as well. Japanese industrial firms have invested heavily in Thailand, which has resulted in a transfer of operational technology; however, Japanese firms have not fully imported their HR and other non-technical management practices to the country (Onishi 2006).

While there are a significant number of large foreign firms in Thailand, there are also a number of smaller foreign entrepreneurial firms. For example, White Lotus Press out of Pattaya is a smaller "foreign" firm with majority Thai ownership. In a similar fashion to many businesses in Thailand, the owners of the company are directly involved in the management. The company uses a niche strategy as it primarily concentrates on printing specialized books on Southeast Asia, mostly in English, aimed toward foreigners with an interest in the region. At the tactical level, the company has similar characteristics to other SMEs in the region, for example, it mostly relies on on-the-job training as opposed to having formal training programs for staff. At the operational level, the company outsources the typesetting, editing, and printing in order to concentrate on what it does best, selecting and marketing books that will appeal to its target market. This strategy, focusing on a particular part of the value chain, is known and advocated by many business educators and researchers. In a similar fashion to those seen in the earlier case studies of small firms, there is no clear separation between the skills and knowledge of the company and its owner-manager,

Mr. Diethard Ande. While international business is normally thought of as an arena dominated by huge multinationals, White Lotus Press shows that small entrepreneurial companies, often first companies labeled "born foreign firms" by Hipsher (2008), can find markets and success outside the borders of the nation in which the entrepreneur was issued a passport.

In Laos, there has been very little investment by Western businesses; however, private companies from Thailand, Vietnam, and China have become extremely important factors in shaping the business environment in the country. De Valk (2003) believed foreign firms can create a more dynamic business environment, which is important in creating economic growth. De Valk also found that the limited exposure to international markets and suppliers was limiting improvements in efficiency in firms within Laos PDR. Western relations with Laos are primarily associated with the handing out of aid (Linter 2008: 179) and therefore hierarchical in nature, with the Western countries being able to dictate conditions the Laotians must accept to receive the aid. Therefore, there has been minimal direct Western influence on Laotian business practices while contact with businesses originating from other countries in Asia is having considerable effect on what Laotian businesses learn and how they operate.

The situation in Cambodia is similar to the one found in Laos PDR. Western influence in Cambodia is mainly through NGOs and other international agencies while most foreign investment comes from nearby Asian countries. Whether Western foreign aid is helping to alleviate the effects of poverty on the country is open to debate. Critics of foreign aid often point to the increase in corruption that has accompanied the influx of money into the public sector and the creation of a dependency on foreign aid which distorts the economy. Many well-paid jobs are created by NGOs, which may rob the private sector of valuable talent. Another criticism is to claim many aid organizations practice a form of cultural imperialism and require recipients of the aid to accept practices based on Western values (e.g., gender equality, egalitarianism, democracy, impersonal justice systems) in order to receive funding, while proponents of foreign aid point out the improvements in health care, education, and other areas which foreign aid has contributed to, and which have improved the lives of a large number of people living in the region. Therefore, the primary foreign influence on the Cambodian business environment has come from companies from nearby Asian countries.

An example of a foreign business operating in Cambodia is TV 5 Cambodia, which is a joint venture between the Royal Cambodian Armed Forces and Mica Media Co. Ltd. (Thailand) which is part of the Kantana Group. The Kantana Group is one of the major producers of television shows and movies in Thailand; however, it does not run any television stations in Thailand. The station was founded in 1995 as a partnership between the Royal Cambodian Armed Forces and a group of investors from Thailand including Dr. Thaksin Shinawatra who would later become the controversial Thai prime minister. Later Mica Media Co. Ltd. (Thailand) bought out the other Thai investors and then Dr. Krisada Manoonwong became the managing director of the company. As the Cambodian economy was decimated by the civil war and the following Khmer Rouge rule, technical knowledge and talent have been in short supply. Therefore, the investors from Thailand were able to bring in experienced and trained experts in television production as well as a professional management team that is now working to provide opportunities for the Khmer employees in the organization to gain exposure of working in a professionally run entertainment and media organization.

To engage with the rest of the world, it might not be necessary for an entire industry to be created within the region, instead firms in the Theravada Buddhist Countries of Southeast Asia may be able to find niches in global value chains. Bonaglia (2006: 31) explained:

> By participating in global value chains, firms in developing countries have an opportunity to overcome the limits imposed by small and less sophisticated domestic markets, access major export markets and gradually expand the range of products and functions they undertake. The structure of rewards and the opportunities to upgrade their technological and managerial skills depend on their capabilities and on their relationships with lead firms in the global value chain.

Foreign influence in the region is nothing new, and the Theravada Buddhist value of impermanence may contribute to the general acceptance of new ideas coming from outside the region. The view that the countries in the region are being primarily influenced by Western business practices and Western-inspired globalization may be misleading. Currently, outside of Thailand, the vast majority of international business is being conducted intra-regionally as opposed to inter-regionally and therefore the business practices in the region may be moving toward becoming more Asian and less "globalized."

Modern and traditional

All societies, in order to survive, need to be able to find a mix between embracing the modern and retaining the traditional. Friedman (2005) claimed the "world is flat" and cultural differences are lessening. While this may be true to some extent, it is equally true that different parts of the world are remaining distinctly different in economic development, adherence to religious philosophies, and social norms. Japan has "modernized," but that has not meant complete convergence of lifestyles and values with other "modern" nations. In a "globalized" world, people and nations choose what to accept from outside and what to retain from their own cultures. For example, many Americans have added Japanese sushi to their diets, but most US companies have rejected Japanese-style HR practices such as seniority-based promotions and guaranteed life-time employment. The same is true with the people of the Theravada Buddhist countries of Southeast Asia and this has been ongoing for centuries. In 1910, Freeman noticed, the Lao peoples of northern Thailand were eager to accept foreign medicine, but less eager to accept the religion of the missionaries dispensing the medicine and medical care. We can still see today how a mixing of the "modern" and traditional handed down from times past is an integral part of modern life in Thailand and the region.

These days, religious rituals aimed at magically improving one's life are a common feature (Jackson 2003), which shows that when the Thais and others in the region adopted the "modern" religion of Theravada Buddhism in centuries past, the modern aspects of the religion were mixed with the more traditional animist practices that were practiced in the region before the conversion of the people to the new modern religion. These traditional pre-Buddhist practices continue to exist alongside the more modern adherence to the teachings of the Buddha.

While Buddhist monastic life is ideally a continuation of a tradition began during the life of the Buddha, "Theravada ethical notions are defined more in terms of attitudes than actions" (Jackson 2003: 220); therefore, the religion is not a major impediment to change in actions for lay people, as long as the fundamental Buddhist principles are followed. Also, the teachings of the acceptance of impermanence foster a willingness to change. This was evident when Dautremer (1913: 358) noticed the Theravada Buddhist Burmese eagerly abandoned traditional methods of manufacturing clothing when exposed to new methods that saved time, while the Animist and Christian Shans and Karens were more likely to hold onto their traditional ways.

Theravada Buddhism has had to adapt and change to survive for over 2,500 years. It is human nature to think of our times as being modern, but Theravada Buddhism has survived through hundreds of "modern" generations. The Theravada Buddhist countries of Southeast Asia have gone through many extreme political changes, including the fall of the Khmer Empire at Angkor, both British and French colonialism, the end of the absolute monarchy in Thailand, and numerous other turning point events, and yet many of the core values of Theravada Buddhism have remained despite all the changes. The cultures of the Theravada Buddhist countries of Southeast Asia have long histories of mixing the modern and the traditional. Today, changes are also happening. We see the introduction of new technologies, moves away from agricultural dominated societies, and increases in contacts with people from other cultures. Will the people of the region be able to blend their traditional values with life in the twenty-first century? History would appear to indicate that modern business and other new practices will continue to be adopted while traditional values and principles will be able to survive and thrive alongside all the changes that are happening during these modern times.

> Unlike Islamic and Christian fundamentalists, Buddhist leaders in Myanmar, as well as in Thailand and Laos, deal with the issue of globalization in a much more neutral way. That is, they prefer to promote peace and harmony which is the Buddhist tradition to accept the flow of change. Change, in Buddhist philosophy is the most certain thing in the world. Certainty is uncertainty. Therefore, globalization does not bring a degree of hostility into Buddhist ideology.
>
> (Chanthanom 1998: 104)

Future of business

Diamond (1997) hypothesized the differences in economic development and cultures are historical reflections of the cultural evolution of societies that come from operating in the differing physical environments found around the world. Therefore, a case could be made that the future of economic development and business practices in the region will continue to be a reflection of the changing external environments in which businesses, governments, and individuals will evolve within. It can be expected the business practices in the region will change in response to the changes in the economic, socio-cultural, political, and technological environments. Boyd and Richerson (2005) felt cultures evolved faster through social learning than through individual experience; therefore, it could be theorized that increasing contact with the outside world will result in an increased amount of social learning and faster changing sectors of the environment will result in faster changes in business practices. Tang and Koveos (2008) proposed rapid economic development leads to faster cultural evolution, which could be leading to a more globalized Thailand and less rapid globalization in other locations in the region. In the most industrial areas of Thailand, spillover effects and the learning that happens in Thai firms from interactions with foreign firms supports this concept that increased contacts and globalization appear to be having a converging effect on local with global business practices (Sajarattanachote 2006).

However, "Globalization does not bring convergence to all societies.... It is shown that the juxtaposition of the western ideas and Buddhism still plays an important role in the interpretation of globalization in countries like Burma, Laos and Thailand" (Chanthanom 1998: 6). Modernization and change in Asia has not meant wholesale Westernization of societies. The Japan of today is both modern and very Japanese, the standard of living in South Korea today is similar to the standard of living of most individuals living in Western societies, however Korean culture is alive and well and its uniqueness is a key feature driving the internationalization of the Korean entertainment industry. Taipei and Hong Kong are modern cities filled with the latest technological gadgets; however, both are easily identifiable as Chinese cities. The countries of the region will continue to modernize and change, but there is little reason to believe these changes will result in the countries becoming less Burmese, Khmer, Lao, or Thai in the future.

Rehbein (2007b: 82) felt globalization was having an effect in Laos PDR; however, it was not felt there was an immediate threat to the current political leadership because of it. While foreign aid and economic development are having an impact on the lives of individuals, traditional-style social and professional networks continue to dominate throughout the country. The traditional client-patron system survives in communist Laos, as it does in the military dictatorship in Myanmar/Burma, and as it does in the theoretically democratic countries of Cambodia and Thailand.

While globalization is often thought of as the Westernization of the world, in the future China will likely have a major influence on world events and cultures.

The rise of China and how to accommodate this will be one of the major international relations challenges of the twenty-first century. Whether or not this can be achieved peacefully is of particular importance for China's neighbors, and none more so than for the countries of Southeast Asia.

(Stuart-Fox 2003: 224)

In Laos, the government has limited the activities of Western NGOs in many provinces over concerns about the promotion of foreign values (such as democratic values) while allowing Chinese enterprises to operate in the same locations unhindered (Linter 2008: 181). It is felt that while both Western NGOs and Chinese businesses bring in money, the Chinese businesses are less likely to promote values that would threaten the existing political system and therefore have found a warmer welcome. In Cambodia, China is investing in many infrastructural development projects (Um 2008) and China has also been investing in Myanmar/Burma for a number of years. It would appear likely the influence of China in the region will continue to grow in the future, most likely at the expense of Western influence.

National identity in the region continues to place a high emphasis on Buddhism as being an identifying characteristic. Chanthanom (1998: 174) reported, "When they asked what makes a person uniquely Burmese, they all said 'practicing Buddhism.'" Chanthanom (1998: 177) also reported, in Thailand, "All religions must be equally recognized under the national constitution. Buddhism, however is the 'national' religion. The King of Thailand must be a Buddhist;" while Su (2003: 61), in reporting on cultural identity characteristics, found the people of Cambodia believed "to be Khmer is to be Buddhist." Therefore, it would appear globalization and modernization will affect many aspects of life in the region in the future, but the central role Theravada Buddhism plays in shaping individual attitudes and identity appears likely to remain for the foreseeable future. However, what it means to be Buddhist would appear likely to change as each of these societies change.

An interesting experiment in different ownership patterns is being seen in the creation of "social enterprises" in Cambodia by NGOs. These social organizations are a blend of non-profit structures, Buddhist values, and capitalist philosophies that attempt to create sustainable institutions that allow employees to gain skills and experience and therefore increase the human capital of the nation (Ty *et al.* 2008). It will be interesting to see if these NGO-private enterprise partnerships will be able to stand the test of time.

On the other hand, in Thailand, there had been a trend toward privatization of state-owned firms (Sriboonlue 2007), however, the military coup of 2006 and political uncertainty have slowed moves toward privatization. Also, it should be kept in mind a large portion of the most valuable real estate in Bangkok continues to be controlled by the royal-owned Crown Property Bureau, therefore a considerable "government" control of the economy remains despite the country's stated capitalist ideology. In Laos, foreign direct investment is seeping in bringing new ownership structures in some larger firms; however, the majority of the nation's economy continues to be controlled by the informal sector, while in Myanmar/Burma, the military continues to control many of the nation's larger businesses.

Economic growth has brought many benefits to the region. For example, in Thailand the number of women dying during childbirth has dramatically decreased, literacy has significantly increased, and life expectancy has been dramatically extended during the period of the rapid economic growth and poverty reduction seen in the last 50 years (Warr 2007). Laos is starting to see significant reductions in poverty in the country through economic growth; however, this has come at a cost to the environment (Linter 2008: 180). Cambodia has been experiencing a very slow rate of poverty reduction compared to other regional economies (Um 2008: 112), while Myanmar/Burma's economy has stagnated due to the isolationist and central planning policies of the government. Parts of the region have benefited from economic growth, but there are still many further benefits possible for the people if the countries of the region can accelerate economic growth.

To continue to achieve economic growth, the nations will need to overcome many obstacles. Corruption remains rampant throughout the region (Linter 2008: 180; Um 2008: 112). Laos PDR has a significant shortage of skilled workers and, with only a single university, it does not currently have the capacity to generate internally a workforce with the skills needed to grow a modern economy (Linter 2008: 182). In Thailand, the ongoing political division and the uncertainty over the government's support of the principles of moving toward a "sufficiency economy" as promoted by King Bhumibol have prompted concerns among international investors (McCargo 2008). While in Myanmar/Burma, the lack of infrastructure and personnel experienced in working in environments controlled by market forces is a major obstacle for economic growth. Also, the inequalities in the region are resulting in large numbers of workers migrating from Myanmar/Burma, Cambodia, and Laos PDR, which could result in political tensions especially during difficult economic times (Warr 2007: 160).

Predictions for the future with or without the aid of a *Maw Do* (fortune teller) are unlikely to be entirely accurate. However, current trends would appear to indicate with the rise of China as an economic, military, and political power, the economies of the region will likely become more integrated regionally and will rely less on exports, investment, and aid from Western nations. It is also predicted that companies in the region will increasingly use globally available technology while continuing to have internal human relations practices influenced by Theravada Buddhist values. Growth is likely to continue, but will most likely be tied closely to global economic trends, yet poverty will most likely continue to plague the region for decades to come. While change is inevitable, it is expected the business environments in the region will continue to be influenced by Theravada Buddhist values and will remain distinctly different from the business environments found in other regions of the world.

Beyond profitability

"Terms such as 'developed,' 'modern,' or 'newly industrialized' nations could be used to identify a hierarchy of nations" (Chanthanom 1998). These terms would seem to imply richer is better. However, whether it is a nation's economic development or a company's profit, the concept that more is better regardless of the costs may not be universal. Ambition is generally considered to be an extremely positive attribute in most Western societies, while ambition and desire for more in Theravada Buddhism teaching is seen as the cause of all human suffering. That is not to say all lay Theravada Buddhists live lives devoid of the desire for material possession and social position, but a case could be made that by following the middle path, professional success usually does not become an all-consuming passion for most workers in the region. For example, Rehbein (2007a: 65) discovered villagers in Laos viewed labor-saving technology as a way to increase their freetime as opposed to being tools to use to increase productivity and profits.

Buddhist ethics are primarily concerned with making people happy with their lot in life as opposed to attempting to change an individual's material condition or improving the world's situation (Jackson 2003: 220). In fact, many scholars have believed Theravada Buddhist values limit economic growth (Piker 1993: 966). On the other hand, Thailand's overall strong economic growth during the past 40 years may support the idea that the lack of economic development in Cambodia, Laos, and Myanmar/Burma has more to do with international and internal politics than the religious values of the population.

The easy-going and non-competitive nature of the citizens of the region has often been observed.

> The Burman neither flatters nor cringes. He is usually very lively and overflowing with high spirits, full of banter and quizzicality. He is never cast down by bad luck and never overcome by abundant riches: sometimes he heaps together a fortune, but it is not a common occurrence, for he lives from day to day and takes little care for the future. He has no idea either of discipline or of perseverance, but he is very whimsical and very independent.
>
> (Dautremer 1913: 78)

> The Laos are often called lazy, unjustly I think.
>
> (Freeman 1910: 102)

In northern Thailand, "Life is lived from day to day and from year to year without looking into the future, striving to build a name or business to leave behind when dead" (Curtis 1903: 163).

> They [Siamese children] are very merry, continually contented, easily pleased and most unselfish in their dealings with one another. Their almost absolute lack of selfishness is one of the most pleasing features in their very

lovable characters. The boys at school lend their property to their fellow-scholars with the greatest readiness. Watches, knives, pencils, and other schoolboy treasures circulate sometimes to such an extent that one is inclined to fancy they must be common property.

(Young 1900: 48)

More recently, a small business owner in Cambodia was quoted as saying, "My plans were more like dreams, not really fixed plans. More like I will become better in the future and that things will be better (Hawks 2005: 134).

If one considers that most Lao were born and raised as peasants under socialism and still work at least part-time as farmers, it is not surprising that many elements of subsistence ethics persist, even in downtown Vientiane. There are plenty of petty traders who are unconcerned about such matters as productivity and time management; they sit around the whole day, even if only a single client shows up and virtually no money changes hands. This is regarded as perfectly acceptable as long as it allows the traders to buy the things they need. In most instances, they still divide the market among themselves in the manner of medieval guilds so that everyone gets a share of business.

(Rehbein 2007a: 54)

Today, Thailand is well known as the land of smiles and visitors often find the laid-back *mai bpen rai* attitude of the Thais adds a relaxing backdrop to an enjoyable vacation. However, many an expatriate manager finds working with Thais can be exceedingly frustrating because of this very same attitude. Avoidance of conflict often is a higher priority in the Thai workplace than efficiency and profitability. Holmes, Tangtongtavy, and Tomizawa, (1996: 21) reported Thais:

Have to find some way of reaching their goals so that the relationship remains intact and cordial, and that everyone likes the plan, whether it is technically the best or not. One could say that compromise is a principle in itself, and is often instrumental in avoiding conflict.

Persons (2008) explored the concept of "face" in the Thai context. It was found gaining and maintaining face was very important to all Thais. Persons found there were five distinct but interrelated phrases used in Thai to refer to face, which can be roughly translated as: appearance to the outside world, honor, fame, dignity, and virtue. Avoidance of loss of face is of utmost importance to Thais, and therefore constructive criticism and competition of ideas, which can result both in loss of face for some and improved decision making, are infrequently used. Often a trade-off of accepting lower effectiveness in working situations is made in order to ensure the face of all participates is maintained. A significant loss of face by a client often results in the seeking out of a new patron; therefore, managers who pursue policies that encourage confrontations may find turnover of key personnel will be at an unacceptable level.

Another important feature of work life is the concept of *Kreng Jai*. Holmes, Tangtongtavy, and Tomizawa (1996: 46–7) explained

> *Kreng Jai* refers to an attitude whereby an individual tries to restrain his own interest or desire, in situations where there is the potential for discomfort or conflict, and where there is a need to maintain a pleasant and cooperative relationship.

Kreng Jai has an element of submission to higher authority in it, but the concept is much broader and also includes an expectation that those higher in the organization and social hierarchy are expected to repay the loyalty of subordinates with protection, support, and opportunities. The dual responsibilities are often referred to as the client-patron relationship. In Thai organizations, loyalty is usually to an individual, one's patron, and normally not focused on an impersonal organization. One does not expect one's impersonal company to take care of oneself, instead it is expected one's patrons in the organization will individually hold that responsibility.

From a Western management perspective, it is easy to find faults in the "inefficient" methods that are often used in businesses in Southeast Asia, but the Western viewpoint normally assumes productivity, profits, and the achievement of goals are the primary objectives of organizations. While these goals are also important in organizations in Southeast Asia, the acceptance of the value of the middle path often moderates the drive to achieve materialistic goals and places a higher emphasis on quality of life. Most workers in the Theravada Buddhist countries are willing to give up some level of material possessions for a low-stress fun workplace. It has often been noticed that workers in the region think of their work efforts as meeting their social as well as physical needs.

Rehbein (2007a: 72) reported

> One might think consumerism would come easily to Lao, and, to a degree, this is the case. But one must not forget that the good life can hardly be imagined outside the group. For a Lao, to be alone or lonely is almost the definition of unhappiness – whereas capitalism and consumerism embody competition and individualism.

Taking the middle path in one's professional life offers obvious attractions, and may often be a viable alternative for individuals living in the region to the ultra-competitive nature of climbing the corporate ladder that is such a prominent feature of the work-life found in many large multinational enterprises.

References

Abbasi, S.M., Hollman, K.W., and Murrey, J.H. (1989) "Islamic economics: Foundations and practices," *International Journal of Social Economics*, 16(5): 5–17.

Abimbola, T. (2006) "Market access for developing economies: Branding in Africa," *Place Branding*, 2(2): 108–17.

Adams, W.H.D. (1879) *In the Far East: A Narrative of Exploration and Adventure in Cochin-China, Cambodia, Laos and Siam*, London: Thomas Nelson and Sons.

Agrawal, P. (2007) "Economic growth and poverty reduction: Evidence from Kazakhstan," *Asian Development Review*, 24(2): 90–115.

Ahmad, K. (2001) "Corporate leadership and workplace motivation in Malaysia," *International Journal of Commerce & Management*, 11(1): 82–101.

Ahmed, A. (2007) *Journey into Islam: The Crisis of Globalization*, Washington D.C.: Brookings Institution Press.

Alamgir, J. (2008) "Myanmar's foreign trade and its political consequences," *Asian Survey*, 48(6): 977–96.

Alexander, D. (2008) "Burma in urgent need of change," *Forced Migration Review*, 30: 6.

Ali, A.J. and Gibbs, M. (1998) "Foundations of business ethics in contemporary religious thought: The Ten Commandments perspective," *International Journal of Social Economics*, 25(10): 1552–62.

Ali, A.J. and Al-Owaihan, A. (2008) "Islamic work ethic: A critical review," *Cross Cultural Management*, 15(1): 5–19.

Ali, I. (2007) "Inequality and the imperative for inclusive growth in Asia," *Asian Development Review*, 24(2): 1–16.

Alvesson, M. and Sveningsson, S. (2003) "Managers doing leadership: The extraordinarization of the mundane," *Human Relations*, 56(12): 1435–59.

Andaya, B.W. (2002) "Localising the universal: Women, motherhood and the appeal of early Theravada Buddhism," *Journal of Southeast Asian Studies*, 33(1): 1–30.

Anderson, A.R., Drakopoulou-Dodd, S.L. and Scott, M.G. (2000) "Religion as an environmental influence on enterprise culture: The case of Britain in the 1980s," *International Journal of Entrepreneurial Behaviour & Research*, 6(1): 5–20.

Andersson, S., Gabrielsson, J., and Wictor, I. (2004) "International activities in small firms: Examining factors influencing the export growth of small firms," *Canadian Journal of Administrative Science*, 21(1): 22–34.

Areethamsirikul, S. (2008) "The impact of ASEAN enlargement on economic integration: Successes and impediments under ASEAN political institution," Doctoral Dissertation, University of Wisconsin-Madison, UMI No. 3314276.

Aribarg, R. (2005) "Thai border town businessmen and the state: An examination of their influence on Thai foreign policy toward Burma," Doctoral Dissertation, Boston University, UMI No. 3157351.

Arnold, D. and Hewison, K. (2005) "Exploitation in global supply chains: Burmese workers in Mae Sot," *Journal of Contemporary Asia*, 35(3): 319–40.

Asian Development Bank. (2008a) *Emerging Asian Regionalism: A Partnership for Shared Prosperity*, Mandaluyong City, Philippines: Asian Development Bank.

Asian Development Bank. (2008b) *Outlook 2008: Workers in Asia*, Mandaluyong City, Philippines: Asian Development Bank.

Asian Development Bank. (2009) *Asian Development Outlook 2009: Rebalancing Asia's Growth*, Mandaluyong City, Philippines: Asian Development Bank.

Askew, M. (2009) "Landscapes of fear, horizons of trust: Villagers dealing with danger in Thailand's insurgent south," *Journal of Southeast Asian Studies*, 40(1): 59–86.

Aung-Thwin, M. (1996) "The myth of the 'Three Shan Brothers' and the Ava period in Burmese history," *The Journal of Asian Studies*, 55(4): 881–901.

Bang, V.V. and Joshi, S.L. (2008) "Conceptualization of market expansion strategies in developing economies," *Academy of Marketing Science Review*, 12(4): 1–26.

Banki, S. and Lang, H. (2008) "Difficult to remain: The impact on mass resettlement," *Forced Migration Review*, 30: 42–4.

Banomyong, R. (2004) "Assessing import channels for a land-locked country: The case of Lao PDR," *Asia Pacific Journal of Marketing and Logistics*, 16(2): 62–81.

Bartlett, C.A. and Ghoshal, S. (1998). *Managing Across Borders: The Transnational Solution*, 2nd edn., Boston: Harvard Business School Press.

Basly, S. (2007) "The internationalization of family SME: An organizational learning and knowledge perspective," *Baltic Journal of Management*, 2(2): 154–80.

Bass, B.M. and Avolio, B.J. (1993) "Transformational leadership and organizational culture," *Public Administration Quarterly*, 17(1): 112–21.

Bass, B.M. and Steidlmeier, P. (1999) "Ethics, character, and authentic transformational leadership behavior," *Leadership Quarterly*, 10(2): 281–317.

Baumann, M. (2001) "Global Buddhism: Developmental periods, regional histories and a new analytical perspective," *Journal of Global Buddhism*, 2: 1–43.

Bechert, H. (1970) "Theravada Buddhist Sangha: Some general observations on historical and political factors in its development," *The Journal of Asian Studies*, 29(4): 761–77.

Beer, M. and Katz, N. (2003) "Do incentives work? The perceptions of a worldwide sample of senior executives," *HR: Human Resource Planning*, 26(3): 30–44.

Beeson, M. (2003) "ASEAN plus three and the rise of reactionary regionalism," *Contemporary Southeast Asia*, 25(2): 251–68.

Biers, D., Vatikiotis, M., Tasker, R., and Dairueng, P. (1999) "Back to school," *Far East Economic Review*, 162: 14.

Bishop, J. (2008) "Greening globalization," *World Conservation*, 38(2): 4–5.

Bitzenis, A. (2003) "Universal model of theories determining FDI. Is there any dominant theory? Are the FDI inflows in the CEE countries and especially in Bulgaria a myth?" *European Business Review*, 15(2): 94–104.

Bjerke, B.V. (2000) "A typified, culture-based, interpretation of management of SMEs in Southeast Asia," *Asia Pacific Journal of Management*, 17(1): 103–32.

Bjorkman, I. and Kock, S. (1997) "Inward international activities in service firms – illustrated by three cases from the tourism industry," *International Journal of Service Industry Management*, 8(5): 362–76.

Bjorkman, I., Fey, C.F., and Park, H.J. (2007) "Institutional theory and MNC subsidiary

HRM practices: Evidence from a three-country study," *Journal of International Business Studies*, 38(3): 430–46.

Bode, M.H. (1898) *A Burmese Historian of Buddhism*, Doctoral Dissertation: University of Berne.

Bonaglia, F. (2006) *Meeting the Challenge of Private Sector Development: Evidence from the Mekong Subregion*, Paris: Organisation for Economic Co-operation and Development (OECD) Publishing.

Bordo, M.D., Eichengreen, B., and Irwin, D.A. "Is globalization today really different than globalization a hundred years ago?" paper presented at the Brookings Trade Policy Forum on Governing in a Global Economy, Washington, D.C., May 1999.

Bowen, H.P. and De Clercq, D. (2008) "Institutional context and the allocation of entrepreneurial effort," *Journal of International Business Studies*, 39(4): 747–67.

Boyd, R. and Richerson, P.J. (2005) *The Origin and Evolution of Cultures*, Oxford: Oxford University Press.

Breazeale, K. (2002) "The Lao-Tay-son alliance, 1792 and 1793," in M. Ngaosrivathana and K. Breazeale (eds.), *Breaking New Ground in Lao History: Essays on the Seventh to Twentieth Centuries*, Chiang Mai, Thailand: Silkworm Books, 261–80.

Brees, I. (2008) "Forced displacement of Burmese people," *Forced Migration Review*, 30: 4–5.

Brothers, K.D. (2002) "Institutional, cultural and transaction cost influences on entry mode choice and performance," *Journal of International Business Studies*, 33(2): 203–21.

Buger, C. and Villumsen, T. (2007) "Beyond the gap: Relevance, fields of practice and the securitizing consequences of (democratic peace) research," *Journal of International Relations and Development*, 10(4): 417–48.

Cai, J., Ung, L., Setboonsarng, S., and Leung, P.S. (2008) "Rice contract farming in Cambodia: Empowering farmers to move beyond the contract towards independence," *Asian Development Bank Institute Discussion Paper*, No. 109.

Carbine, J. (2004) *An Ethic of Continuity: Shwegyin Monks and the Sasana in Contemporary Burma/Myanmar*, Doctoral Dissertation, University of Chicago. UMI No. 314931.

Carney, M. (2004) "The institutions of industrial restructuring in Southeast Asia," *Asia Pacific Journal of Management*, 21(1–2): 171–88.

Carney, M. and Gedailovic, E. (2003) "Strategic innovation and the administrative heritage of East Asian family business groups," *Asia Pacific Journal of Management*, 20(1): 5–26.

Chalk, P. (2008) "The Malay-Muslim insurgency in Southern Thailand: Understanding the conflict's evolving dynamic," *Rand Counterinsurgency Study*, Paper 5.

Chandler, D. (2000) *A History of Cambodia*, 3rd edn., Chiang Mai: Thailand: Silkworm Books.

Chandprapalert, A. (2000) "The determinants of US direct investment in Thailand: A survey on managerial perspectives," *Multinational Business Review*, 8(2): 82–8.

Chanthanom, S. (1998) *Globalization of the Golden Triangle: Cultural Transformation in Burma, Laos and Thailand*, Doctoral Dissertation, University of Pittsburgh. UMI No. 9919264.

Chen, S. and Wilson, M. (2003) "Standardization and localization of human resource management in Sino-foreign joint ventures," *Asia Pacific Journal of Management*, 20(3): 397–408.

Chen, X.P. and Peng, S. (2008) "Guanxi dynamics: Shifts in the closeness of ties between Chinese coworkers," *Management and Organization Review*, 4(1): 63–80.

Cheng, J.Y. (2004) "The ASEAN-China free trade area: Genesis and implications," *Australian Journal of International Affairs*, 50(2): 257–77.

Chew, I. and Goh, M. (1997) "Some future directions of human resources practices in Singapore," *Career Development International*, 2(5): 238–53.

Chirakiti, P. (2001) "Developing democratic institutions and processes in Thailand," in U. Johannen and J. Gomez (eds.), *Democratic Transitions in Asia*, Singapore: Select Books, 67–72.

Chong, L.M. and Thomas, D.C. (1997) "Leadership perceptions in cross-cultural context: Pakeha and Pacific Islanders in New Zealand," *Leadership Quarterly*, 8(3): 275–93.

Choo, S. and Wong, M. (2006) "Entrepreneurial intention: Triggers and barriers to new venture creation in Singapore," *Singapore Management Review*, 28(2): 47–64.

Chortareas, G.E. and Pelagidis, T. (2004) "Trade flows: A facet of regionalism or globalization?" *Cambridge Journal of Economics*, 28(2): 253–71.

Chui, A. and Kwok, C. (2008) "National culture and life insurance consumption," *Journal of International Business Studies*, 39(1): 88–101.

Chung, W.C. and Yuen, P.K. (2003) "Management succession: A case for Chinese family-owned business," *Management Decision*, 41(7): 643–55.

Claessens, S. (2006) "Access to financial services: A review of the issues and public policy objectives," *The World Bank Research Observer*, 21(2): 207–40.

Clarke, L.D. (1998) *The Role of Overseas Chinese Investment in the Emerging Countries of Southeast and East Asia: A Confucian Model of the Foreign Direct Investment Decision-Making Process using Factors Unconsidered in the West*, doctoral dissertation, Florida International University. UMI No. 9835704.

Coase, R.H. (1937) "The nature of the firm," *Economica*, 4: 386–405.

Cochrane, A. and Pain, K. (2004) "A globalizing society?" in D. Held (ed.), *A Globalized World? Culture, Economics and Politics*, 2nd edn., London: Routledge, 5–43.

Collinson, S. and Rugman, A.M. (2008) "The regional nature of Japanese multinational business," *Journal of International Business Studies*, 39(2): 215–30.

Constable, P. and Kuasirikun, N. (2007) "Accounting for the nation-state in mid nineteenth-century Thailand," *Accounting, Auditing and Accountability Journal*, 20(4): 574–619.

Cornwell, B., Cui, C.C., Mitchell, V., Schlegelmilch, B., Dzulkiflee, A., and Chan, J. (2005) "A cross-cultural study of the role of religion in consumers' ethical positions," *International Marketing Review*, 22(5): 531–46.

Cowell, N.M. (2007) "Human resource development and enterprise competitiveness in Jamaica," *Journal of Eastern Caribbean Studies*, 32(4): 25–51.

Crosby, K. (2006) "A Theravada code of conduct for good Buddhists: The Upasaka-manussavinaya," *Journal of the American Oriental Society*, 126(2): 177–87.

Cuervo-Cazurra, A. and Genc, M. (2008) "Transforming disadvantages into advantages: Developing-country MNEs in the least developed countries," *Journal of International Business Studies*, 30(6): 957–79.

Cummings, S. (2007). "Shifting foundations: Redrawing strategic management's military heritage," *Critical Perspectives on International Business*, 3(1): 41–62.

Curtis, L.J. (1903) *The Laos of Northern Thailand*, Philadelphia: The Westminster Press.

D'Souza, C. and Peretiatko, R. (2005) "Cultural impact on investment destination choice of US-multinational corporations," *Cross Cultural Management*, 12(3): 14–31.

Daft, R.L. and Marcic, D. (2004) *Understanding Management*, 4th edn., Mason, OH: Thomson South-Western.

Dai, Y. (2004) "A disguised defeat: The Myanmar campaign of the Qing dynasty," *Modern Asian Studies*, 38(1): 145–89.

Dalton, J. (2007) "Before the EEOC: How management integrated the workplace," *Business History Review*, 81(2): 269–96.

Darusman, M. (2001) "Lessons from Indonesia's democratisation for ASEAN," in U. Johannen and J. Gomez (eds.), *Democratic Transitions in Asia*, Singapore: Select Books, 45–7.

Dautremer, J. (1913) *Burma under British Rule*, trans. Sir George Scott, London: T. Fisher Unwin Ltd.

Davids, T.W.R. (1894) *Buddhism: A Sketch of the Life and Teachings of Gautama, the Buddha*, London: Society for Promoting Christian Knowledge.

Davis, P.S., Desai, A.B., and Francis, J.D. (2000) "Mode of international entry: An isomorphism perspective," *Journal of International Business Studies*, 31(2): 239–58.

Dellios, R. (1996) "Mandala-building in international relations as a paradigm for peace," paper presented at the 16th General Conference of International Peace Research Association, Brisbane, Australia, June 8–12.

Deng, P. (2003) "Foreign investment by multinationals from emerging countries: The case of China," *Journal of Leadership & Organizational Studies*, 10(2): 113–24.

Dess, G.G. and Davis, P.S. (1984) "Porter's (1980) generic strategies as determinants of strategic group membership and organizational performance," *Academy of Management Journal*, 27(3): 467–88.

Dessler, G. (2003) *Human Resource Management*, 9th edn., Upper Saddle River, NJ: Prentice Hall.

De Valk, P. (2003) "How do firms learn? With case studies from Lao PDR," *Working Paper series*, Institute of Social Studies, The Hague. (385).

Dewett, T., Whittier, N.C., and Williams, S.D. (2007) "Internal diffusion: The conceptualizing innovation implementation," *Competitive Review: An International Business Journal*, 17(1/2): 8–25.

Dhammapia, A. (2003) *Nibbana in Theravada Perspective with Special Reference to Buddhism in Burma*, doctoral dissertation, California Institute of Integral Studies. UMI No. 3093559.

Diamond, J. (1997) *Guns, Germs, and Steel: The Fates of Human Societies*, New York: W.W. Norton & Company.

Dittmer, L. (2008) "Burma vs. Myanmar: What's in a name?" *Asian Survey*, 48(6): 885–8.

Downie, S. and Kingsbury, D. (2001) "Political development and the re-emergence of civil society in Cambodia," *Contemporary Southeast Asia*, 23(1): 43–64.

Dunning, J.H. (1973) "The determinants of international production," *Oxford Economic Papers*, 25(3): 289–336.

Dunning, J.H. (1980) "Toward an eclectic theory of international production: Some empirical tests," *Journal of International Business Studies*, 11(1): 9–31.

Duong, C.M. and Swierczek, F.W. (2008) "Corporate culture, leadership competencies, job satisfaction, job commitment, and job performance: A comparison of companies in Vietnam and Thailand," *Journal of American Academy of Business, Cambridge*, 13(1): 159–65.

Eanes, J. (2002) "The rise and fall of the Khmer Rouge," master's thesis, California State University, Fresno. UMI No. 1412792.

Ear, S. (1995) "The Khmer Rouge canon 1975–1979: The standard academic view on Cambodia," undergraduate political science honors thesis, University of California, Berkeley.

Ear, S. (2009) "Sowing and sewing growth: The political economy of rice and garments in Cambodia," *Stanford Center for International Development Working Paper*, No. 384.

The Economist. (2008a) "A right royal mess," December 4, 2008.

The Economist. (2008b) "The king and them," December 4, 2008.

Egreteau, R. (2008) "India's Ambitions in Burma: More frustration than success?" *Asian Survey*, 48(6): 936–57.

Ekachai, S. (2008) "Leading the way," *Bangkok Post*, April 25, 2008, O1.

Eldridge, K. (2008) "The Thai psyche, Thailand's messy politics: Is culture the culprit?" *Bangkok Post*, November 29, 2008.

El-Kot, G. and Leat, M. (2008) "A survey of recruitment and selection practices in Egypt," *Education, Business and Society: Contemporary Middle Eastern Issues*, 1(3): 200–12.

Ellis, P. (2000) "Social ties and foreign market entry," *Journal of International Business Studies*, 31(3): 443–69.

Ellis, P. (2008) "Does psychic distance moderate the market size-entry sequence relationship?" *Journal of International Business Studies*, 39(3): 351–69.

Emmerson, D.K. (2007) "Challenging ASEAN: A 'topological' view," *Contemporary Southeast Asia*, 29(2): 424–46.

Endres, G.M. and Mancheno-Smoak, L. (2008) "The human resource craze: Human performance improvements and employee engagement," *Organization Development Journal*, 26(1): 69–78.

Erdilek, A. (2008) "Internationalization of Turkish MNE's," *Journal of Management Development*, 27(7): 744–60.

Evans, G. (2002) *A Short History of Laos: A Land in Between*, Crows Nest, Australia: Allen and Unwin.

Fairlie, R.W. and Robb, A. (2007) "Families, human capital, and small business: Evidence from the characteristics of business owners' survey," *Industrial and Labor Relations Review*, 60(2): 225–45.

Fajnzylber, P., Maloney, W., and Rojas, G.M. (2006) "Microenterprise dynamics in developing countries: How similar are they to those in the industrialized world? Evidence from Mexico," *The World Bank Review*, 20(3): 389–419.

Fam, K. and Grohs, R. (2007) "Cultural values and effective executional techniques in advertising: A cross-country and product category study of urban young adults in Asia," *International Marketing Review*, 24(5): 519–38.

Fauver, L., Houston, J., and Naranjo, A. (2003) "Capital market development, international integration, legal systems, and the value of corporate diversification: A cross-country analysis," *Journal of Financial and Quantitative Analysis*, 38(1): 135–57.

Ferguson, J. (2004) "ASEAN Concord II: Policy prospects for participant regional 'development,'" *Contemporary Southeast Asia*, 26(3): 393–415.

Fernandez, Z. and Nieto, M. (2005) "Internationalization strategy of small and medium-sized family businesses: Some influential factors," *Family Business Review*, 18(1): 77–89.

Freeman, J.H. (1910) *An Oriental Land of the Free: or, Life and Mission Work among the Laos of Siam, Burma, China and Indo-China*, Philadelphia: The Westminster Press.

Freeman, N.J. "Foreign direct investment in Cambodia, Laos and Vietnam," paper presented at the Conference on Foreign Direct Investment Opportunities and Challenges for Cambodia, Laos and Vietnam, Hanoi, Vietnam, August, 2002.

Friedman, T.L. (2005) *The World is Flat: A Brief History of the Twenty-First Century*, New York: Farrar, Straus & Giroux.

Gabrielsson, M., Sasi, V., and Darling, J. (2004) "Finance strategies of rapidly-growing Finnish SMEs: Born international and born globals," *European Business Review*, 16(6): 590–604.

Gallo, M.A., Tapies, J., and Cappuyns, K. (2004) "Comparison of family and nonfamily business: Financial logic and personal preferences," *Family Business Review*, 17(4): 303–18.

Garrison, J.A. (2005) "China's prudent cultivation of 'soft' power and implications for U.S. policy in East Asia," *Asian Affairs: An American Review*, 32(1): 25–30.

Gay, B. (2002) "Millenarian movements in Laos, 1895–1936: Depictions by modern Lao historians," in M. Ngaosrivathana and K. Breazeale (eds.), *Breaking New Ground in Lao History: Essays on the Seventh to Twentieth Centuries*, Chiang Mai, Thailand: Silkworm Books, 281–97.

George, J.M. and Jones, G.R. (2008) *Understanding and Managing Organizational Behavior*, 5th edn., Upper Saddle River, NJ: Pearson Prentice Hall.

Ghebregiorgis, F. and Karsten, L. (2007) "Employee reaction to human resource management and performance in a developing country: Evidence from Eritrea," *Personnel Review*, 38(5): 722–38.

Ghemawat, P. (2003) "Semiglobalization and international business strategy," *Journal of International Business Studies*, 34(2): 138–52.

Giampetro-Meyer, A., Brown, T., Browne, M.N., and Kubasek, N. (1998) "Do we really want more leaders in business?" *Journal of Business Ethics*, 17(15): 1728–37.

Gleason, G., Kerimbekova, A., and Kozhirova, S. (2008) "Realism and the small state: Evidence from Kyrgyzstan," *International Politics*, 45: 40–51.

Goddard, C. (2005) *The Languages of East and Southeast Asia*, New York: Oxford University Press.

Goh, G.Y. (2007) *Cakkrvatiy Anuruddha and the Buddhist Oikoumene: Historical Narratives of Kingship and Religious Networks in Burma, Northern Thailand and Sri Lanka (11th–14th centuries)*, doctoral dissertation, University of Hawaii. UMI No. 328813.

Goh, M. and Ang, A. (2000) "Some logistics realities in Indochina," *International Journal of Physical Distribution & Logistics Management*, 30(10): 887–911.

Griffin, R.W. and Putsay, M.W. (2005) *International Business*, 4th edn., Upper Saddle River, NJ: Pearson Education.

Gunn, G.C. (2008) "Laos in 2007: Regional integration and international fallout," *Asian Survey*, 48(1): 62–8.

Hadiz, V.R. (2002) "Globalization, labour, and economic crisis: Insights from Southeast Asia," *Asian Business & Management* 1: 249–66.

Harrigan, F. (2007) "Technology and Development in Asia," *Asian Development Bank's Economics Policy Brief*, No. 49.

Harris, R.L. (2008, March–April) "Latin America's response to neoliberalism and globalization," *Nueva Sociedad*, No. 214.

Harveston, P.D., Kedia, B.L., and Davis, P.S. (2000) "Internationalization of born global and gradual globalizing firms: The impact of the manager," *Advances in Competitiveness Research*, 8(1): 92–9.

Harvey, P. (2007) "'Freedom of the will' in the light of Theravada Buddhist teaching," *Journal of Buddhist Ethics*, 14: 35–98.

Hasan, R., Mitra, D., and Ulubasoglu, M. (2007) "Institutions and policies for growth and poverty reduction: The role of private sector development," *Asian Development Bank Review*, 24(1): 69–116.

Hatcher, C. and Terjesen, S. "Towards a new theory of entrepreneurship in culture and gender: A grounded study of Thailand's most successful female entrepreneurs," paper presented at the Fourth AGSE International Entrepreneurship Research Exchange, February 6–9, 2007, Brisbane, Australia.

Hawks, V.D. (2005) *Observations of Small Manufacturing Enterprise Owners in Phnom Penh Cambodia*, doctoral dissertation, Gonzaga University, Washington. UMI No. 3170688.

Head, K. and Ries, J. (2004) "Exporting and FDI as alternative strategies," *Oxford Review of Economic Policy*, 20(3): 409–23.

Header, S. (2005) "Hun Sen's consolidation: Death or beginning of reform?" in *Southeast Asian Affairs 2005*, Singapore: Institute for Southeast Asian Studies, 113–30.

Helms, M.M. (2003) "The challenge of entrepreneurship in a developed economy: The problematic case of Japan," *Journal of Development Entrepreneurship*, 8(3): 247–63.

Hengkietisak, K. (2008) "PPP must step carefully," *Bangkok Post*, January 26, 2008, Section 1, 10.

Higham, C.F.W. (2001) "Commentary: Archaeology in Myanmar: Past, present and future," *Asian Perspectives*, 40(1): 127–38.

Hill, R. (2002) *Southeast Asia: People, Land and Economy*, Crows Nest, Australia: Allen & Unwin.

Hipsher, S.A. (2005) "Leadership: Style or substance," *Bangkok University's Executive Journal*, Third Quarter.

Hipsher, S.A. (2007) "Creating market size: Regional strategies for the world's least developed areas," in J. Stoner and C. Wankel (eds.), *Innovative Approaches to Reducing Global Poverty*, Charlotte, NC: Information Age Publishing.

Hipsher, S.A. (2008a) "Born foreign firms in Cambodia: exploration of mode of entry decisions of firms originating from the Greater Mekong Subregion," *International Journal of Emerging Markets*, 3(1): 104–15.

Hipsher, S.A. (2008b) "Burma, repressions and (in)humane sanctions," *European Courier*, www.europeancourier.org/60.htm.

Hipsher, S.A. "Reexamining and revaluating underlying assumption in business education in developing economies," paper presented at 1st Bangkok International Forum on Indigenous Management Practices, Kasetsart University, Bangkok, February 2–6, 2009.

Hitt, M.A., Ireland, R.D., and Hoskisson, R.E. (2005) *Strategic Management: Competitiveness and Globalization*, 6th edn., Mason, OH: Thomson.

Hlaing, K.Y. (2005) "Myanmar in 2004: Why military rule continues," *Southeast Asian Affairs 2005*, 231–56.

Hlaing, K.Y. (2007) "Aung San Suu Kyi of Myanmar: A review of the Lady's biographies," *Contemporary Southeast Asia*, 29(2): 359–76.

Hlaing, K.Y. (2008) "Power and factional struggles in post-independence Burmese governments," *Journal of Southeast Asian Studies*, 39(1): 149–77.

Hofstede, G. (1980) "Motivation, leadership, and organization: Do American theories apply abroad?" *Organizational Dynamics*, 9(1): 42–63.

Hofstede, G. (1983) "The cultural relativity of organizational practices and theories," *Journal of International Business Studies*, 14(1): 75–89.

Holliday, I. (2008) "Voting and violence in Myanmar: Nation building for a transition to democracy," *Asian Survey*, 48(6): 1038–58.

Holmes, H., Tangtongtavy, S., and Tomizawa, R. (1996) *Working with the Thais: A Guide to Managing in Thailand*, 3rd edn., Bangkok: White Lotus.

Hooi, L.W. (2008) "The adoption of Japanese recruitment practices in Malaysia," *International Journal of Manpower*, 29(4): 362–78.

Hoshino, T. (2002) "Wen Dan and its neighbors: The Central Mekong Valley in the seventh and eighth centuries," in M. Ngaosrivathana and K. Breazeale (eds.), *Breaking New Ground in Lao History: Essays on the Seventh to Twentieth Centuries*, Chiang Mai, Thailand: Silkworm Books, 25–72.

Hudson, B. (2006) "The origins of Bagan: The archaeological landscape of Upper Burma to AD 1300," *University of Sydney Digital Theses*, http://hdl.handle.net/2123/638.

Hudson-Rodd, N. and Hunt, M. (2005) "The military occupation of Burma," *Geopolitics*, 10(3): 500–21.

Hui, M.K., Au, K., and Fock, H. (2004) "Empowerment effects across cultures," *Journal of International Business Studies*, 35(1): 41–60.

Human Rights Watch. (2007a) *Human Rights Watch Report*, 19(18c).

Human Rights Watch. (2007b) "Sold to be soldiers: The recruitment and use of child soldiers in Burma," *Human Rights Watch Report*, 19(15).

Hutzschenreuter, T. and Voll, J.C. (2008) "Performance effects of 'added cultural distance' in the path of international expansion: The case of German multinational enterprises," *Journal of International Business Studies*, 39(1): 53–70.

Hyakumura, K. and Inoue, M. (2006) "The significance of social capital in local forest management in Laos: Overcoming latent conflict between local people and forestry officials," *International Journal of Sustainable Development and World Ecology*, 13(1): 16–24.

Ibeh, K. and Young, S. (2001) "Exporting as an entrepreneurial act: An empirical study of Nigerian firms," *European Journal of Marketing*, 35(5/6): 566–86.

Ibrahim, N.A., Angelidis, J.P., and Parsa, F. (2008) "Strategic management of family businesses: Current findings and directions for future research," *International Journal of Management*, 25(1): 95–110.

Imai, Y. and Kawagoe, M. (2000) "Business start-ups in Japan: Problems and policies," *Oxford Review of Economic Policy*, 16(2): 114–23.

Ismail, A. (2001) "Democracy in Asia: Riding the wave," in U. Johannen and J. Gomez (eds.), *Democratic Transitions in Asia*, Singapore: Select Books, 51–5.

Ivarsson, S. and Goscha, C.E. (2007) "Prince Phetsarath (1890–1959): Nationalism and royalty in the making of modern Laos," *Journal of Southeast Asian Studies*, 38(1): 55–81.

Jackson, P.A. (2003) *Buddhadasa: Theravada Buddhism and the Modernist Reform in Thailand*, Chiang Mai, Thailand: Silkworm.

Jagan, L. (2009) "Eradicating opium has become a pipe dream," *Bangkok Post*, February 15, 2009.

James, H. (2004) "King Solomon's judgment," *NBR Analysis*, 15(1): 55–66.

Jeldres, J.A. (1993) "The UN and the Cambodian transition," *Journal of Democracy*, 4(4): 104–16.

Jerryson, M. (2009) "Appropriating a space for violence: State Buddhism in southern Thailand," *Journal of Southeast Asian Studies*, 40(1): 33–57.

Jitpiromsri, S. and McCargo, D. (2008) "A ministry for the South: New governance proposals for Thailand's Southern Region," *Contemporary Southeast Asia*, 30(3): 403–28.

Johannen, U. and Gomez, J. (2001) "Introduction," in U. Johannen and J. Gomez (eds.), *Democratic Transitions in Asia*, Singapore: Select Books.

Johnsen, R.E. (2007) "The role of focal suppliers in strategic networks for internationalization: Perspectives from small and medium-sized Italian and Thai silk suppliers," *Journal of Fashion Marketing and Management*, 11(1): 135–47.

Jumsai, M. (2000) *History of Laos*, Bangkok: Chalermnit.

Jumsai, M. (2001) *History of Thailand and Cambodia*, Bangkok: Chalermnit.

Kainzbauer, A. "Buddhism, 'sanuk' and intuition – making sense of Thai realities," paper delivered at 1st Bangkok International Forum on Indigenous Management Practices, Kasetsart University, Bangkok, February 2–6, 2009.

Kalantaridis, C. and Labrianidis, L. (2004) "Rural entrepreneurs in Russia and the Ukraine: Origins, motivations, and institutional change," *Journal of Economic Issues*, 38(3): 659–81.

Kamrava, M. (1999) *Cultural Politics in the Third World*, London: Routledge.

Kanungo, R.N. and Wright, R.W. (1983) "A cross-cultural comparative study of managerial job attitudes," *Journal of International Business Studies*, 14(2): 115–29.

Kao, C., Wu, W.Y., Hsieh, W.J., Wang, T.Y., Lin, C., and Chen, L.H. (2008) "Measuring the national competitiveness of Southeast Asian countries," *European Journal of Operational Research*, 187: 613–28.

Kaosa-ard, M. (2006) "Tourism: Blessing for all?" *Journal of Greater Mekong Subregion Studies*, 3(1): 1–24.

Karadeniz, E.E. and Gocer, K. (2007) "Internationalization of small firms: A case study of Turkish small- and medium-sized enterprises," *European Business Review*, 19(5): 387–403.

Kaw, E. (2005) *Buddhism and Education in Burma: Varying Conditions for a Social Ethos in the Path to "Nibbana*," doctoral dissertation, Princeton University. UMI No. 3169805.

Kawai, M. and Wignaraja, G. (2007) "ASEAN+3 or ASEAN+6: Which way forward?" *Asian Development Bank Institute Discussion Paper*, No. 77.

Kaweevisultrakul, T. and Chan, P. (2007) "Impact of cultural barriers on knowledge management implementation: Evidence from Thailand," *Journal of American Academy of Business, Cambridge*, 11(1): 303–08.

Keller, G.F. & Kronstedt, C.R. (2005) "Connecting Confucianism, communism, and the Chinese culture of commerce," *The Journal of Language for International Business*, 16(1): 60–75.

Kelly, B. and Prokhovnik, R. (2004) "Economic globalization?" in D. Held (ed.), *A Globalized World? Culture, Economics and Politics*, 2nd edn., London: Routledge, 82–122.

Keyes, C.F. (1977) "Millennialism, Theravada Buddhism, and Thai society," *The Journal of Asian Studies*, 36(2): 283–302.

Keyes, C.F. (2002) "Presidential address: 'The peoples of Asia' – Science and politics in the classification of ethnic groups in Thailand, China, and Vietnam," *The Journal of Asian Studies*, 61(4): 1163–203.

Khanal, B.R. and Souksavath, B. (2005) "Environmental management measures and current practices in solid waste management: A case study from Vientiane, Lao People's Democratic Republic," *Journal of Greater Mekong Subregion Development Studies*, 2(1): 69–89.

King, W.L. (1964) *In the Hope of Nibbana*, LaSalle, IL: Open Court.

Knight, G.S. and Cavusgil, S.T. (2004). "Innovation, organizational capabilities and the born-global firm," *Journal of International Business Studies*, 35(2), 124–41.

Knight, G.S. and Cavusgil, S.T. (2005) "A taxonomy of born-global firms," *Management International Review*, 45: 15–35.

Knight, G.S., Madson, T.K., and Servais, P. (2004) "An inquiry into born-global firms in Europe and the USA," *International Marketing Review*, 21(6): 645–65.

Kniveton, B.H. (2008) "Recruitment/selectors' perceptions of male and female trainee managers," *Journal of European Industrial Training*, 32(6): 404–17.

Koh, T. (2008) "ASEAN at forty: Perceptions and reality," in D. Nair and L.P. Onn (eds.), *Regional Outlook, Southeast Asia, 2008–2009*, Singapore: Institute of Southeast Asian Studies.

Kraft, H. (2001) "Human rights, ASEAN and constructivism: Revisiting the 'Asian Values' discourse," *Philippine Political Science Journal*, 22(45): 33–54.

Kristiansen, S. (2002) "Individual perception of business contexts: The case of small scale entrepreneurs in Tanzania," *Journal of Development Entrepreneurship*, 7(3): 283–304.

Krongkaew, M. (2004) "The development of the Greater Mekong Subregion (GMS): Real promise of false hope?" *Journal of Asian Economics*, 15:(5): 977–98.

Kuik, C.C. (2005) "Multilateralism in China's ASEAN policy: Its evolution, characteristics, and aspiration," *Contemporary Southeast Asia*, 27(1): 102–22.

Kuo, H.C. and Li, Y. (2003) "A dynamic decision model of SMEs' FDI," *Small Business Economics*, 20(3): 219–31.

Kurlantzick, J. (2005) "Laos: Still communist after all these years," *Current History*, 104(680): 114–19.

Kusakabe, K. (2004) "Women and men's perceptions of borders and states: The case of fish trade on the Thai–Cambodian border," *Journal of Greater Mekong Subregion Development Studies*, 1(1): 45–66.

Lau, H.K. (1992) "Internationalization, internalization, or a new theory for small, low-technology multinational enterprise?" *European Journal of Marketing*, 26(10): 17–31.

Li, L., Li, D., and Dalgic, T. (2004) "Internationalization process of small and medium-sized enterprises: Toward a hybrid model of experiential learning and planning," *Management International Review*, 44(1): 93–116.

Limsombunchai, V., Gan, G., and Lee, M. (2006) "Determinants of bank lending in Thailand rural financial markets," *Journal of Greater Mekong Subregion Development Studies*, 3(2): 63–76.

Linter, B. (2008) "Laos at the crossroads," *Southeast Asian Affairs 2008*, 171–83.

London, T. and Hart, S.T. (2004) "Perspective: Reinventing strategies for emerging markets: Beyond the transnational model," *Journal of International Business Studies*, 35(5): 350–70.

Longo, M. and Mura, M. (2008) "Stakeholder management and human resources: Development and implementation of a performance measurement system," *Corporate Governance*, 8(2): 191–213.

Lorch, J. (2008) "Stopgap or change agent? The role of Burma's civil society after the crackdown," *Internationales Asienforum*, 39(1/2): 21–54.

Luk, C., Yau, O., Sin, L., Tse, A., Chow, R., and Lee, J. (2008) "The effects of social capital and organizational innovativeness in different institutional contexts," *Journal of International Business Studies*, 39(4): 589–612.

Luo, Y. (2003) "Market-seeking MNEs in an emerging market: How parent-subsidiary links shape overseas success," *Journal of International Business Studies*, 34(3): 290–309.

Luo, Y. (2005) "Transactional characteristics, institutional environment and joint venture contracts," *Journal of International Business Studies*, 36(2): 209–30.

Lychack, W. (2008) "Captives of the Junta," *The American Scholar*, 17(2): 9–17.

Mackay, H. (2004) "The globalization of culture?" in D. Held (ed.), *A Globalized World? Culture, Economics and Politics*, 2nd edn., London: Routledge, 44–81.

Maekawa, T. (2004) "Cooperation pays, conflict doesn't," *Asian Development Bank Review*, 36(6): 4–5.

Mahmood, M. (2005) "Getting decent work for poverty reduction for Cambodia," *International Labour Organization (Geneva) Working Paper*, 48.

Maneepong, C. and Wu, C.T. (2004) "Comparative borderland developments in Thailand," *ASEAN Economic Bulletin*, 21(2): 135–66.

Mangahas, M. (2001) "Strong civil society needed to ensure a free media," in U. Johannen and J. Gomez (eds.), *Democratic Transitions in Asia*, Singapore: Select Books, 122–31.

Masson, P. (2001) "Globalization: Facts and figures," *International Monetary Fund Policy Discussion Paper*, PDP/01/04.

Masviriyakul, S. (2004) "Sino-Thai strategic economic development in the Greater Mekong Subregion (1992–2003)," *Contemporary Southeast Asia*, 26(2): 302–19.

McCargo, D. (2005) "Cambodia: Getting away with authoritarianism?" *Journal of Democracy*, 16(4): 98–112.

McCargo, D. (2008) "Thailand: State of anxiety," *Southeast Asian Affairs*, 2008: 333–56.

McCargo, D. (2009) "The politics of Buddhist identity in Thailand's deep south: The demise of civil religion?" *Journal of Southeast Asian Studies*, 40(1): 11–31.

McCarthy, S. (2008) "Burma and ASEAN: Estranged bedfellows," *Asian Survey*, 48(6): 911–35.

McGrath-Champ, S. and Carter, S. (2001) "The art of selling corporate culture: Management and human resources in Australian construction companies operating in Malaysia," *International Journal of Manpower*, 22(4): 349–68.

McGrew, A. (2004) "Power shift: From national government to global governance?" in D. Held (ed.), *A Globalized World? Culture, Economics and Politics*, 2nd edn., London: Routledge, 123–59.

Menon, J. (2005) "Can subregionalism or regionalism aid multilateralism? The case of the Greater Mekong Subregion and the Association of Southeast Asian Nations Free Trade Area," *Journal of Greater Mekong Subregion Development Studies*, 2(1): 21–36.

Menon, J. (2006) "Would you like to pay in Dollars, Baht, or Kip?: Economic consequences of multiple currencies in the Lao People's Democratic Republic," *Journal of Greater Mekong Subregion Development Studies*, 3(2): 35–47.

Menon, J. (2007) "Dealing with dollarization: What options for the transitional economics of Southeast Asia?" *Asian Development Bank Institute Discussion Paper*, No. 63.

Mills, G.F., Askwith, J.E., Abrillo, H., and Howe, J. (2004) "Training needs analysis for development in the Greater Mekong Subregion," *Journal of Greater Mekong Subregion Development Studies*, 1(1): 1–30.

Min, W. (2009) "Looking inside the Burmese military," *Asian Survey*, 48(6): 1018–37.

Model, D. (2005) *Lying for Empire: How to Commit War Crimes with a Straight Face*, Monroe, ME: Common Courage Press.

Moeller, J.O. (2007) "ASEAN's relations with the European Union: Obstacles and opportunities," *Contemporary Southeast Asia*, 29(3): 465–82.

Moen, O. (2002) "The born globals: A new generation of small European exporters," *International Marketing Review*, 19(2/3): 156–75.

Moen, O. and Servais, P. (2002) "Born global or gradual global? Examining the export behavior of small- and medium-sized enterprises," *Journal of International Marketing*, 10(3): 49–72.

Mohrman, S.A. (2008) "Designing organizations for growth: The human resource contribution," *Human Resource Planning*, 30(4): 34–45.

Mon, M. (2005) "Burmese migrants in Thailand," *Review of Indonesian and Malaysian Affairs*, 39(2): 129–50.

Montesano, M. (2005) "Beyond the assimilation fixation: Skinner and the possibility of a spatial approach to twentieth-century Thai history," *Journal of Chinese Overseas*, 1(2): 184–216.

Montlake, S. (2008) "Vanishing Asia: A written thread; How exiles keep the Shan language alive," *The Wall Street Journal Asia*, October 10, 2008: W.9.

Moran, R., Harris, P., and Moran, S. (2007) *Managing Cultural Differences: Global Leadership Strategies for the 21st century*, 7th edn., Burlington, MA: Butterworth Heinemann.

Morck, R. and Yeung, B. (2007) "History in perspective: Comment on Jones and Khanna 'bringing history (back) into international business,'" *Journal of International Business Studies*, 38(3): 357–60.

Moy, J, Luk, V., and Wright, P.C. (2003) "Perceptions of entrepreneurship as a career: Views of young people in Hong Kong," *Equal Opportunities International*, 22(4): 16–40.

Murray, A.I. (1986) "A contingency view of Porter's generic strategies," *The Academy of Management Review*, 13(3): 390–400.

Myint-U, T. (2006) *The River of Lost Footprints: A History of Burma*, New York: Farrar, Straus and Giroux.

Myoe, M.A. (2007a) "Sino-Myanmar economic relations since 1988," *Asia Research Institute Working Paper series* (National University of Singapore), No. 86.

Myoe, M.A. (2007b) "A historical overview of political transition in Myanmar since 1998," *Asia Research Institute Working Paper series* (National University of Singapore), No. 95.

Naisbitt, J. (1997) *Megatrends Asia: Eight Asian Megatrends that are Reshaping our World*, New York: Touchstone.

Neelankavil, J.P., Mathur, A., and Zhang, Y. (2000) "Determinants of managerial performance: A cross-cultural comparison of the perceptions of middle-level managers in four countries," *Journal of International Business Studies*, 31(1): 121–40.

Nelson, M.H. (2007). "'People's sector politics' (*Kanmueang Phak Prachachon*) in Thailand: Problems of democracy in ousting Prime Minister Thaksin Shinawatra," *Southeast Asia Research (City University of Hong Kong) Centre Working Paper*, No. 87.

Neupert, K.E., Baughn, C.C., and Dao, T. (2006) "SME exporting challenges in transitional and developed economies," *Journal of Small Business and Enterprise Development*, 13(4): 535–45.

Newburry, W. and Yakova, N. (2006) "Standardized preferences: A function of national culture, work interdependence and local embeddedness," *Journal of International Business Studies*, 37(1): 44–60.

Ng, E.S. and Wiesner, W.H. (2007) "Are men always picked over women? The effects of employment equity directives on selection decisions," *Journal of Business Ethics*, 76(2): 177–87.

Ngaosrivathana, M. and Ngaosrivathana, P. (2002) "Early European impression of the Lao," in M. Ngaosrivathana and K. Breazeale (eds.), *Breaking New Ground in Lao History: Essays on the Seventh to Twentieth Centuries*, Chiang Mai, Thailand: Silkworm Books, 95–150.

Nopkhun, T. (2005) *Globalization, Growth, and Regional Disparity: Testing Thailand's Experience 1981–2003*, doctoral dissertation, Northern Illinois University. UMI No. 3205111.

O'Connor, R.A. (1995) "Agricultural change and ethnic succession in Southeast Asian States: A case for regional anthropology," *The Journal of Asian Studies*, 54(4): 968–96.

Okpara, J.O. and Wynn, P. (2008) "Human resource management practices in a transition economy," *Management Research News*, 31(1): 57–76.

Oldfield, D.D. (1998) *The Restructuring of Thailand's Foreign Policy Towards Laos 1988–1991*, doctoral dissertation, Northern Illinois University. UMI No. 9906440.

Ong, E.C. (2003) "Anchor East Asian free trade in ASEAN," *The Washington Quarterly*, 26(2): 57–72.

Onishi, J. (2006) "The transferability of Japanese HRM practices to Thailand," *Asia Pacific Journal of Human Resource Management*, 44(3): 260–75.

Oviatt, B.M. and McDougall, P.P. (1994) "Toward a theory of international new ventures," *Journal of International Business Studies*, 25(1): 45–64.

Paulson, A.L. and Townsend, R.M. (2005) "Financial constraints and entrepreneurship: Evidence from the Thai financial crisis," *Economic Perspectives*, 29(3): 34–48.

Peng, M.W. (2002) "Towards an institution-based view of business strategy," *Asia Pacific Journal of Management*, 19(2/3): 251–67.

Peng, M.W., Wang, D., and Jiang, Y. (2008) "Perspective: An institution-based view of international business strategy: A focus on emerging economies," *Journal of International Business Studies*, 39(5): 920–36.

Penny, D., Hua, Q., Pottier, C., Fletcher, R., and Barbetti, M. (2007) "The use of AMS 14C dating to explore issues of occupation and demist at the medieval city of Angkor, Cambodia," *Nuclear Instruments and Methods in Physics Research*, B 259: 388–94.

Persons, L.S. (2008) *Face Dynamics, Social Power and Virtue Among Thai Leaders: A Cultural Analysis*, doctoral dissertation, Fuller Graduate Schools, School of Intercultural Studies.

Petison, P. and Johri, L.M. (2008) "Dynamics of the manufacturer-supplier relationships in emerging markets: A case of Thailand," *Asia Pacific Journal of Marketing and Logistics*, 20(1): 76–96.

Petry, J. (1993) *The Sword of the Spirit: Christians, Karens, Colonialists, and the Creation of a Nation of Burma*, doctoral dissertation, Rice University, Houston. UMI No. 9408655.

Pholsena, V. (2004) "The changing historiographies of Laos: A focus on the early period," *Journal of Southeast Asian Studies*, 35(2): 235–59.

Phongpaichit, P. and Baker, C. (2008) "Commentary: Thailand: Fighting over democracy," *Economic and Political Weekly*, December 13, 2008, 18–21.

Phothisane, S. (2002) "Evolution of the chronicle of Luang Prabang: A comparison of sixteen versions," in M. Ngaosrivathana and K. Breazeale (eds.), *Breaking New Ground in Lao History: Essays on the Seventh to Twentieth Centuries*, Chiang Mai, Thailand: Silkworm Books.

Piker, S. (1993) "Theravada Buddhism and Catholicism: A social historical perspective on religious change, with special reference to *Centesimus Annus*," *Journal of Business Ethics*, 12(12): 965–73.

Pinfold, J.F. (2001) "The expectations of new business founders: The New Zealand case," *Journal of Small Business Management*, 39(3): 279–85.

Pitamber, S. (2000) "Accessing financial resources and entrepreneurial motivations amongst the female informal sector micro-entrepreneurs in Sudan," *Ahfad Journal*, 17(1): 4–21.

Polaski, S. (2006) "Combining global and local forces: The case of labor rights in Cambodia," *World Development*, 34(5): 919–32.

Porter, M.E. (1980) *Competitive strategy*, New York: Free Press.

Porter, M.E. (1996) "What is strategy?" *Harvard Business Review*, 74(6): 61–78.

Pounder, J.S. (2001) " 'New leadership' and university organisational effectiveness: Exploring the relationship," *Leadership & Organization Development Journal*, 22(5/6): 281–90.

Prachvuthy, M. (2006) "Tourism, poverty, and income distribution: Chambok community-based ecotourism development, Kirirom National Park, Kompong Speu Province, Cambodia," *Journal of Greater Mekong Subregion Development Studies*, 3(1): 25–40.

Prajogo, D.I., Laosirihongthing, T., Sohal. A., and Boon-itt, S. (2007) "Manufacturing strategies and innovation performance in newly industrialized countries," *Industrial Management and Data Systems*, 107(1): 52–68.

Prakoonheang, K. (2001) "Political ideologies and development in the Lao People's Democratic Republic since 1975," master's thesis, University of Western Sydney, Macarthur.

Prasertrungruang, T. and Hadikusumo, B.H.W. (2007) "Heavy equipment management practices and problems in Thai highway contractors," *Engineering, Construction and Architectural Management*, 14(3): 228–41.

Prebish, C.S. (2008) "Cooking the Buddhist books: The implications of the new dating of the Buddha for the history of early Indian Buddhism," *Journal of Buddhist Ethics*, 15: 1–21.

Pribbenow, M.L. (2006) "Vietnam's invasion of Cambodia," *The Journal of Military History*, 70(2): 459–86.

Pride, W.M., Hughes, R.J., and Kapoor, J.R. (2008) *Business*, Boston: Houghton Mifflin.

Qian, G., Li, L., Li, J., and Qian, Z. (2008) "Regional diversification and firm performance," *Journal of International Business Studies*, 39(2): 197–214.

Quy, T.V. (2002) "The Quy Hop archive: Vietnamese-Lao relations reflected in border-post documents dating from 1619–1880," in M. Ngaosrivathana and K. Breazeale (eds.), *Breaking New Ground in Lao History: Essays on the Seventh to Twentieth Centuries*, Chiang Mai, Thailand: Silkworm Books, 239–60.

Rajah, A. (2008) *Remaining Karen: A Study of Cultural Reproduction and the Maintenance of Identity*, Canberra: Australian National University Press.

Ralston, D.A. (2008) "The crossvergence perspective: Reflections and projections," *Journal of International Business Studies*, 39(1): 27–40.

Ralston, D.A., Holt, D.H., Terpstra, R.H., and Cheng, Y.K. (1997) "The impact of national culture and economic ideology on managerial work values: A study of the United States, Russia, Japan, and China," *Journal of International Business Studies*, 28: 177–207.

Rasmussan, E.K., Madson, T.K., and Evangelista, F. (2001) "The founding of the born global company in Denmark and Australia: Sensemaking and networking," *Asia Pacific Journal of Marketing and Logistics*, 13(3): 75–107.

Raszelenberg, P. (1999) "The Khmers Rouges and the final solution," *History and Memory*, 11(2): 62–93.

Rehbein, B. (2007a) *Globalization, Culture and Society in Laos*, Oxford: Routledge.

Rehbein, B. (2007b) "Configurations of Globalization in Laos and Cambodia," *Internationales Asienforum*, 38(1/2): 67–85.

Reynolds, P.L. and Lancaster, G. (2007) "Predictive strategic marketing management decision in small firms: A possible Bayesian solution," *Management Decision*, 45(6): 1038–57.

Rigg, J., Veeravongs, S., Verravongs, L., and Rohitarachoon, P. (2008) "Reconfiguring rural spaces and remaking rural lives in central Thailand," *Journal of Southeast Asian Studies*, 39(3): 355–81.

Robbins, S. (2003) *Organizational Behavior*, 10th edn.. Upper Saddle River, NJ: Prentice Hall.

Roberts, C. (2006) "Myanmar and the argument for engagement: A clash of contending moralities," *East Asia*, 23(2): 34–62.

Roman, F. (2004) "Building competitiveness through cross-border cooperation in Cambodia and Thailand," *Journal of Greater Mekong Subregion Development Studies*, 1(1): 31–44.

Rubesch, E. and Banomyong, R. (2005) "In emerging markets, sometimes it is better to let 'gray' point the way," *Proceeding of the 10th International Symposium on Logistics*, July 3–5: 237–42.

Rugman, A.M. and Brain, C. (2003) "Multinational enterprises are regional, not global," *Multinational Business Review*, 11(1): 3–12.

Rugman, A.M. and Verbeke, A. (2004) "A perspective on regional and global strategies of multinational enterprises," *Journal of International Business Studies*, 35(1): 3–18.

Rugman, A.M. and Verbeke, A. (2008) "The theory and practice of regional strategy: A response to Osegowitsch and Sammartino," *Journal of International Business Studies*, 39(3): 326–32.

Saicheua, S. (2008) "Volatile times ahead," *Bangkok Post*, July 30, 2008, A1.

Sajarattanachote, S. (2006) *The Role of Multinational Enterprises and Geographical Spillovers on Regional Development in Thailand*, doctoral dissertation, State University of New York at Buffalo. UMI No. 3226677.

Sangkhawasi, T. and Johri, L.M. (2007) "Impact of status brand strategy on materialism in Thailand," *Journal of Consumer Marketing*, 24(5): 275–82.

Sarkar, M. and Cavusgil, T.S. (1996) "Trends in international business thought and literature: A review of international market entry mode research: Integration and synthesis," *The International Executive*, 38(6): 825–47.

Saunder, K.J. (1922) *Buddhism in the Modern World*, London: Society for Promoting Christian Knowledge.

Schmidt, S.W. and Akdere, M. (2007) "Measuring the effects of employee orientation training on employee perceptions of vision and leadership: Implications for human resources," *The Business Review, Cambridge*, 7(1): 322–7.

Schober, J.S. (1989) *Paths to Enlightenment: Theravada Buddhism in Upper Burma*, doctoral dissertation, University of Illinois. UMI No. 9011007.

Seekins, D.M. (2009) "Myanmar in 2008: Hardship, compounded," *Asian Survey*, 49(1): 166–73.

Sengupta, K. and Chattopadhyay, A. (2006) "Importance of appropriate marketing strategies for sustainability of small businesses in a developing country: Case of bakery chains in Kolkata, India," *Asia Pacific Journal of Marketing*, 18(4): 328–41.

Setboonsarng, S. (2008) "Global Partnership in poverty reduction: Contract farming and regional cooperation," *Asian Development Bank Institute Discussion Paper*, No. 89.

Setboonsarng, S., Leung, P.S., and Stefan, A. (2008) "Rice contract farming in Lao PDR: Moving from subsistence to commercial agriculture," *Asian Development Bank Institute Discussion Paper*, No. 90.

Severino, R.C. (2007) "ASEAN beyond forty: Towards political and economic integration," *Contemporary Southeast Asia*, 29(3): 406–23.

Shahidi, M. and Smagulova, A. (2007) "The challenges of entrepreneurship in dynamic society," *Central Asia Business*, 1(1): 34–46.

Shapiro, D.M., Gedaijlovis, E., and Erdener, C. (2003) "The Chinese family firm as a multinational enterprise," *International Journal of Organizational Analysis*, 11(2): 105–22.

Sharrock, P.D. (2009) "Garuda, Vajrapani and religious change in Jayavarman VII's Angkor," *Journal of Southeast Asian Studies*, 40(1): 111–51.

Shukla, K. (2008) "The international community's responsibility to protect," *Forced Migration Review*, 30: 7–9.

Sim, A.B. and Pandian, J.R. (2007) "An exploratory study of internationalization strategies of Malaysian and Taiwanese firms," *International Journal of Emerging Markets*, 2(3): 252–73.

Simola, S.K., Taggar, S., and Smith G.W. (2007) "The employment selection interview: Disparity among research-based recommendations, current practices and what matters to human rights tribunals," *Canadian Journal of Administrative Sciences*, 24(1): 30–44.

Siriphon, A. (2006) "Local knowledge, dynamism and the politics of struggle: A case study of the Hmong in Northern Thailand," *Journal of Southeast Asian Studies*, 37(1): 65–81.

Slangen, A. and Hennart, J. (2008) "Do multinationals really prefer to enter culturally distant countries through greenfields rather than through acquisitions? The role of parent experience and subsidiary autonomy," *Journal of International Business Studies*, 39(3): 472–90.

Smeaton, D.M. (1920) *Loyal Karens of Burma*, 2nd edn., London: Kegan Paul, Trench, Trubner & Co. Ltd.

Smith, A.L. (2004) "ASEAN's Ninth Summit: Solidifying regional cohesion, advancing external linkages," *Contemporary Southeast Asia*, 26(3): 416–33.

Sokheng, V. (2008) "F'pec rattled by more defections," *The Phnom Penh Post*, December 30, 2008.

Son, H.H. (2007) "Interrelationship between growth, inequality and poverty: The Asian experience," *Asian Development Review*, 24(2): 37–63.

South, A. (2007) "Karen nationalist communities: the 'problem' of diversity," *Contemporary Southeast Asia*, 29(1): 55–76.

Southiseng, N. and Walsh, J. (2008) "Competition and management issues in SEM entrepreneurs in Laos: Evidence from empirical studies in Vientiane Municipality, Savannakhet and Luang Prabang," *Proceedings of the 2nd International Colloquium on Business & Management* (ICBM) in conjunction with the *International Colloquium on Business & Management Education* 2008.

Sriboonlue, O. (2007) *Privatization and Performance of Formally State-owned Enterprises in Thailand: A Strategic Management Study*, doctoral dissertation, Alliant International University. UMI No. 3273264.

Srivastava, P. (2005) "Poverty targeting in India," in J. Weiss (ed.), *Poverty Targeting in Asia*, Cheltenham: Edward Elgar, 34–78.

Srivastava, P. (2009) "Myanmar," in *Asian Development Outlook 2009: Rebalancing Asia's Growth*, Mandaluyong City, Philippines: Asian Development Bank.

Stads, G.J. and Kam, P.S. (2007) "Myanmar," *Agricultural Science and Technology Indicators (ASTI) Country Brief*, No. 38.

Steinberg, D.I. (2004) "A guide for the perplexed?" *NBR Analysis*, 15(1): 41–54.

Strutt, A. and Lim, S. (2005) "Trade liberalization and poverty alleviation in the Greater Mekong Subregion," *Journal of GMS Development Studies*, 2(1): 1–20.

Stuart-Fox, M. (2002) "On writing of Lao history: Continuities and discontinuities," in M. Ngaosrivathana and K. Breazeale (eds.), *Breaking New Ground in Lao History: Essays on the Seventh to Twentieth Centuries*, Chiang Mai, Thailand: Silkworm Books.

Stuart-Fox, M. (2003) *A Short History of China and Southeast Asia: Tribute, Trade and Influence*, Crows Nest, Australia: Allen & Unwin.

Styles, C., Patterson, P.G., and Ahmed, F. (2008) "A relational model of export performance," *Journal of International Business Studies*, 39(5): 880–900.

Su, C.M. (2003) *Tradition and Change: Khmer Identity and Democracy in the 20th Century and Beyond*, doctoral dissertation, University of Hawaii. UMI No. 3110036.

Su, Y., Xu, D., and Phan, P.H. (2007) "Principal-principal conflict in the governance of the Chinese public corporation," *Management and Organization Review*, 4(1): 17–38.

Suehiro, A. and Wailerdsak, N. (2004) "Family business in Thailand: Its management, governance, and future challenges," *ASEAN Economic Bulletin*, 21(1): 81–93.

Suh, T. and Kwon, I.G. (2002) "Globalization and reluctant buyers," *International Marketing Review*, 19(6): 663–80.

Sumedho, A. (1992) *The Four Noble Truths*, Hertfordshire, UK: Amaravati Publications.

Suutari, V., Raharjo, K., and Riikkila, T. (2002) "The challenge of cross-cultural leadership interaction: Finnish expatriates in Indonesia," *Career Development International*, 7(6/7): 415–29.

Swierczek, F.W. and Onishi, J. (2003) "Culture and conflict: Japanese managers and Thai subordinates," *Personnel Review*, 32(1/2): 187–210.

Syamananda, R. (1993) *A History of Thailand*, Bangkok: Thai Watana Panich.

Tahir, R. and Larimo, J. (2004) "Understanding the location strategies of the European firms in Asian countries," *Journal of American Academy of Business, Cambridge*, 5(1/2): 102–9.

Tan, C. (2007) "Education reforms in Cambodia: Issues and concerns," *Educational Research for Policy and Practice*, 6(1): 5–24.

Tang, L. and Koveos, P.E. (2008) "A framework to update Hofstede's cultural value indices: Economic dynamics and institutional stability," *Journal of International Business Studies*, 39(6): 1045–63.

Tappe, O. (2007) "A new banknote in the People's Republic: The iconography of the Kip and ideological transformation in Laos, 1957–2006," *Internationales Asienforum*, 38(1–2): 87–108.

Taylor, R.H. (2008) "Myanmar in 2007: Growing pressure for change but the regime remains obdurate," *Southeast Asian Affairs 2008*: 247–73.

Than, M. (2005) "Myanmar's cross-border economic relations and cooperation with the people's republic of China and Thailand in the Greater Mekong Subregion," *Journal of Greater Mekong Subregion Development Studies*, 2(1): 37–54.

Thawnghmung, A.M. (2008) "Responding to strategies and programmes of Myanmar's military regime: An economic viewpoint," *Southeast Asian Affairs 2008*: 274–90.

Thomas, A.S. and Mueller, S.L. (2000) "A case for comparative entrepreneurship: Assessing the relevance of culture," *Journal of International Business Studies*, 31(2): 287–301.

Thomas, D.E. (2001) *Who Goes Abroad? International Diversification by Emerging Market Firms*, doctoral dissertation, Texas A&M University. UMI No. 3033889.

Thompson, M.R. (2001) "Whatever happened to 'Asian Values'?" *Journal of Democracy*, 12(4): 154–65.

Tipper, J. (2004) "How to increase diversity through recruitment practices," *Industrial and Commercial Training*, 36(4): 158–61.

Tong, T.W., Alessandri, T.M., Reuer, J.J., and Chintakananda, A. (2008) "How does country matter? An analysis of firms' growth options," *Journal of International Business Studies*, 39(3): 387–405.

Tsai, M. and Cheng, Y. (2004) "Asset specificity, culture, experience, firm size and entry mode strategy: Taiwanese manufacturing firms in China, Southeast Asia and Western Europe," *International Journal of Commerce & Management*, 14(3/4): 1–27.

Tsang, E. (2001) "Internationalizing the family firm: A case study of a Chinese family business," *Journal of Small Business Management*, 39(2): 88–94.

Tully, J. (2005) *A Short History of Cambodia: From Empire to Survival*, Crow Nest, Australia: Allen & Unwin.

Ty, M., Walsh, J., and Anurit, P. (2008) "Training and development in social enterprises in Cambodia," *Proceedings of the 2nd International Colloquium on Business & Management* (ICBM) in conjunction with the *International Colloquium on Business & Management Education* 2008, Bangkok, November 10–12, 2008.

Um, K. (2008) "Cambodia: A decade after the coup," *Southeast Asia Affairs 2008*: 107–20.

Ungpakorn, G.J. (2007) *A Coup for the Rich. Thailand's Political Crisis*, Bangkok: Workers Democracy Publishing.

United Nations Development Programme. (2007) "Raising rural incomes in Cambodia: Beyond sectoral policy, *UNDP Funded Discussion Paper*, No. 4, Phnom Penh: United Nations Development Programme.

United Nations Economic and Social Commission for Asia and the Pacific. (2003) "Transit transport issues in landlocked and transit developing countries," *Landlocked Developing Countries Series*, No. 1, New York: United Nations.

Vallaster, C. and Hasenohrl, S. (2006) "Assessing new product potential in an international context: Lessons learned in Thailand," *Journal of Consumer Marketing*, 23(2): 69–78.

Vatikiotis, M. (2001) "Freedom and truth: Cultivating the free press in emerging democracies," in U. Johannen and J. Gomez (eds.), *Democratic Transitions in Asia*, Singapore, Select Books: 143–9.

Venkatraman, M. and Nelson, T. (2008) "From servicescape to consumptionscape: A photo-elicitation study of Starbucks in New China," *Journal of International Business Studies*, 39(6): 1010–26.

Vernon, R. (1966) "International investment and international trade in the product cycle," *Quarterly Journal of Economics*, 80: 190–207.

Vickery, M. (2004) "Cambodia and its neighbors in the 15th Century," *Asia Research Institute Working Paper series*, No. 27.

Vinten, G. (2000) "Business theology," *Management Decision*, 38(3): 209–15.

Wallerstein, I. (2000) "Globalization or the age of transition: A long-term view of the trajectory of the world system," *International Sociology*, 15(2): 251–67.

Walton, M.J. (2008) "Ethnicity, conflict, and history in Burma: The myths of Panglong," *Asian Survey*, 48(6): 889–910.

Wang, M.C. (2004) "Greater China: Powerhouse of East Asian regional cooperation," *East Asia*, 21(4): 38–63.

Wang, S. (2005) "Poverty targeting in the People's Republic of China," in J. Weiss (ed.), *Poverty Targeting in Asia*, Cheltenham: Edward Elgar, 136–85.

Wang, T. and Chien, S. (2007) "The influences of technology development on economic performance: The example of ASEAN countries," *Technovation*, 27(8): 471–88.

Warr, P. (2007) "Long-term economic performance in Thailand," *Asian Economic Bulletin*, 24(1): 138–63.

Warr, P. and Sarntisart, I. (2005) "Poverty targeting in Thailand," in J. Weiss (ed.), *Poverty Targeting in Asia*, Cheltenham: Edward Elgar, 186–218.

Wattanapruttipaisan, T. (2003) "ASEAN-China Free trade area: Advantages, challenges, and implications for the newer ASEAN member countries," *ASEAN Economic Bulletin*, 20(1): 31–44.

Wattanapruttipaisan, T. (2007) "Priority integration sectors in ASEAN: Supply side implications and options," *Asian Development Review*, 24(2): 64–89.

Wei, L.Q. and Lau, C.M. (2008) "The impact of market orientation and strategic HRM on firm performance: The case of Chinese enterprises," *The Journal of International Business Studies*, 39(6): 980–95.

Weiss, J. (2005) "Experiences with poverty targeting in Asia: An overview," in J. Weiss (ed.), *Poverty Targeting in Asia*, Cheltenham: Edward Elgar, 1–33.

Weng, L. (2008) "An enduring culture," *The Irrawaddy*, 16(4): 28–9.

Westhead, P., Ucbasaran, D., and Binks, M. (2004) "Internationalization strategies selected by established rural and urban SMEs," *Journal of Small Business and Enterprise Development*, 11(1): 8–22.

Win, S. (2001) "Human rights abuses and violations in Burma in emerging democracies," in U. Johannen and J. Gomez (eds.), *Democratic Transitions in Asia*, Singapore, Select Books: 113–19.

Wolters, O.W. (1982) "History, culture and region," in *Southeast Asian Perspectives*, Singapore: Institute for Southeast Asian Studies.

Wong, C.S. and Wong I.C. (2003) "The role of perceived quality of social relationships within organizations in Chinese societies," *International Journal of Management*, 20(2): 216–22.

Wu, C., Lawler, J.J., and Yi, X. (2008) "Overt employment discrimination in MNC affiliates: Home-country cultural and institutional effects," *Journal of International Business Studies*, 39(5): 772–94.

Wyatt, D.K. (2003) *Thailand: A Short History*, 2nd edn., Chiang Mai, Thailand: Silkworm.

Yan, J. and Sorenson, R.L. (2004) "The Influence of Confucian ideology on conflict in Chinese family business," *International Journal of Cross Cultural Management*, 4(1): 5–17.

Yang, D. (2003) *Foreign Direct Investment from Developing Countries: A Case Study of China's Outward Investment*, doctoral dissertation, Victoria University, Melbourne, Australia.

Yeung, H.W. (2005) "Organizational space: A new frontier in international business strategy," *Critical Perspectives on International Business*, 1(4): 219–40.

Yokoyama, S., Tanaka, K., and Phalakhone, K. "Forest Policy and Swidden Agriculture in Laos," paper presented at the SEAGA Conference, Singapore, November 28–30, 2006.

Young, E. (1900) *The Kingdom of the Yellow Robe*, 2nd edn., Westminster, UK: Archibald Constable & Co.

Zajac, E.J. and Shortell, S.M. (1989) "Changing generic strategies: Likelihood, direction and performance implications," *Strategic Management Journal*, 10(3): 413–30.

Zaleska, K.J. and Menezes, L.M. (2007) "Human resource development practices and their association with employee attitudes: Between traditional and new careers," *Human Relations*, 60(7): 987–1018.

Zamroni "Thailand's agricultural sector and free trade agreements," *Asia-Pacific Trade and Investment Review*, 2(2): 51–70.

Zhang, W., Huang, Y., and Zuh, W. (2006) "The People's Republic of China factor in Mekong tourism," *Journal of Greater Mekong Subregion Development*, 3(2): 1–22.

Zhang, X. (2002) "China's involvement in Laos during the Vietnam War, 1963–1975," *The Journal of Military History*, 66(4): 1141–66.

Zhou, K.Z., Brown, J.R., Dev, C.S., and Agarwal, S. (2007) "The effects of customer and competitor orientations on performance in global markets: A contingency analysis," *Journal of International Business Studies*, 38(2): 303–19.

Zitta, S.J. and Power, T.L. (2003) "Motives for foreign direct investments in the United States," *Thunderbird International Business Review*, 45(3): 275–88.

Index